PADDLING WITH SPIRITS
A Solo Kayak Journey

∼

PADDLING

with

GREEN WRITERS PRESS *Brattleboro, Vermont*

SPIRITS

A Solo Kayak Journey

Irene Skyriver

Printed in the United States

10 9 8 7 6 5 4 3 2

DISCLAIMER: The family portions of this book, although based on what is known of the author's ancestors, are their stories told in fiction form. Any references to historical events, real people, or real places are used fictitiously. Other names, characters, places and events are products of the author's imagination, and any resemblance to actual events, places or persons, living or dead, is entirely coincidental.

Green Writers Press is a Vermont-based publisher whose mission is to spread a message of hope and renewal through the words and images we publish. Throughout we will adhere to our commitment to preserving and protecting the natural resources of the earth. To that end, a percentage of our proceeds will be donated to environmental activist groups. A percentage of sales from *Paddling With Spirits* will go to Planned Parenthood. Green Writers Press gratefully acknowledges support from individual donors, friends, and readers to help support the environment and our publishing initiative.

GReen
wriTers
press

Giving Voice to Writers Who Will Make the World a Better Place
Green Writers Press | Brattleboro, Vermont
www.greenwriterspress.com

ISBN: 978-0-9987012-4-0

COVER ART: PAMELA MARESTEN
BLOCK PRINTS: MIKE RUST
NW COAST OTTER DESIGN: CHARLIE PRINCE

PRINTED ON PAPER WITH PULP THAT COMES FROM FSC (FOREST STEWARDSHIP COUNCIL)-CERTI-FIED, MANAGED FORESTS THAT GUARANTEE RESPONSIBLE ENVIRONMENTAL, SOCIAL, AND ECONOMIC PRACTICES BY LIGHTNING SOURCE. ALL WOOD-PRODUCT COMPONENTS USED IN BLACK & WHITE OR STANDARD COLOR PAPERBACK BOOKS, UTILIZING EITHER CREAM OR WHITE BOOKBLOCK PAPER, THAT ARE MANUFACTURED IN THE LAVERGNE, TENNESSEE, PRODUCTION CENTER ARE SUSTAINABLE FORESTRY INITIATIVE® (SFI®) CERTIFIED SOURCING.

There's a haunting quiet
A vicious void
Totems decayed
Skulls growing moss

There's a scoured seascape
No canoe or paddler in sight
Rotting remains of tooled wood
Lying in dark caves of the dead

Breezes breathing soul-filled sighs
As they push at my back
Urging me onward
Along the watery route
Of a time lost

IN LOVING MEMORY OF

My Mom and Dad—

Mary Ann Fahrenkopf and Don Petroleum Barrett II

❧

Contents

Prince William Sound

Katalla

Kayak Island

Yakutat Bay

Gulf of Alaska

Prince of Wales Islar

Queen Charlotte Isla

PACIFIC OCEAN

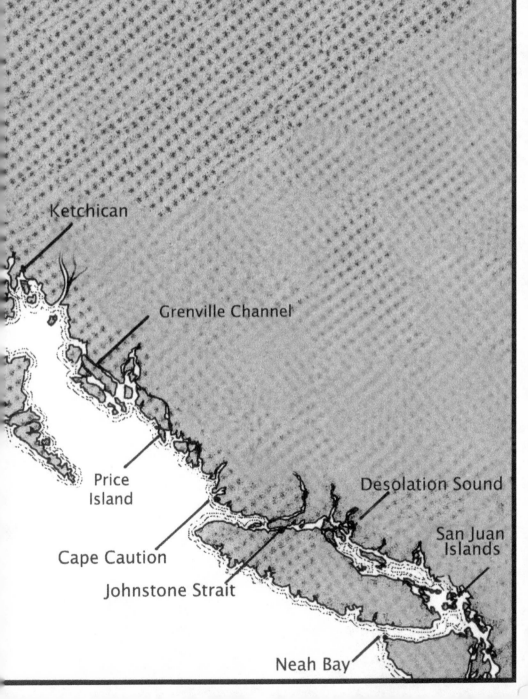

Ketchican

Grenville Channel

Price
Island

Cape Caution

Johnstone Strait

Desolation Sound

San Juan
Islands

Neah Bay

A Solo Journey

I AM ONE IN THE CONTINUUM of family born on these shores of the Pacific Northwest. My soul is connected to their spirits by the very sea waters we have each stepped into, through the generations.

My earliest coastal ancestors paddled these same waters in war canoes, whaling canoes, move-the-whole-village canoes. My ancestor mothers paddled smaller women's canoes to their berry-picking and clam-digging sites or to the trading posts. The sea that carried them was vast and incomprehensible. It could be devastatingly violent or serenely calm. They drew endless nourishment from it, but it could also be their unintended grave. Every stroke of the paddle away from shore was as much a risk as it was a chance at life.

My immigrant ancestors, who found their way to the Pacific Northwest Coast and intermarried with the original peoples of this land, were their own kind of renegades. In seeking their dreams, they distanced themselves as far as possible from their East Coast families and risked hardships for a chance to rise above their origins, not just to live, but to have a *real* life. I am also of their rebel ilk.

It is this call to *life*, and need for freedom—the gamble my ancestors took to experience a more authentic and vital path—that has served me as both example and guidance. Never was this more directly the case than when I decided to embark on a solo kayak journey from Alaska to my home in the San Juan Islands of Washington State. For we are never more alive than when we are defying death. This would be the magic edge I would travel, that fine line my kayak bow cut as I paddled alone—save for the spirits on either side—for over seven-hundred and fifty miles, in forty paddling days.

Thankfully I paddled a kayak and not a canoe. My modern vessel kept my gear dry and contained. It would protect me from lashing winds and waves as I wove through the coastal labyrinth from the Alaskan waters of my father's coastal ancestors, the Tlingit, to the Washington waters of my mother's coastal ancestors, the Makah. These starting and ending points were only symbolic, for the true territories of my father's people were further northwest and my mother's people slightly further southwest, but both native groups skillfully plied the coast, ranging far into each other's provinces. In essence, I would paddle in their spirit tracks.

I grew up on the Olympic Peninsula surrounded by forests. The dark woods were my playgrounds. The skies were my father's. When I was five, he took a job at a grass strip airfield improbably called the *Jefferson County International Airport*, and in his off hours he navigated the skies. My brother and I flew with him on joy rides, dipping, diving, buzzing and barrel-rolling. From those thrilling heights, I could see the Earth below, slightly curved at the edges, as if I were looking down into a crystal ball. The emerald waterways reached northward like fingers wrapping around the green jewels of islands. Even as I was being propelled wildly through the air in my dad's small plane, I was instinctively drawn down toward that liquid element. Where did those water paths lead? Did people live on those islands? It would be years before I would come to know answers to those questions, but spirit was moving me slowly toward the water and the islands.

My first detour was teen pregnancy. My children were always a joyful part of my journey, and the choices I made were based as much on what I wanted to create for them as what I wanted to create for myself. There were, however, some bumps along that path.

An innocent, youthful heart easily falls in love and that is what happened when I met the father of my children. My love of his kind spirit blinded me to his alcoholism. His parents were both heavy drinkers and he was already following their path. Before long, he began to come home late at night, drunk but demanding his dinner. He threw things and punched holes in the walls. After three years of pleading with him for change, I had to harden my heart and leave with the children. In the same truck we'd often used to escape his violence, we left for the last time. We were set adrift, looking for a safe home.

Our first retreat was a rundown rental farmhouse near a highway overpass. But I knew that what I wanted most for us was a home in the peace and beauty of nature. I'd heard of Stuart Island, in the San Juans. With a small population, a one-room schoolhouse, and no ferry service, it seemed idyllic. One night by candle-light I composed a letter to a woman living there. I finished, and got out of bed to check on my children. When I returned, my letter lay transmuted into a small pile of ash. A breeze coming through my open window had blown it onto the candle flame. Believing in spirit guidance, I took this as a sign that Stuart Island was *not* the right choice.

Our rental house was about to be sold and I still hadn't found a home. But when friends suggested that we travel with them to Mexico I decided to push our problems aside and go. This was our first time traveling south of the border. We rode the train about a thousand miles down the west coast, drinking in the beauty of the land and its people. We hitched rides from the train station toward the village of San Blas. At a palm-lined beach on the Sea of Cortez, we tossed our packs into the edge of the jungle and spent the entire day in the water. Having only ever experienced the frigid waters of Washington, we were in a state of bliss.

I had never known the sea to be such a caress. We could not force ourselves out of the waves until near sundown.

When we finally went to retrieve our backpacks, we found they had been stolen, along with our money. This was our first day and suddenly we had nothing but the clothing we had taken off to go in the water.

We sat in the sand with rays of the sinking sun intensifying the red burns on our virgin skin. I shook my head, slipping from disbelief to anger.

"How could someone do that, even taking *children's* packs?"

Almost as soon as I spoke these words, I realized we would be okay. We were not going to die by the roadside simply because we had nothing. We would get along. Suddenly I felt light and free, unburdened by backpacks and changes of clothing. However I still would need to hitch to the city of Tepic to make a long-distance call back home to see about a loan.

The next day, my kids stayed with my friends and I hitched a ride to the city to make the call. When the operator finally patched me through, I listened in disbelief again as the voice on the other end of the line told me that our house had burned to the ground, my dog was dead, and our belongings were nothing more than a pile of ash. A violent wind storm had sent a power surge through the ancient wires of our farmhouse. Witnesses claimed the entire three-story house had fallen over and collapsed in twenty minutes. The young man I had left to care-take the house and animals had narrowly escaped with his life, saving only his fiddle.

Once again, after disbelief came anger. As if being a single parent were not difficult enough, now, everything we owned was destroyed, including generations of photographs and films for which I had been the family's keeper. We had not one stick of furniture or item of clothing besides what was on our backs. Bringing the sad news back to my kids was difficult, but together we progressed through the identical series of thoughts we'd had just the day before. We realized that we probably would not have survived the midnight house fire and were therefore lucky to be alive. We were survivors, and about as free of worldly encumbrances as any pilgrim or pauper. My traveling companions in Mexico helped us out with cash so that we could finish our month-long tropical camp-out.

On our return, we stayed with friends. I worked on their farm until I made some money and re-collected the bare necessities to set up a home.

Now more than ever, I was drawn to those islands I had never set foot on, and managed to wrangle a $50 rental on Lopez Island. The one possession not destroyed by the fire was my old 1965 Ford pickup. The taillights were melted out and the paint was scorched on one side but she still purred like a kitten. My two horses had been pastured next to the house, and they had also survived. With a rental horse trailer and small assortment of household goods we were finally able to make it to our new home.

Lopez Island was one of those jewels held in the sea I had first spied as a girl. And even though we seemed to have been pushed aggressively by Forces Unseen towards this home, it felt like we had made the perfect touchdown landing from that flight of my childhood.

It was here on Lopez, for the first time, that I connected with the salty, kelp-forested waters of the sea in an intimate way. My children and I passed many hours of our youth (for I, too, was still young) at the tide's edge, with the waters rhythmically lapping and frothing. It was gentle, like foreplay, nothing bold, nothing dangerous. It was just a love affair maturing, with so many secrets yet to learn.

Here my third child was born in our cabin home. One season, while picking apples in eastern Washington to earn money, I fell in love again, with a Brazilian man. Together we hatched a plan to fly with my two children, Summer and Cody, to northern Brazil. We would buy a horse and cart and drive it down the coast to his family home in Sao Paulo. In the heat of our beautiful dream I had called out to the universe for another child to come to me, even if it did not seem rational. Though we got as far as Florida, we found we were short of the funds for our flight to Brazil and it was not easy to find work. We ended up flying back to Washington. There our travel dream faded away, but by that time stirrings of my dream baby were coming to life and my Brazilian lover had returned to his home.

We lived on our lovely island surrounded by gentle people of like mind, sharing good music, food, dance and ritual. We sang songs in celebration of the Earth and Sea, of the Sky and Fire. We watched the moon have her way with the tides. We dove into the icy sea after the searing heat of sweat baths. As a community surrounded on all sides by water, we experimented, at first timidly in small boats, hugging the shore with our babies, landing for picnics and small excursions. As we began to learn the currents and winds, we wandered further. We would travel in flotillas of gypsy revelers to May Day celebrations on distant islands. I was gathering and bringing back to the surface of my consciousness that ancient collective knowledge of my water-navigating ancestors and honing the skills necessary to carry me on my future journey.

I also initiated myself with a solo spirit quest. In the late 1980s, I paddled to a small uninhabited island where I spent three days fasting, drinking only water. My hope was to cleanse and purify my mind and body enough that I might make contact with my very own spirit helper. There are many tangible and ethereal gifts that come to one who intentionally goes to spend time alone in nature, but to actually be blessed with a spirit guide is not a certain thing. However, I was lucky enough to be granted this most magical experience, on my second evening.

I sat beside the fire. Stars lit the sky and sea, and trees stood behind me in black jagged silhouettes. At last I raked sand over the coals to make a warm bed to lie on. I woke from a light sleep to slithering, slinking forms, bumbling from the tide's soft edge. Playing by starlight on the beach right at my feet, nine otters! Like dark, glistening serpent spirit-dancers of an aquatic dream, they intertwined like Celtic knots on the starlit beach. Then, disentangling, they slipped one by one back into their mysterious, cold, wet world.

My spirit animal had come to me. I had acquired a new power for my sea travels: the slick, playful and buoyant River Otter. At home in both fresh and saltwater, this animal was considered sacred by the Shamans of my native ancestors and was never killed, unlike its larger cousin the Sea Otter. It would still be eight years before I would be ready for my solo paddle, yet when that time arrived, I would have this source of strength to draw on.

In the time between, Gregg, an island resident and friend, was the first man to come into my life who seemed not to be challenged by loving me and all three of my children. Initially, I was not as interested in him as he seemed in me. He was more than ten years older than I was, for one thing, and for another, he and his former wife were an institution in the island community. I wanted no part in causing something that iconic to crumble, but there he stood one day at my door, with his pillow, of all things, in hand. At least it wasn't a teddy bear! Who can say what drives a person away from a marriage? In my youthful three-year marriage it had been alcoholism, but in some cases love just dies inexplicably. Like a beautiful bird, stopped dead by a transparent window, nothing can revive it.

Gregg, it is said by some, is a true Renaissance man. He had made a name early for himself as a designer and maker of mountaineering equipment in Boulder, Colorado, and then was expedition leader on the first winter summit of Alaska's Mount McKinley in 1967. Later he and his wife, Edi, traveled and lived aboard their sailboat, and in the late 60's they bought twenty acres on Lopez Island, where they homesteaded, and raised two children while he developed a business making carving tools. I had to agree there was little this man could not undertake with success. Most attractive to me was his rebel spirit and love of the outdoors. So, on that day as he stood there with pillow in hand, I made the choice to let him into my house and my heart, and have never regretted it.

My children light-heartedly referred to Gregg as their "father figure." My third child, Raven, was five years old when Gregg came along, and had never known his father. Gregg embraced them each as his own.

He also introduced me to the full-on wilds of the West Coast. Paddling off the coast of Vancouver Island with the force of the open Pacific meeting my kayak served as my first truly exhilarating love affair with a wild man and the wild sea. These journeys whetted my appetite for more fish, more bear, more cougar, more wolves and more wilderness. My true happiness was in the wild. I also felt nostalgia for the indigenous people of the coast as we paddled into abandoned and even prehistoric village sites. These were my people! But where were they now? They seemed to have been erased from their homelands. They had not just *visited* these wild far flung areas, they had *lived* here. They were comfortable in this environment and so was I.

More and more, these experiences on the coast brought back childhood memories and raised long-held questions about my family. I remembered my father flying off to Alaska in his two-seat Luscombe airplane to find summer work. He returned months later with gifts of beaded, fur-trimmed moccasins that smelled of wood smoke and told stories of Alaskan relatives I had never met. There were also secrets he hadn't told. A mysterious grandfather existed, mentioned only in hushed tones amongst the adults. It had been clear to me that Alaska held excitement and mystery. It had also been clear that my dad was the one who got to have the adventures while mom stayed home and cared for six children. As a young girl, this inequality had never sat well with me.

As a mother myself, I had no problem with domesticity. I thought of motherhood as a sacred act. I'd raised my three children and had spent half of those twenty-two years as a single parent. But by the time I'd fledged my two older children, I realized that perhaps I could allow myself an extended adventure. The waters surrounding me were my obvious route to adventure. No need for a jet or a car to take me to some far flung corner of the world. Here from this island, the sea could be my highway. Alaska now tugged on me like the gravitational pull of the moon. It had pulled my father to fly there but *I could paddle!*

The paddle filled my daydreams. Still, I kept the idea to myself. Raven was only thirteen, and would be most affected by my absence, but he shared a close and loving relationship with Gregg. I knew they would be okay for a couple of months on their own.

Then, one day as I worked in the flower fields for my friend Susan, I was visited by a pure white hummingbird. My father had died not long before, and I understood this bird immediately to be his spirit, coming to tell me he would watch over me on my solo adventure. It made perfect sense that he would come in the form of a bird, especially one as agile and acrobatic as a hummingbird, because his playful flights had been so much like that bird.

When I told Gregg about the visitation by the amazing albino hummingbird, I also confessed my desire to do a solo paddle from Alaska back to Lopez. He just nodded politely. No comment. I wondered what he'd do if I told him I wanted to become a nun? Just nod and make no comment? Did he think I was too crazy to even warrant a response? Later he told me that he did believe me from the start but was afraid to encourage me because of the inherent danger. In the next few months, as I began to make plans and found sponsors to help pay for a kayak and gear, he saw that my heart was set and backed me 100%.

Although I had done no real conditioning for my paddle, I had worked in my large garden: tilling, hoeing, planting, weeding, (repeat repeat), until by the time I was ready to leave home, it was meticulously clean and growing nicely. This work had my arms and back in shape, but I had not been in my boat since the summer before and had never really practiced the roll maneuver. It was my philosophy that in a fully loaded boat, with seas rough enough to turn me over, it would be near impossible to right myself by performing a roll. I did have means of attaching flotation to my paddles for aiding a re-entry and felt confident in using them. In all ways, I felt as ready as I would ever be.

Finally, in June at the age of forty and surrounded by my three children, my partner and the tribe-like community of Lopez, I was ready to jump into my solo endeavor.

Our friend Patrick, setting off for another season of fishing in southeast Alaska, had kindly offered to give me and my kayak a lift on his salmon seiner, the *Saint Janet*. My daughter Summer Moon asked if she might come along for that part of the adventure.

Patrick, having known Summer since she was a wee girl, sweetly obliged.

Gregg invited family and friends to bid us farewell. He held me tight, giving me the confidence of his love and strength. He pressed an envelope into my hands just before I boarded, with instructions not to read it until the first night of my paddle. As we pulled away from the dock, with loved ones waving and blowing kisses, I was glad to have Summer's shoulder to cry on. They'd sent me on my way with prayers, gifts and talismans. One gift was a poem:

Lowly faithful, banish fear
Right onward, paddle unharmed
The Port, well-worth the cruise, is near
And every wave is charmed.
—RALPH WALDO EMERSON

✦

At 4:00 the next morning I woke in my bunk to a violent pitching and rolling. If the *Saint Janet* was going down, I wanted to be up top, so I climbed to the wheelhouse. A "May Day!" was coming over the VHF, and for the next hours we listened as the drama unfolded in Semour Narrows. The boat in distress, the *Courageous*, had overturned. We must have passed it in the dim light before dawn, even as its surviving crew of five still clung to the hull. A sixth, we heard, was hopelessly trapped inside.

It was a grave reminder of the seriousness of these waterways. If the tide rips and notorious *williwas* could do that to a commercial fishing vessel, what, I wondered, could they do to my kayak?

Patrick and the crew of his boat were all lovely fellows, generous and kind. Sam, the cook, kept plying me with high calorie gourmet meals. Each time he handed me a plate of beautiful food he said, "This will be your last—for months. Eat!" And so I indulged, worrying all the while whether I'd fit into my kayak when the moment came to depart.

As we motored northwest, I watched the coastline, making mental notes about what I saw. My general sense was, "I can do

Gregg and I just before I departed from Lopez for my journey.

Getting some kayaking experience on the West coast of Vancouver Island, before my solo.

this," but it was only based on gut feeling. I'd gathered a random collection of charts from different mariner friends, but their scale didn't offer much detail and I knew that, for the most part, they were inadequate for kayaking. I'd be navigating by the seat of my pants and without any means of communication.

We pulled into Ketchikan at 8:00 A.M. in a spitting, wind-driven rain. It was blowing from the south. This was not how I was hoping to begin my journey, but it also didn't surprise me much.

Patrick, being protective, offered to stay the night so that I could get an early start the next morning, when the weather would be better. He needed to work on the boat anyway, he assured me, before they shoved off for Petersburg.

With time to kill, we thought we'd run around Ketchikan. This small town, normally sleepy and slow in other seasons, was transformed at the start of summer into something close to madness. The cruise ships, like floating skyscrapers, lay docked along the waterfront streets. Tourists from all over the world had streamed out of these behemoths and now choked the sidewalks and souvenir shops. Float planes roared in and out. Smaller boats of all kinds scuttled and maneuvered around one another, and an endless flow of car traffic made crossing the street nearly impossible. Ketchikan was a zoo!

That evening, we gathered at the Sea Breeze Diner, and our dinners had just arrived when we got word that the *Saint Janet* had been rammed, accidentally by another fishing boat. The boat had been motoring in to tie up alongside when something went wrong and it T-boned her instead. The damage was bad enough that Patrick would have to set out straight away for Petersburg, where repair work could be done. Suddenly, instead of a sweet little morning send-off, I was to be dumped at night on a pier at the edge of town.

The pier was actually a pre-arranged location near the water-side home of one of Gregg's customers, a woman by the name of Sy Painter. The crew felt as bad about ditching me as I did to be so suddenly severed from their hospitality. Summer felt the worst. She offered to stay behind. I felt especially blessed by her love and support. With light in her eyes and a powerful spirit of her own, she offered me great strength and a sense of well-being just from her presence.

The Old Ones, those ancestors, really came through in her. She'd been born with black hair and bruise-like splotches down her back. My doctor had called this the "Mongolian Mark" which people of native blood often have, especially in infancy. All through her childhood, I'd been humbled by her goodness and wisdom, her tenderness and sensitivity to living things. As a three year old with me in the greenhouse, she'd once asked with great concern, "How do these plants live without wind?"

In so many ways, I could not imagine my life without her, and now as she stood there on the pier hugging and kissing me good-bye, I knew she was a direct conduit to the ancestor spirits whose guidance I would be calling on. Her pureness and her prayers were imbued with a great power that I knew would help carry me along the way. But as much as I loved her, I now insisted. She should go on with the *Saint Janet* as she'd planned.

Saint Janet pulled away with her rigging lights flashing a farewell with all hands on deck waving until they disappeared into the inky blackness. Sy was not home, so I bedded down next to my gear under her covered deck and fell quickly to sleep.

The morning was damp and heavy. Sy had returned, and insisted on making me a fruit smoothie. She was very hospitable and helpful as I prepared to launch. She sensed my eagerness and didn't keep me long, but snapped a few photos as she gave my boat a shove and sent me gliding out onto the stippled surface of the morning water.

After my first few strokes out into the channel, I stopped to look behind. On the Ketchikan skyline loomed the enormous sky-scraping cruise ships. They seemed such beasts of human creation. They represented everything I wished to escape. As I looked ahead toward the gray mist-enshrouded channel, I had no idea what encounters might lie ahead, but there a salmon jumped and splashed on the surface of the water. I chose the way of the salmon and paddled off.

On this first day, my plan was to take it easy. I felt reasonably strong and confident, but after the excitement and distractions of the past few days, I needed to find my center. As essential as my kayak was for carrying me on my journey, so too was my need to be clear and focused. An early camp would allow me to unscramble. A south wind strengthened and stung my face and made my decision even easier.

I had never set eyes on this coast from the perspective of a paddler. The unknown was around every curve and headland. I could paddle close enough to touch the mussel-encrusted rocks and smell the earthy aroma wafting from the virgin stands of evergreens. Fern fronds and berry vines dripping with rain hung close to the water's edge. Charts, for all their usefulness, cannot even hint at this beauty. They also couldn't inform me of the steepness of the coastal terrain through which an abundance of crashing creeks spilled into the sea. I saw that it would almost be possible to fill my water bottle without getting out of my kayak. I was relieved to find drinking water so abundant, since I could only carry small amounts in my boat, but it seemed as though finding a place to camp might be difficult. What looked on the chart like a promising indent or cove could turn out to be as steep sided as a bathtub, with no means of coming ashore. Soon, islands within the short range I was looking for would run out, and then there would be a wide channel to cross. I reluctantly decided to choose the final cove available on a gumdrop-shaped island.

The beach was small and strewn with creosote logs. I found a rusty cable anchored securely to the beach and tied my boat to it. As I looked for a place to pitch my tent, I saw the only flat ground available was well above the pebble beach in a dry, high-tide salt marsh. Because the solstice tides are extreme and because Alaskan tides are some of the biggest in the world, I knew that even this site was endangered. I would just have to hope for the best.

This was not the homiest of places for my first camp, but it did have its charms. As I unpacked my duffels and found my dinner, a beautiful hummingbird buzzed down by me and then perched on a cedar branch above, watching me as I ate the care-package meal given to me by the fishing crew. "Thanks for checking on me Dad," I said, remembering the white hummingbird on Lopez Island. He buzzed around me before darting away and I laughed, comforted by his playful presence. While I finished eating I opened the letter Gregg had given me on my departure. His loving words moved me.

> *Irene my queen. You are my soul mate and the love of my life and I can't wait to have you back in my arms. There is no one for me but you so please paddle safe. . .*

✦

I was so thankful for him and his unfailing love and support. I knew he understood my need for this adventure, having been an expedition leader himself. A team member had died on the Denali ascent, so he also knew how things could go terribly wrong. I tucked his letter into my new journal for safekeeping. Now, with the important elements of both the spirit world and this letter, I felt embraced and grounded, ready for my journey. Only a long solid sleep could make things more perfect, and it was just mid-afternoon when I crawled into my sleeping bag and dozed off.

I awoke to the tide surging under my tent. It seemed luck was *not* on my side. Peering out, I saw the water's reflection right at my door. One of my waterproof duffels and a pair of my sandals were just starting to float away. I tried to assess the time. It looked to me like the soft light of dawn. The solution to the problem at hand seemed simple: pack up and leave. After all, by the time I was ready to leave the beach, it would be completely light. As I scurried around packing up, I had the sinking realization that in fact I had awakened to twilight, not dawn. I'd been so sure that it was morning that I'd never bothered to look at my watch. Now I pulled it out of my duffle. It was 10:45 at night!

I walked to the kayak and, to my dismay, saw my next problem. The cable I found so convenient on the beach and had cleverly tied my boat to now stretched my bowline straight into the depths. My lessons were coming in rapid succession! I waded out to grab my bow but when I tugged on the line it did not budge. I had no choice but to strip and go under the dark, icy water to untie my knot.

By the time I dried off, packed my kayak and left the beach, it was totally dark, under a thick cloud cover. At this point I didn't care. The conditions were calm now, and it wasn't raining, and I could vaguely discern the silhouettes of the distant hills and islands. It would be such a relief to be off shore away from the menacing tide.

My spirits were oddly buoyant, setting off into the peace of a midnight paddle. As I crossed a two-mile inlet, lime-green phosphorescence burst with each stroke and peeled in ribbons from the kayak's hull. This aquatic light show seemed a manifestation of my spirit guides, comforting and other-worldly through my night flight to a more hospitable shore. Sunrise would be at 3:00 A.M., on this short Alaskan night. I reached the other side of the inlet and paddled on for another hour or more, until at last I tied my bow line to an overhanging tree limb to wait until it was light enough to find a morning camp. As I sat bobbing in my kayak, the rain began to fall. I pulled out my poncho and tried to nap until sunrise.

My next camp had all the amenities: a sandy beach, a high berm, firewood, and shelter from the southerly wind that had started up again. I pitched my tent in a steady rain and at last peeled off my soggy clothes and crawled into the sleeping bag to get warm. From my snug tent, I could hear my little spirit-guide hummingbird buzz back and forth to let me know he was there.

When the rains let up, I crawled from my tent and looked at my saturated surroundings. I decided half-heartedly to start a fire. Split cedar sticks and shavings were usually all I needed, but now that I was in a part of Alaska that got twelve annual feet of rain, lighting a successful fire seemed less like a sure thing. Because of that, I'd bought some paraffin fire-starting sticks in Ketchikan. The wood on this beach was so soggy, I doubted that even these would be enough, and was surprised how quickly I had a peppy fire to cook my first hot meal and a cup of tea. I kept the fire burning hot and hung my wet clothes on sticks to dry.

Looking out on the dark green little cove, it seemed like it could be a good fishing hole. This would be a chance to try the new rod that I carried on top of my kayak. I had a trusty lure, a *Buzz Bomb*, attached and ready to go. I paddled about thirty strokes from shore and dropped the line into the emerald depths. It hadn't even hit bottom when I had a fish on. The tug and fight on the line told me this fish was not too small. I reeled in a black and frisky rock cod, thanked it, and gave it a hit with a stick before carefully placing the spiny fish on the deck between my legs. Each time I sent the line down, a fish was on the hook before it hit bottom. They were as plentiful as the rain, it seemed. It was hard to want to stop but finally, I kept the two largest ones and returned to my fire for my first wild-caught meal. The juicy white fillets sizzled in the pan with fresh garlic, a pot of rice steamed away, and I was nearly swooning with hunger.

I woke the next morning feeling well rested and ready to begin my paddling in earnest. I was off the beach a couple of hours after sunrise, happy to "make tracks" before the southerly winds kicked back up.

My route took me across the wide maw of Behm Canal, a stretch open to the outside waters of Dixon Entrance. Half of the day's paddle was spent in this crossing, which could have been hellish, but soon the winds died and the water turned as calm as a mill pond. Nevertheless, my still-acclimating body was sore by the time I pulled into a white-sand crescent beach just north of Foggy Bay. As I stepped from the kayak, the sun burst out in a cheery welcome, so I stripped off my clothes and allowed the rays to warm my stiff muscles as I unpacked and began to make dinner.

I was cooking my fish when to my disbelief a helicopter appeared in the sky, heading straight for the beach I was on. I rushed for my clothes as it dropped out of the sky and landed just a hundred yards down the beach! I tried to ignore my fellow visitors, and went on cooking. I never could ascertain the reason for their stop. Soon they were gone but I laughed about the irony of thinking I'd finally escaped civilization and was *really* in the wilds!

The next morning dawned clear and serene, and I was on the water early. I paddled along the shore and across a wide body of water. Then, when a slight NW wind rose behind me, I decided to sail. I had an inverted triangular sail with tethers that attached to either side of my paddle. So all I needed to do was hold the paddle and spill-off extra wind or adjust for direction by turning the sail to the degree that I was able. This had limited applications but was a fun break from paddling. It was my first try at sailing on the journey, and I found it relaxing after the exertion of the crossing. At first the going was slow but then the wind picked up enough to move me right across the bay to Foggy Point. It was late morning when I reached the other side and went ashore for a snack. Because I was well rested from sailing, I decided to head back out. Now the gill netters were out in full force, fishing from Foggy Point all the way down to the Alaskan-Canadian border.

I found the glut of fishing vessels very interesting. Earlier in the summer when I was planning my trip, my friend Bob Lyon, who'd done a solo paddle around Vancouver Island, told me about a psychic he'd consulted before his voyage. Her name was Laurie McQuary and she came highly recommended. Since she lived in Idaho, I assumed she was unfamiliar with the Northwest coast, so I'd been a little skeptical about her ability to divine my route with any degree of accuracy. However, if *I* would travel on faith that my ancestor spirits were with me, why not put merit in a psychic's skills? I sent my itinerary by mail and she returned it marked with comments that I had, in some cases, questioned as I read. Her first warning along my route was here at Foggy Point. She wrote I would have some sort of "interference or slight inconvenience with heavy boat traffic." How, I thought, could I have "heavy boat traffic" in the middle of nowhere? But sure enough, her predictions were accurate. Gill netters with cork lines stretched out, made it impossible to not paddle right over their gear. As she had noted, it really was not much of an inconvenience. But it certainly encouraged me to take her other predictions seriously.

Far from being a problem, really, the fishermen hailed me with well-wishes as I paddled by, and when I stopped to talk to one he offered to let me use his marine radio to put a call through to Gregg back on Lopez. I went aboard and soon an operator had me patched through, loud and clear to Gregg and my son Raven. What a joy it was to talk to them! It had been eight days since I'd left Lopez, but it felt like so much more. Not only did I feel triumphant at having spoken to my family, but the kind fisherman gave me a pair of sunglasses too, which I happily received, since mine had sunk to the sea floor earlier in the day. And to top it all off, he sent me away with a gorgeous slab of fresh caught king salmon.

After many heartfelt thanks I paddled another five miles in choppy water and ducked into a last-chance sort of cove with a wonderful shell beach covered with deer and cougar tracks. The water of the cove was a brilliant blue-green. In this lovely setting I made a feast of my salmon fillet. A logger would have been hard-pressed to eat as much as I did that night, but, then again, I had traveled about fifteen miles that day. It was fun to relax on the beach and watch the deer come check me out. When they first jumped down from the edge of the woods onto their beach and saw me they were shocked and perplexed. Slowly they came closer and closer, sniffing my fire and trying to figure out who or what I was. They ran a little way off and then circled back a couple of times. I hoped they were as entertained by me as I was by them.

The next day the water was calm in the morning and the weather radio predicted winds again out of the NW, so I didn't hurry off the beach. I left Laketa Point at 7:00 A.M. and headed for Cape Fox, paddling the first hour and sailing the next. I was absolutely flying along the shore, maybe going five knots or better, when the wind died at the tip of the cape. I paddled most of the four miles across Nakat Inlet and was then able to put my sail back up and blast the last mile to the nearest island. I rested and ate lunch there and found my first wild salmonberries. I was tempted to stay at this nice beach but decided to move on so that I could be poised and ready to cross the open waters of Dixon Entrance. I had five more miles to paddle before reaching that jump-off point. Along the way some guys on a fish-buying boat told me where I could replenish my water supply at a pair of floating docks. I could paddle right up to the fresh water spigot! The floats were in the middle of a narrow channel between two small islands.

I soon found them, and filled my water containers for the first time on the paddle. It was easier here than if I was filling them at home with the hand pump at my kitchen sink. It seemed wrong somehow to be turning on a faucet in the middle of a saltwater channel, but I wasn't complaining.

I'd traveled about twenty miles that day and my body was spent. As I paddled through big swells and whitecaps, searching the coastline in vain for an evening camp, I began to regret leaving the lunch beach. I had no choice but to keep the faith and push on.

And then, there it was! Thank you spirits! So sweet to behold, a small sandy slot beach with lots of firewood and a great view of my next morning's crossing to the Tsimpsean Peninsula. From my camp I could contemplate the fifteen-mile stretch of potentially treacherous waters. I was told that some of the largest known "sea spouts" happen here. This phenomenon is like a small hurricane that forms strongly enough to suck a column of water into the sky, but from my tiny beach it looked calm. I would have to see what the morning brought.

That night I had a dream. I was flying, soaring just over the tree-tops. I was able to do this by simply bounding upwards. I often had flying dreams, but this time the reason I took off above the trees was to escape some very evil force. The "force" appeared as a sort of wild energy, throwing off intense light and moving at super-human speed through the woods below me. Finally I realized that I had to come down and confront the energy because it was about to harm someone innocent.

I tossed in my tent and awoke wondering: were my ancestors

trying to communicate a looming danger? Unfortunately the dream had begun to blur right away. I couldn't remember more details, and I fell back to sleep.

✦

I left the beach bright and early. The weather was so calm that any dreams of danger seemed unfounded. I'd considered the safer option of heading northeast to Wales Island, but now that longer route seemed unnecessary. I would paddle a straight track across to Port Simpson. The water was perfectly still. Dixon Entrance and Chatham Sound must seldom see such serenity as that morning. Other than the actual miles to put behind me, I had the luxury to let my mind wander.

As I paddled that day, leaving my dad's beloved Alaska behind, I found myself thinking about him again. His father, Don Petroleum Barrett Sr., was an alcoholic, and had abandoned him and his brother when they were boys. As a young man, my father had gone searching for him in Alaska, expecting little, but still was not prepared for the wreck of a man he found. This perhaps gave him some closure about his Native father, but it hadn't ended his infatuation with this wild northern land.

Aside from the annual flights north in his small plane to find work, my father had also once attempted to reach Alaska by boat from our home in Snohomish. One summer when my younger brother was about ten or eleven, my dad hatched a crazy plan. He loaded his aluminum skiff to the gunnels with supplies, and, with almost no room left for the two of them, he set off down the Snohomish River. My mom and I had innocently waved them off, thinking how pleasant and uncomplicated our summer would be. They motored that day until they got to Everett, where the river spilled into the turbulent Puget Sound. Dad took one look at the big sea and his small, over-loaded boat, and turned back.

At the age of 70 he had been diagnosed with asbestos-related lung cancer. The doctors believed he had one year to live, but in fact he lived for three more good years. Not long before he passed away, I visited, where he lived at that time, in Eastern Washington at my sister's home. In this final year of life, he'd decided to learn to play the accordion, of all things! I found him in his bed, his body diminished and wracked by cancer. At some point, to make conversation, I asked if he had learned to play anything on the accordion. He said he'd learned one song. He leaned toward the bed stand where it sat and dragged the heavy instrument across the bed. He labored to get his arms through the straps and positioned to play. Then, to my surprise, he played a lovely unfaltering rendition of *Irene Good Night*, the song he and mom had sung to me so many times when they had tucked me into bed at night.

As I sat on the edge of his bed sobbing from his beautiful gift to me of this song, I realized that even though he was so near death, he was also still very alive. Since I had to end my visit to travel the 200 miles back home, that was my parting and final sweet memory of him.

Now, as I was leaving Alaska behind, I thought of all the reasons he loved this land. I thought of the Irish ancestors and my Tlingit Native great-grandmother Ann Andrusha, who had no doubt imbued both my father and myself with strength, courage and passion. My dad seemed to be branded from birth with these traits. I had also sensed an underlying melancholy. Something drove him forward while also something impeded him. I had heard so many stories of his forebears. How had those from the past formed him and what mark had the generations left on me?

On this long and tranquil paddle, as if held in suspended animation, with the spirits gently tugging, my paternal past came to me.

My Father

And I thought over again
My small adventures
As with a shore-wind I drifted out
In my kayak
And thought I was in danger,

My fears,
Those small ones
That I thought so big
For all the vital things
I had to get and reach.

And yet there is only
One great thing,
The only thing:
To live to see in huts and on journeys
The great day that dawns,
And the light that fills the world.

—INUIT SONG

I IMAGINE THE LAND STILL LOCKED in the talons of glaciers, with not a breath of a human. The great Trickster Raven whirled in the dark cosmos of a sky yet without sun. Only because of Raven's loneliness and selfish nature did my earliest ancestors appear at all, for without humans, who could Raven play tricks on? So I was told that Raven, having already created all land formations, created humans as well.

However, light still did not exist for those *Taat Kwaani* People of the Dark. They lived in the hellish realm, dank and dreary. Seeing their misery, Raven took pity and through trickery, stole the sun from its keeper and thrust it into the sky, bringing light and warmth. Still deeply suspicious of the powerful magic that had so recently given breath to them, the First People struggled in small bands, praying and seeking protection from all of the natural forces around them. A glacier could swallow them, waves could drag them under, bears could devour them. These were not easy times. They were new, and had only their intuition to guide them. Perhaps they could sense a more comfortable existence to the south-east. Slowly, slowly, the persistent warmth of the sun caused the ice to recede and the determined people began to make their homes in villages along the shores.

Generations slowly unfolded and still, in 1890, the village of Katalla appeared as only a tiny cluster of human dwellings set against the primeval grandeur of the Alaskan wilderness. The vast delta of the Copper River spread out to the northwest. To the southeast, beyond the protective arm of Oklee Spit, the coast continued for hundreds of miles. In front of their clan houses, the mercurial sea stretched to the horizon. This was *Lingít aaní'* "land of human beings," belonging to these, the northernmost Tlingit.

The Trickster Raven still filled the gray Katalla mornings with his guttural taunting and reprimands. One early morning, not long after he had pulled Ann Andrusha from her sleep, she slipped out of the house before her mother could ask her to take her little brother.

She'd been waiting for this chance. Walking briskly past the rows of tents where the white men still slept, Ann had only one wild propelling purpose in mind. It gave her butterflies to imagine that she was actually going to do what she'd only daydreamed about for so long.

Out there on Strawberry Point grew the 'love' flower, a powerful *Wooch sixáni náakw* or 'dope,' as her mother called it. She had personally witnessed the effect of the Starflower when her uncle had used it to win Nellie Goodlataw. The Starflower had cast its spell. Auntie Nellie and Ann's uncle had been together many years now and had four children.

Strawberry Point was two miles away. And though she often went out with other women to berry-pick or collect wild rhubarb or greens, almost no young woman would run off that far down the coast alone. But even though it was bear country, Ann didn't feel particularly reckless. She took comfort in the common-sense ways passed on to her by the older women for convincing bears to leave them be. The simple act of lifting the shirt to reveal their breasts would show the bear that they were only women collecting food, and posed no threat. Ann would do the same if needed; her breasts were surely big enough for a bear to notice.

On the point, thick tangles of strawberry plants were blooming, but Ann stepped through them. She was here to collect this far more important thing. The Starflower also had a delicate white blossom but was easy to distinguish from the strawberry flower. Her eyes fell on a plant that seemed to radiate light. It might indicate strong medicine, or maybe it was just that the clouds had parted ever so briefly. Ann knelt and offered a brief but heartfelt prayer before digging gently around the base of the plant. She broke the stem away and shook the soil free from the roots and poked them into her pocket, and almost as an afterthought, stuck the small flower behind her ear. She repeated this three more times. Then, with the first step in her bold scheme accomplished, she hurried back to the village.

It felt like mid-day as she reached the beach in front of Katalla. She picked up as much beach wood as she could carry, hoping that an armload of firewood might hide her long absence. She was glad to find William Henderson, the visiting Reverend from Yakutat, deep in conversation with her mother over a cup of tea. She picked up Little John, bouncing him on her narrow hip, and sang his favorite song, about the beaver.

Who will stop the building of the den?
But they built it just the same.
That's why all my uncles died
And left me alone
Because there was no one there to warn them
They are just as much to blame as the river
And the people who destroyed their den.

Ann saw the Reverend's disapproving look. She knew he would much prefer a Bible song, but this man did not intimidate her. She repeated the song to her brother's delight. Her mother, on the other hand, always seemed under his spell. It disturbed Ann that she was seriously considering sending Little John off to a mission school in Yakutat. This wasn't the first visit he'd made to persuade her. He paid visits to all the homes, tempting the mothers with his promises of education, nice clothes and meals; but Ann had already lost two younger siblings to diphtheria and whooping cough, and couldn't bear the thought of Little John being sent away. She squeezed him close and Little John reached up and pulled the flower from behind her ear. She'd forgotten it. He dropped it to the floor. Ann was fast, but not fast enough to snatch it up before her mother noticed. She knew her mother would wait to ask her until the Reverend was gone.

Ann stood Little John near a bucket of halibut fillets that her father had set in the kitchen and went out into the salty freshness of the day. At the clothesline, she tugged at the hem of her old blue calico dress. The fabric was so old and thin that it was easy enough to tear a piece from the tattered hem. She stuffed the cloth into her pocket and hoped her mother wouldn't notice.

Down at the beach, her uncle and father were working on a new canoe. Ann had grown up paddling with her family to and from the trading post on Little Kayak Island and to their clam-digging beds and berry-picking places. She was as comfortable on the water as she was on land. She even had her own small canoe. Today they had filled the new canoe with water and were adding hot rocks. The rocks made steam, and the men wedged in crosspieces that slowly splayed the softened wood into graceful lines.

"Don't just stand there little *Daguntu-tla*, help grab the edge of the canvas and put a lid on this." Ann could hardly see her uncle and father for the thick cloud of steam that surrounded them. Between the three of them they covered the canoe hull over to let it steam. *Daguntu-tla,*—Poor Little Rich Girl—is what her father liked to call her to tease her about how easy her life was.

"Don'tchya got some chores you oughta be doing for mother up at the house?"

"She's busy with the Reverend. She wants me to paddle out to the Commercial Company for some coffee and spruce pitch gum." It wasn't in her nature to lie, but today she needed to. "*Káak,*" she called her mother's brother, "Please come help push my boat in?" He looked at her skeptically and then out across the water to Kayak Island. Kaak had always been more of the authority in her life than her father and ultimately, he could forbid her to paddle. "The water's calm," he said, "but it's late to be goin' out."

Ann assured her uncle that she was planning to camp out on the nearer island, Kanak, to break the distance, and that she'd spend a night there on her return to Katalla as well.

"Still, don't waste no time out there. Get back before weather changes." He asked if she had provisions, and when she said no, he gave her some dried salmon flakes, wrapped in a handkerchief.

Then with a shove, he sent the canoe gliding out. The swift and sudden release from solid land to the slick water was, Ann imagined, like a fall from a cliff just before discovering she could fly. The fear she felt as she dove into the unknown of her quest instantly transformed into a freedom flight of confidence. She paddled like a fledgling that had just discovered the joy and power of its own beating wings.

Little Kayak Island seemed to float in the distance on the still water, and Big Kayak Island loomed beyond. Ann had the tide with her. A curious harbor seal followed in her wake, popping up every so often, its round wet eyes keeping watch over her journey. She traversed the shore of Katalla Bay past Strawberry Point, then crossed the channel to the western end of Kanak Island. Controller Bay was shallow and could easily whip into white caps, but today it was flat, the glassy water reflecting the low white clouds standing bright against the dark steel sky.

Ann paddled easily, losing herself in her plan. Surely, there would be activity at the Post. Perhaps the Swede brothers had arrived with new trade goods from Sitka. It was always exciting to see the shelves stocked with new supplies. But what she really wanted was to see and speak to the man who ran the post, a tall gray-eyed Irishman, George Barrett.

Ann had seen this man since she was about eight years old. She came with her family to trade her mother's beautifully woven baskets and her father's beaver pelts for tea, sugar, tobacco, cloth and other supplies. He was the first white man to stay in their area, but to Ann he was nothing like the crude, wild-eyed land-grabbers who had arrived in Katalla since.

How different he seemed. She remembered a desperate paddle with her parents out to the Post; her weak and fevered younger sister lay wrapped in a blanket in the bottom of the canoe. Colonel George had consulted his medical books and gently administered to her sister. His remedy hadn't saved her, and she'd died the following week, but Ann remembered the true sorrow in his eyes when he heard the news.

Colonel George was not the very first white man to appear on their coast. She'd heard stories about those who had appeared on ships generations earlier, the *Gus'k'iyee Kwáan*—Horizon People—Russians, who valued otter pelts more than gold. They'd enslaved the Tlingit and forced them to scour the sea for pelts. A Russian slaver, Andrusha, had passed his name to Ann's grand-fathers and grand-uncles as proof these men were his property. Now both the hated Russians and the sea otter were gone, but her name was from that difficult time. Ann was thankful that George was a *Gus'k'iyee Kwáan* that she *and* her parents admired.

At last she pulled ashore on the sandy beach of Kanak island. She rolled her canoe over to protect her from the wind if it kicked up. With a blanket wrapped around her and the dried salmon to enjoy, she lay comfortably in the lee of it. In this month of June, the nights were brief, and she lay for a long time and watched the wind pushing away the ceiling of clouds until sleep finally pulled her back to Earth.

She woke to a lapping tide so high that she could stretch out her arm and dangle her fingers in the sea. A perfect time to launch her canoe! She freshened herself with a quick dip in the icy water but was too preoccupied to think of eating. With a couple of easy tugs, she was back in her boat heading towards the Post.

Just beyond her destination stretched the far larger Big Kayak Island. It ran perpendicular to Little Kayak Island, with a steep ridge of mountains along its length and a pinnacle of bare rock known as Cape Saint Elias at its southern tip. Ann was grateful for the calming effect Big Kayak Island had on the waters as she neared the smaller island. She was astonished by how swiftly she reached it. The pebbles of the shore rolled gently under her canoe as she leapt out and pulled the boat up the beach.

The smell of wood smoke was a promising sign that Colonel George was at the post. Following the trail up the bank, she saw the simple cabin of thick, hand-hewn timbers. Colonel George, as if he had known she was coming, sat in the doorway, tall and straight and smoking a pipe. He pulled it from his mouth and greeted her with a nod and a warm smile.

"Say, Lass, what would bring ya all the way out this time o' day? You come alone, did you?"

Ann strode up to meet him face-to-face and with him sitting, they were in fact nearly eye-to-eye. She marveled once again at the smoky-gray of his eyes that were at the same time kind and mysterious. "Mother sent me on an errand to git her some coffee and I hope the Athabaskans have brought you spruce pitch gum from the sticks. We want some of that too. But we don't got the money so we thought maybe we could work a trade, like do some clothes washin' for you."

George stood and motioned her to follow. Inside it was warm and smelled of smoke-tanned hides, dried salmon, coffee and boiled potatoes. He poured her a cup of coffee without asking. It was his tradition to offer coffee to any visitor. She wasn't used to drinking the brew but with a generous helping of sugar she politely sipped it, looking around. Supplies seemed low. "When's the Swede brothers due in from Sitka?"

George, wrapping a ball of spruce pitch in newsprint, said, "I heard from some Eyaks that the ship is in down at Yakutat, so it will be any day now."

Ann was beginning to feel anxious about how long she'd been away from home, and butterflies were replacing her bravery. What did she think she was doing anyway? This man was about seventeen years older than she, and no doubt would prefer a white wife.

George brought her a bundle of wash, a tin of coffee and the wrapped gum. "It's a hopeless lot I'm in out here with no wife to do me washin' so I guess it's a fair trade. Just don't be long. They're all I got."

Ann snatched the items from his hands and headed for the door. "I'll have them back in 'bout four days, if the weather allows. Mother's got some bluing that'll do a real nice job, you'll see."

She felt a little sick to her stomach as she scampered down the bank to the beach with her armload. She had gotten *so* close; she had smelled him, almost touched him and had successfully left with some of his clothing! It took the entire paddle back to Kanak Island before her nerves settled. That night she lay next to her boat contemplating all of the mysterious nuances of Colonel George. It was not until morning that reality started to sink in. She'd have a lot to explain to her mother.

By the time Ann saw her beach at Katalla, the canoe steaming fire was out and the men had left. She tugged hard on her canoe to get it up high enough on the berm to keep it away from tide and surge.

Running now with her arms loaded, some of the white trappers and prospectors called from their tents in mocking humor, "Hey! Little squaw, you wantum white man? Wantum hooch? We show you some fun."

Ann did not give them the pleasure of showing her disgust and hurried along. Outside of her home, she stopped to catch her breath.

She saw her mother's grave look, when she entered. "Why you paddle out to the Commercial Company and what are them things you got?"

Ann dropped the bundle to the floor. "I had a good idea 'bout how I could get sumpthin' special for brother and you. I get so sad when I think that the Reverend might take Little John away that I decided to go out to Kayak Island and offer to do Colonel George's wash in trade for some spruce pitch gum for him and I got you some coffee too."

She handed the ball of pitch to her little brother, who squealed and ran around the room, pulling the paper off.

Mother's anger was fading, and by the time Ann offered the tin of coffee to her, she completely relented. She smiled and went back to weaving her spruce root basket. Without looking up from the twining of her gnarled hands, she said. "So, you still got some explainin' 'bout why you had that flower the other mornin'. You think I don't remember but I do."

Ann heaved a sigh and plunged in. "I'm also doin' sumpthin' special for me. I'm using some love magic on Colonel George. I'm old enough to be a wife and he's a good man."

Ann knew that even in her mother's generation, husbands were always chosen for their daughters: always men who would bring as much wealth and prestige as possible, and always men from the opposing Tlingit clan. But now so many people of the great clan houses from the Controller Bay area had died of diseases brought by the Horizon People, that there were very few to consider as potential mates. Her mother also could not deny that Colonel George was as wealthy as he was gentlemanly. If Ann married him, she would be able to stay in Katalla rather than having to move more than a hundred miles down the coast to be with the Tlingit in Yakutat. Ann hoped that this argument alone would persuade her mother. Their age difference also was not an issue. After all, her mother's first husband had been an old man. When he died, not long after they married, she'd been in line to marry his nephew, as was the custom, and he was closer to her age. This is the way it had always been. No, the battle would not be about Colonel George, but about whether her mother would recognize that she was not longer a little girl.

"You don't even know how to cook for a white man. You'll end up eatin' so much potatoes; you'll turn as white as him! Who will be here to help with brother?"

Ann felt guilty. She had taken her mother completely by surprise. But she couldn't have kept her love a secret much longer. Lately, with George on her mind, she'd been almost worthless.

Mother set aside her basket and poured some seal oil from a tin into a chipped, yellowed china cup and pulled a dried salmon filet down from the rack over the wood stove. She set the two things side by side and motioned Ann to sit and eat.

She said, "When them Russians first come, we hate them. But before them come a white woman, the only survivor from a shipwreck out in Controller Bay. Two white mens was with her too but they fell under the glacier after they went ashore and died. One of my mother's uncles took that woman for his wife. She lived to be old and ate all the same food as Indians. I never seen her, only heard stories of her. Mixing, now it happens more and more but so much getting lost 'bout our people now when Tlingit marries a white man."

Ann had heard the old people talk of how it was before. Her people had ruled the coast for hundreds of miles, but now she could scarcely imagine it. They were so few in Katalla. It was like an overturned canoe, she thought. Some of the stowed items sank and others floated, to be salvaged and used again. That was how Ann saw herself: the survivor. She would gather up what stayed afloat from her troubled people and use that to create a new life, her life!

She dredged pieces of salmon through the rich, mild seal oil, and savored them. The more she chewed, the more the flavors came to life, but she was finding it hard to remember to chew. In all her excitement she'd forgotten to eat, and now realized what her mother had already noticed, that she was famished.

"Mother," Ann said, "please help tell Kaak that I made a good choice. Tell father Colonel George will give me a good life. Make them not angry with me."

Mother pulled the trade blanket over little brother where he had fallen asleep and gave Ann a small nod. Ann finished her meal and hugged her mother.

"He may not even want me to be his wife." She said as she scooped her brother up and carried him back to the bed they shared. Her body felt completely spent. Now that she'd revealed her secret, the activity of the past two days seemed like a week. She moved her sleeping brother next to the wall, shed her dress and fell into bed beside him.

Her sleep was oceans deep and in that depth she was brought to the terrifying place she seemed to visit all too often. She was holding the large steersman's paddle in the stern of an immense canoe. Ten other paddlers stroked in unison in front of her. Who were they? Maybe the grandparents she had hardly known. She saw her sisters who had died. They seemed more grown-up than they had been in life. In the bow stood a man wearing a chief's hat, stacked high with basketry-cylinders. There were other strong men at the paddles but she couldn't see who they were. The boat was loaded with steam-bent chests and baskets and blankets. A fog had closed in so that all she could see was a broiling sea of white caps gnashing like wolves' teeth at the gunwales. Large swells rolled from behind them. She was afraid of what might suddenly appear as they hurtled forward. Yet she also had a disturbing sense that the boat was not moving ahead at all as it tossed in the blinding fog. The chief seemed fearless, he was singing, but no sound came from his moving lips. It seemed they might be trying to escape some evil, or were they rushing toward it? Suddenly a large rock loomed and without a moment to correct or prepare for disaster, the canoe smashed onto it, and they were in the black water. Floating, floating, so many things pitched around her, hard to grab. She was alone. Everyone had disappeared. She reached again for floating cargo and held tight to a cedar box. Clutching, she kicked.

Her slight kick woke her to the relief of her own bed. She heard the soft voices of her mother and father, and her name spoken, but couldn't fight her fatigue, and drifted back to sleep.

The next time she opened her eyes, the morning was well advanced. Somehow her little brother had squirmed right over her without waking her. Ann rose and helped herself to a bowl of boiled salmon eggs with seaweed. The salmon eggs popped in her mouth and seemed to give her instant energy. A breeze blew light fog through pools of morning sun. She saw her mother standing out in the mists hanging clean, white bear intestines on the clothesline to dry. She was going to split them into strips and sew them to make Little John a rain parka. Ann gathered up the pile of Colonel George's laundry and joined her mother outside and soon lost herself in the task of scrubbing.

She could not help herself from lifting each item to smell the essence of the man she desired. Sweet, stale pipe smoke and sweat permeated his shirts and trousers. She liked these scents and really didn't even want to wash them out. She added the bluing to his yellowed shirts. As she picked through his assortment, she kept her eye open for an item that she could tear a small piece from without his noticing. A comically stretched-out pair of wool long-johns with tattered cuffs seemed like the perfect choice for a slight alteration. She decided to cut the cuffs off of both legs and replace them with the good upper parts of some old wool socks. She hoped he wouldn't mind that there were now black wool cuffs on his white long johns. After the darning job was complete, she washed them too, and hung his laundry in the cool breeze next to the lengths of bear gut. Then she gathered the tattered cuffs and the piece of hem from her blue calico dress, as well as the lucky roots of the Starflower, and walked the path to the woods.

The woods were like a loving home. The bite of the wind ceased. Here were lush cushions of moss and a comforting quiet, broken by the powerful beat of Raven's wing and his loud voice, letting her know that he would be her cohort in this bit of mischief and magic. Her family's knowledge, and Raven's support, gave her confidence as she walked. She nimbly crossed a fallen hemlock spanning a grotto. On the opposite side, among moss and ferns, was a rotted stump. She knelt and took all the items from her pocket and began to prepare two small bundles as she made up a song, and sang it:

I look around
Very lonesome it is
I feel so sad
Give me your hand
Still loving you

Ann sang in the haunting minor notes she'd learned from her mother's songs. She laid a strip of her dress over a strip of Colonel George's long john cuffs and then placed half of the roots at one end of the layered fabrics and rolled it up. She tied the little bundle with a thread and then repeated the ritual, completing the second bundle just before rain began to patter down through the canopy. She buried one of the bundles in the loose duff of the rotten stump and then ran quickly back across the hemlock bridge, wanting to get home to the clothesline before her laundry was soaked by the rain.

For four days, late spring winds and rain whipped in from Controller Bay with force enough to knock down a few of the white men's sturdy canvas tents. Ann was delighted. But aside from that comic relief, she was sick with impatience. Reverently, she'd hand-dried George's laundry, turning each item by the stove and meticulously folding them like the new shirts she had seen on the Commercial Company shelves. Now she waited. Even Little John's silly antics couldn't make her smile. She did the chores, singing under her breath the song she'd composed while making the love bundles. Alone, she sang it aloud.

On the fourth night, again she dreamed. This time she was alone digging clams and lost in singing her song when she saw Raven swoop down. He was hopping along the beach toward her, clucking and croaking as he picked through the clam-hole tailings. Then stopping before her, he spoke.

"This man you love will love you too but in having him you will be like a raven among gulls." With one big hop, he flew off into a thick gray sky.

In the pre-morning dark, she lay awake trying to remember the dream, but it had faded. What did he say? She tried to whisper his words, so not to wake her brother. All she remembered for certain was that the man she loved would love her too.

From outside she heard no sound of wind or rain. She lay awake, hardly able to stay in bed until light, but when she did rise she found her mother already up. She'd packed Ann some dried salmon and biscuits in an old flour sack, tied closed with a string.

"Deliver them clothes to Colonel George and don'tchya think about stayin' too long. Just do your business with that Love Dope and get back home. You hear me?" Her mother's voice was unconvincingly stern.

Ann gave her a quick hug, grabbed up her bundles. The morning air was washed crisp and clean. Sunbeams bounced off every blade of wet grass. Was it coincidence that Kaak just happened to be on the beach to help send her off?

Although there was not a breath of wind left over from the bluster of the previous days, the water still remembered it. A washboard of wavelets stretched before her and greeted each stride forward with a slap against the bow. Ann met the challenge by focusing her attention on the glowing green of Kayak Island, though she knew she would only paddle today as far as Kanak. She was pleased that she'd thought to wrap George's laundry in oiled canvas as an occasional wave sprayed onto it.

On Kanak Island, she passed the evening practicing. "I've given much thought to the possibility of becoming your wife." No, that would be much too bold. "I've come to notice you seem so lonely out here." No, she couldn't have him think she pitied him. "Have you ever considered taking a squaw for a wife?" She used the word she had heard the other white men call her in Katalla but somehow this did not seem right either. In the end, she could only laugh at her own rehearsals.

The paddle to Little Kayak took longer than she hoped, but finally a wisp of smoke rising from behind the trees gave her an extra surge of energy. Before she knew it, she was landing her canoe. The love potion in her pocket made her equally nervous and determined. She hadn't thought about where or when she would deal with it, but it now seemed that she should take care of it before she went up the bank to the Commercial Company.

She found a deer path where the alder brush, Devils Club, and salmonberry bushes met the gravel beach and squeezed through it to a clearing. She found a rotten spruce and knelt and once more sang her song as she dug in the rich, fragrant earth. She buried the bundle with a prayer to her ancestors. Now she could only wait for them to help her, along with the power of the Love Dope.

At the beach again she was surprised to see George walking toward her, looking down as though trying to read her tracks in the gravel. With mock displeasure she blurted out, "George, are you tracking me?" Her words caught him off guard. He jumped straight up like a mountain goat and then she could not control her laughter.

"Good God, Lass, you scared the b'jesus outta me! Whatchya doin' in them woods?"

"It was a very long paddle out."

It was funny to think of a grown man blushing, but an unmistakable shade of crimson washed up his face. "I seen you a-comin' but when I come down, there was no sign of ya. I was startin' to think a bear maybe got you."

Ann walked by him coolly and pulled out the laundry bundle, placed it atop her head and began walking up the trail with George following.

"Here Lass, I'll carry it." George offered.

Ann ignored his gentlemanly gesture and carried it up to the Post. Opening the canvas tarp, she laid the items out on the table.

"I damn near froze out here without me union suit." He shook out his beloved woolies and fell silent when he noticed the new black cuffs on the bottom.

"I fixed your cuffs," she said.

He seemed good natured about the alteration. "Well then, what do you think I owe you for your services?"

"I'd like some coffee is all and maybe a bowl of beans?" She gestured to the pot simmering on the fire.

He gave a wink as he poured her coffee, "You drive a hard bargain, but if you insist, Lass, it's a deal." He folded his long frame into the chair next to her and sipped his own. Feeling the qualities of the man's warmth and strength so near, Ann's breath became so shallow that she inhaled a little coffee and began to cough, and George leapt to his feet. He hit her back with the flat of his hand, saying "Sorry Lass!" When her coughing subsided, his hand still lay on her shoulder.

Ann inwardly gave thanks to the Ancestors. The Love Dope was working already! But outwardly she teased, "Didn'tchya ever learn it's not nice to hit girls?" And then, "You got strong hands." She laid her hand on his and gently ran it down to his finger tips and then pushed back from the table to go stir the pot on the stove.

He followed, and touched her again on the shoulder. "These strong hands would never hurt someone as pretty as you."

The ladle in the beans helped anchor Ann. She felt that if she were not clutching it, she could not trust where her arms would go. He took the ladle from her, leaving it to rest in the pot.

He turned her and ran his hands from her shoulders down the length of her arms and held her hands. "Lass, you're as pretty as a button you are, but I remember you nearly knee high so 'tis a wee bit of a stretch to picture you in me arms."

Ann's knees wanted to give in. She commanded them to be strong, but could do nothing about the flush she felt burning in her cheeks. When he pulled her to him, she did not resist one bit. She said, "But maybe you noticed, I *am* a woman now." She smelled his sweet pipe tobacco scent and wood smoke. His arms felt like the safest place she had ever been.

"To tell ya the truth, Lass, till this moment, I never paid a mind to your womanliness but obviously, it's been a over-lookin' on my part."

All of Ann's daydreaming had not prepared her for the reality and power of this moment with Colonel George. She even heard some bewilderment in his voice.

"They'll never give you over to an old man like me." He held her away from him and looked into her eyes. "Lass, you don't have a notion whatchyer gitten yerself into."

"Mother, Kaak and father all have no objections to me being a wife to you. They respect how you have doctored and been fair with Tlingits. They know you are a good man." Ann felt a need to return to the ladle in the pot and she sensed that George likewise needed to give this situation time to sink in.

He released his hold and found his pipe. He sat in a sturdy chair facing the water, and lit it. He drew and released a plume of smoke along with a sigh as he looked out. "Well, Lass, it's a lonesome life I've been a-livin' and I can't say that the thought of havin' you as me mate sounds all that bad, but you must be sure of yerself and it must be made proper. Are ya sure of yer feelin's' Lass?"

Ann found it easier to look at him directly now that he was across the room. "I'm the one who's made the long paddles out to see you. I've known my feelings for a long time. I *would* like to be your wife but I have to go now." Ann was feeling jittery. "But next time you come to Katalla, can you bring the Reverend Henderson with you?" Ann gathered up the canvas the laundry had been wrapped in, and started for the door.

"Wait, Lass." She saw that he was surprised by the suddenness of what had happened. "What about a bowl of beans?"

When she continued resolutely for the door, she saw that he was desperate for her to stay. She was shaken by the lightening-bolt-speed at which the Love Dope had apparently taken effect, and now fought off the urge to run to his arms. But she knew she would not be able to get back in her canoe if she didn't force herself to leave. "Mother will be waiting my return. I will have nuthin' but you on my mind until we see each other again. Please don't take too long."

She fled almost in a panic to the beach and shoved off, looking back only from a very safe distance offshore. She saw Colonel George standing on the bank. He looked very small from that vantage and suddenly Ann felt guilty for causing such a strong man to become so flustered. She stopped and waved and he waved back at her enthusiastically.

It may as well have been shouted down from the tree tops by Raven himself. Soon everyone knew about the success of Ann's intrepid deed. Aunties and Uncles stopped in just to look at her with admiration, jealousy, and disbelief. Her mother was almost as excited as she. Ann could hear her talking to them in muted tones and occasionally her voice would rise, "Yes! It's true! Yes, the Dope Flower!" Still, no one knew what would happen next, and as days passed, Ann felt a gnawing doubt that Colonel George would ever show up.

It was well into the month of July, *At Gadaxeet Dísi*, the Moon when everything is born. The strawberries out at Strawberry

Point were in their prime. Ann and her mother were out filling baskets. In her mother's generation, the berries would have
been mixed in a paste of salmon roe to keep them through the
winter. Ann much preferred the sugar they used now. Enjoying
the warmth of the day and the hunt for the tiny red berries, she
scarcely heard the far-off steamboat whistle until the second blow,
when she realized it wasn't a bird's cry but a boat from Kayak
Island. She dropped her basket and ran to the edge of the point
by the remains of the old Beaver Clan House, studying the boat
as it grew nearer. By the time her mother arrived beside her,
she could just make out the forms of the people on deck. Yes! It
was Colonel George, and the man in black was the Reverend.
At this, she started hopping up and down, waving her arms, and
her mother jumped with her. Ann looked at her laughing and
thought she'd never seen her look so happy.

As they hurried back, they discussed the preparations they had
already made (in spite of their uncertainties) and details that still
needed to be attended to. Ann didn't run along the path so much
as floated. Would she truly become his wife on this day?

The steamer was anchoring as they reached the village, Mother
tugged on her arm, reminding her that she had to stay out of
George's sight until her father officially gave her over. It was hard
to turn her back on George, but she obediently followed her
mother. Auntie Nellie showed up soon after with her arms full
of hemlock branches covered in smoked, dry herring eggs. Two
months earlier the branches had been submerged in the bay for
the herring to spawn on before they were harvested. The citric
flavor that the hemlock boughs imparted to the herring eggs
was one of Ann's favorites, and she was thankful they would have
them to offer to their guests. From the large steam-bent chest in
the corner of the house, Mother brought out her cherished seal-
oil bowl, carved in the likeness of a beaver. Its wide hollowed-out
body gleamed with generations of use. She filled it, and stacked
dried fillets of salmon on the table next to it.

While other aunties and their children came with offerings
of food, Ann washed herself in a basin of icy water and then had
such jitters that she was unable to braid her long hair. She had

to call for her mother's help. As her mother's strong, steady hands tugged and neatly folded her hair into perfect plaits, Ann began to feel calmed but unexpectedly saddened as well. Tears ran down her cheeks.

"Mother, how can I leave you? How can I leave brother? What will my life with that white man be like?" She wondered for the first time if she wasn't making some grave mistake.

Her mother said, "Colonel George will make you like royalty. I think you will live easy, good life. And I will be near *Ax dachxánk*."

The thought of her mother being near her grandchildren was indeed comforting. Ann turned and hugged her mother as though she might never have the opportunity again.

They could hear the approach of the men and boys. She hurried behind the blanket partition and sat on her bed for what seemed like an eternity as the house filled with guests and family. Her father's voice, normally soft, now resounded as he appointed seats around the room according to status. At last, Ann heard him usher in Reverend Henderson and Colonel George. George, being a long-time family friend, was comfortable, and more than once she could hear good humored laughter amongst the guests. She wanted very much to peek out to see the gathering but she did not, and was beginning to feel the self-pity of banishment by the time her mother came for her.

✦

George was struck by Ann's light stride. He had not wavered for a moment about his decision to wed her, but only wondered why *he* hadn't been the one to pursue *her*. Her hair gleamed like black argillite as she approached. Bright abalone earrings glinted blue and green against her braids but they did not shine as bright as her black eyes. He felt he was reaching for a lifeline as he took her hand and she sat next to him on the cedar-bark mat.

His Irish family would never approve of an Indian wife, but he was not like them. His parents had started having children as soon as they were off the boat in New Brunswick, and before long he had just been one in a swarming houseful. While the rest of the family seemed satisfied to stay close, he was drawn to the wild elements and the great unfolding of discovery westward. Branded with bullet scars from fighting Indians under Custer and Miles, he'd continued west by horse, train and foot to the shores of the great Pacific. From San Francisco he'd come north with a contract and supplies to man the Commercial Company post in this, the northern-most land of the Tlingit. Now, far from his headstrong Catholic family, he still felt the need to make their union "proper," but also wanted to honor the traditions of her people.

He reached around and brought forward a large canvas bag from which he pulled out a shining new shotgun for Ann's father. "You have raised yerself a fine daughter and I know I'm a lucky man to have her, so accept this as a token."

Next, he handed to Kaak an axe. "You have looked after the interests of yer sister's daughter since she was a wee thing. I hope this axe serves you well."

He then passed out a stack of folded lengths of calico with colors and patterns different from any they'd seen. He smiled at the small commotion among the women.

To Ann's father, he said, "I feel a wee bit o' guilt takin' from you yer only daughter, please take these gifts and know I will be a fine husband to her."

"*Gunalchéesh,* Thank you, Colonel George. My people were of the great Tcicqedi House called Eagle House on Bering Lake who 'long with Ann's mother's people, the great Galyix-Kagwantan of the Beaver House, also on Bering Lake, were flooded out and re-established by our Grandfathers and Grandmothers in the places now where you can still see our old clan houses at Okalee Spit, Strawberry Point, Kayak Island, Chilkat and Kaliakh River. We have always sit here at the source of copper and so were once made rich and powerful. Our power is no more here in Katalla. There's few of us left, and I have no nephew to pass this on to so here I give you this important family copper named 'Comes From the Sun'. It was worth eight slaves in the days of my Grandparents. I give this to you so that you know the greatness of the people your wife comes from." The pounded copper was long and shield-like.

Ann's mother then came forward with a basket that she had been working on for the past month. It was no trade basket, but so tight and finely woven it could hold water. "Care for my Annie," she said, "and bring us many grandchildren."

When at last the giving was done, old Reverend Henderson pulled the black book from his robes and married them, and drumming began, and they feasted.

✦

The smell of tobacco was thick in the house. Ann wanted out. Her brother had been sitting in her lap and she now passed him off to Auntie Nellie. She found George talking with the Reverend and gently pulled on his elbow, and he followed her through the room full of guests and out into the dark. Ann could see the silhouettes of some of her younger cousins stumbling and passing a bottle of hooch, but nothing now prevented them from the embrace they'd both been waiting for. George turned her and she felt the press of his warm lips on hers, on her neck, then her ear, more glorious than she ever imagined. Suddenly he stopped. Ann hoped she had not displeased him. He took her by the hand and led her down to the beach and without a word he pulled a small skiff to the water's edge. Ann pretended not to know what his intentions were but she was a willing recruit if it meant more of this. He rowed through the still night, towards the silhouette of the anchored steamboat. When they reached it, he tied off and helped her up the ladder and into the cabin. It smelled of engine oil and grease but was at least warmer than outdoors. He fumbled in the dark until he managed to light a kerosene lamp, then pulled back a curtain to reveal a narrow bunk with blankets. "Lass, will you be me bride and join me in this bunk?"

Ann did not have to affect shyness. The sight of the bed made her uneasy, but George soothed her with more kisses as he unbuttoned the long row of shell buttons on the front of her dress. She slid into the blankets and watched as her husband removed his clothing. By the soft light of the lamp, his pale skin was illuminated like moonlight off a glacier. She marveled at his whiteness.

✦

George lay next to Ann and felt her warmth and smoothness; sensations that had become alien to him in his bachelor's life. He felt like a starving wolf with a fawn in his possession. He wanted to devour her. He wanted to consume her. But, knowing well that she was an untouched maiden, he approached her slowly and gently. It was not long before he saw that the slow advance suited Ann well, and in turn he found himself immersed in pleasure so deep he had almost forgotten it to be the right of man.

✦

The raucous report of the Raven woke Ann. Where was she? Her bed gently tilted. George, beside her, slept soundly. She looked out through the porthole by their bunk. The first rays of sunlight poured over the hills and struck her face and she remembered. She was a woman now! This was a new beginning to her life. She turned toward her husband and spooned into his long body and ran her fingers down his spine and kissed the back of his neck. Her attentions brought George out of his sleep. He turned and wrapped her in his arms.

Enfolded in their intimacies, they were unaware of the canoe paddlers until they heard them all around the boat.

In a clumsy dash, George hit his head on the overhead bunk and Ann buttoned her dress all crooked and followed him out onto the deck. Three canoes were filled with Ann's family, the skipper, crew and Reverend Henderson, all coming aboard.

The Reverend said, "It seems that a storm is brewing and I've got to make it back to Yakutat by this evening for a christening. Sorry to disrupt your honeymoon."

Ann looked out. Sure enough, a menacing front was on the horizon. Little John was handed up, and Mother came to lean over the rail to grab Colonel George's Copper, wrapped in red trade wool. Then, pushing from underneath, Father raised the big steam-bent chest and with her Mother's help, set it aboard. Ann could not believe that Mother would give the chest that had been in her family for generations. Mother turned to her and said, "You are now the keeper of the Beaver House treasures. Don't let no harm come to them things. Some day you give 'em to your daughter."

Ann had seen this chest only in the dark corner of their house. Seeing it now in the brightness of the morning sun was like laying eyes on it for the first time. A Beaver motif was carved in deep relief and painted in worn shades of black and red. Ann ran her hand over the thick, textured lid and then lifted it to see, among other things, the beaver bowl and the goat horn ladle. She hugged her father and mother. She felt such deep appreciation for all the ways they had loved, protected and now standing behind her in her marriage to Colonel George.

The engines of the boat were thudding to life as they said their good-byes. Ann cried again as her parents climbed back over the gunwales and lowered themselves into their canoes. They brought her canoe aboard to bring out to Kayak Island. Ann blew kisses to her brother, who pouted as the boats parted ways. Churning towards her new home, Ann was exhilarated by the unknown.

◆

It was the moon of *Kayaani Dísi,* the time the geese lay their eggs, in the year 1892, one year after Ann and George's marriage, when Ann's mother arrived to assist in the birth of their first child. Ann was round, ripe and ready. Together, they hemmed the edges of flannel squares to use for diapers and made miniature clothing that Ann held up and admired, dreaming of her child soon to arrive.

"I'm sure wishin' for a girl. I get lonely for woman-talk out here with only men," Ann complained as she watched her mother make tiny and precise stitches. Since living on Kayak Island she had come to appreciate her mother's wise and quiet nurturing. "I'm scared I won't be able to get the baby out. Were you scared too?"

Mother, not looking up from her needlework, spoke softly, "Babies don't always live. You love every one, they worth all the hard work. But I think you won't have no problem."

The next morning Ann woke early. The supply ship was due to come in from Sitka. She served George a breakfast of oats and coffee and dusted the nearly empty shelves, making them ready for the new supplies. When the boat arrived, she helped carry goods up from the beach. On her fourth trip up the bank, carrying a bag of flour, she suddenly was gripped with a pain that caused her to set the bag down. After the pain subsided, she picked up the flour and brought it into the post.

She said to her mother, "I miss that food you used to feed me. These white man's beans give me gas pains. I had a big pain carrying this flour."

Ann's mother looked suspiciously and said, "Annie, that ain't gas pain, your babe's comin'."

Ann brushed off her mother's comment and left for another load of supplies. But by the time she experienced the same sensation a second and third time before she had even made it back to the post, she was willing to admit her mother was right. Ann was equally delighted and terrified. She ran down the bank to the beach, cupped her hands to her mouth and yelled to George out on the supply boat, "George, yer child's on its way!"

He hollered back, "Who's gone away?"

Ann made big sweeping gestures, pointing towards her belly. "The BABY's comin'!"

When the news sank in, he and the crew gave a few cheers and then George rowed the skiff in. As she waited on a beach log for him, she had another pain.

He kissed her and led her up to the post, but had to continue offloading the boat. He laid his hand on her belly. "Don't worry Lass, I'll be near, just have mother holler if you desire me presence." He led her to the bed and insisted she lie down.

Once he had gone, her mother told her to get up. "It'll be a long day before baby comes. Walk and stay up, baby will come more easy pointing downward."

Ann did as her mother said and by midafternoon her contractions came at steady intervals. She winced with each pain, wondering how long she could bear the relentless gripping force she was powerless to prevent. She tried to stay on her feet and keep busy. When she thought she could bear no more, the contractions only intensified. By dusk she lay down and looked into her mother's calm eyes. "Is it ever coming out? I'm scared it's not gonna come out!"

Mother stroked her forehead with a cool damp cloth. "First babies come slow. Think of sea anemone, the way it open wide when it's relaxed and the way it close tight when it's scared. Don't be scared. Just open and baby will come."

Ann thought of the beautiful sea anemones she had seen in tidepools since she was a little girl, soft shades of pinks, whites and greens, swaying, undulating and open. This image helped to calm her. Oh, how badly she wanted to see her child!

George looked in as darkness fell. His presence was comforting, but she wanted only mother by her side. Between contractions, she slipped into sleep, but when they returned, she felt like a bear awakened from a winter's den, roaring with power and determination. Suddenly she felt a tremendous need to push. She wished now that she was a mother bear because their cubs are born so tiny. This was no tiny cub. She roared, red in the face as the baby finally came forth, and her mother announced, "You got yer girl, Annie!"

George must have been nearby, for he was at her side by the time her mother placed the rosy, wrinkled infant into Ann's arms.

"Ah, she's a beauty!" George cooed.

Weak with exertion, Ann stroked the baby's velvety, glowing skin. "Let us call her 'Grace,'" she said.

"As long as her middle name be Margaret," George said. "It sits well with me."

◆

Grace Margaret livened up the household and brought out the kindness of many who came to Kayak Island. The Swede brothers always brought her candy from down the coast. They loved to take turns bouncing her on their knees and singing sea chanties. Jack, one of the cannery workers and a regular customer to the post, taught her to count and recite the ABC's. Grace's laughter warmed the souls of those who found themselves in this cold northern land separated from their own families. Best of all, she was Ann's constant companion and source of endless entertainment. For this Ann was grateful. George had taught her to handle the affairs at the post and spent more and more time away with the men who'd moved into the area.

Tom White was one especially close friend. The two of them dreamed up explorations and outings that sometimes kept George away for weeks at a time. Together they explored a cave at Cape Suckling, southeast of Kayak Island, and from there had crossed Controller Bay, where they'd paddled up the Copper River for a week, hunting deer and setting trap lines. When he finally returned home bright and well satisfied, Ann could barely hear of his travel tales.

"Well, I'm glad you had a lot a good times with yer buddy Tom, but it's been lonely here. Jack's the only regular man Grace sees."

She took some pleasure in knowing this comment would hurt him. He only pulled out a little pair of Athabaskan moccasins decorated with flowers stitched in dyed porcupine quills, as well as crystals he'd found in the cave, and gave them to Grace. Seeing Grace's innocent joy made Ann feel a pang of guilt, and through the day she slowly warmed to her husband and by evening she could not deny the joy she felt to be back in his arms.

A second daughter was born from joys they shared through the cold nights of that winter. She was born more easily than Grace. Anne named her for her Auntie, Nellie Edith. Yet, whenever travel was possible, George left them alone again. Though the post and the girls kept her busy, she often felt like a sailor marooned on a ship at sea.

One such melancholy day came when Grace was nearly three and Nellie had just turned two. Ann packed a lunch of canned salmon and, with Nellie strapped to her back and Grace, who sometimes walked and sometimes rode on her hip, she hiked to an overlook on the island. From that height they could see across the water towards Katalla.

Ann pointed to the small village, not quite visible in the distance, and said to the girls, "Grandma. *Tcuca* over there." She could see by the way their eyes wandered left and right that they really had no idea what they were supposed to see or understand about the far off land. They knew they had a grandma but they could not see her.

Ann sat down with them on a soft mossy rock. She said, "When I was a little girl my grandma used to tell me stories of the Trickster Raven."

"Tell us a story!" Grace said.

Ann nestled them to her and began:

"Looong time ago before you, me, Papa, Grandma or any of us lived here, the animals and people had to do everything in the dark. There was no daylight. People had to dig for clams by feel. They were always bumping into each other and having great difficulties. They were cold all the time and that made them grumpy. Raven saw that the work of the creation wasn't complete until the people had light.

"There was an old man who lived in a big house down the coast from here, at the head of the Nass River. He and his wife had a beautiful daughter. In bentwood chests they kept the *Dis*, moon, *kutx.ayanaháa*, stars, and *Gagaan*, the sun. They kept them hidden. They were greedy! Raven turned into a spruce needle floating in the creek outside the big house and when the slave dipped water for the beautiful daughter, the spruce needle was brought into her. She didn't notice it in her water and drank it. She soon grew big with a child inside of her. The family was very upset. The slave swore he hadn't come near her.

"Soon the baby was born but it had unusual eyes, beady and black like a Raven (for of course it *was* Raven in human form). The Grandfather could not help but love his new grandchild (who seemed to grow strangely fast).

"Soon the baby/Raven was demanding the treasures within the chests. At first, the grandfather said 'absolutely not' but Raven wailed and cried so loud and long that finally the box of stars was handed over to quiet the house. Raven opened the box when the family was out of the house and seeing that they were stars and not the sun, threw them out the smoke hole where they scattered into the dark sky.

"Next Raven cried and carried on with demands for the second chest. Finally grandfather could stand it no longer. He opened the chest and there was a glowing moon. He let Raven play with the Moon like a ball but when nobody was looking, Raven threw that moon out the smoke hole too.

"At last the greatest possession of the old man's, the Box of Daylight, was handed over to Raven because he could see that there would be no peace in the house until he gave it up, and besides, he loved his grandchild so very much! At last Raven had possession of the sun and flew out the smoke hole with it. He flew with it out above Dry Bay. It frightened the people so much at first that those who had been wearing seal and otter skins ran into the sea and those wearing deer and bear skins ran into the woods. Even the mountains jumped back and the big rocks rolled into the ocean. That's why Dry Bay is wide and open as it is and why there are animals in the ocean and in the woods. It's because of Raven."

By the time she'd finished the story the girls were both asleep. Ann felt drowsy herself. She was pregnant again, and soon, even walking to this outlook would be difficult. She never imagined she could miss her mother like she now did. Telling the old story made her long for her family and Katalla, more than ever. She'd been away too long. After realizing her loneliness, she resolved to talk to George about a visit home, then she curled up on the moss with the children and drifted off to sleep.

When they returned that afternoon, the sight of Aleut skin kayaks on the beach sent a chill up her spine. It was unreasonable to be afraid, she knew. After all, times had changed. But since childhood, she'd known these people were their enemies. Even before the Russians, the Aleuts had come to hunt otter from the waters near Katalla, and to capture Tlingits as slaves. Heading down to the post, she reminded herself that her own people had taken slaves and hunted and made war, and that through the years, all kinds of people had come to this post to trade. She was a modern woman with no foolish fears. Still, she gripped the children tighter as she came through the door.

George nodded at her and smiled around his pipe, and the Aleuts only glanced at her. They were around the table showing him trade objects they had brought. She saw carved ivory amulets, and a long billed visor made of wood, brightly painted and bristling with sea lion whiskers that bobbed with Russian trade beads. Miniature ivory animals and birds stood along the hat's bill. Even as wildly outlandish as the wooden hat was Ann admired the craftsmanship and could appreciate its hunting magic.

The Aleuts had pooled their offerings in an effort to trade for a gun that George had laid on the table. It was a strange old gun, but in good working condition, and when one of them picked it up and sighted down the barrel, Ann's heart pounded. She ducked and pulled the girls toward the door and only stopped when the man lowered it again and returned to the negotiations. She could see by all the empty coffee cups that they'd already been at the post for some time. At last, to her relief, they settled on a trade for the gun and four boxes of cartridges, and shook hands.

With big toothy grins, they patted Grace and Nellie on their heads as they departed. One of the men pulled a leather thong from around his neck. A yellowed ivory amulet hung from it, carved in the form of a mother otter cradling her baby on her upturned belly. He placed his hunting magic carefully around Grace's neck, gave her cheek a gentle pinch and walked out.

Ann felt the tension drain from her as the Aleuts made their way to the beach. She reached to take the necklace off her child but George said, "Let her keep it, now," and Ann felt ashamed. Her fears were unfounded. Things had changed since she was a girl.

Instead she looked at the carved otter with her baby and appreciated the fine handiwork. She said, "That's real pretty on you, Grace."

That night, when George put his hand on her to feel the delicate kicks from the new baby, Ann used the tender moment to tell him how much she missed her family and Katalla. "Soon there will be five of us and it will be more hard to pay a visit."

To her surprise, he agreed with a sigh. "Aye Lass, it's high time we do it. We'll head over as soon as I can get someone to mind the Post."

Ann rolled atop him, playfully nibbling and kissing at his warm salty neck and soon he was tickling her until she had to bolt from the bed. The growing baby seemed to be dancing a jig on her bladder and she barely made it outdoors in time. She squatted in the light of an enormous full orange moon rising over silhouetted mountains. The night was extraordinarily still with only the haunting call of Loon somewhere off shore. Ann gave a silent thanks to her ancestors for the joy and magic she felt around her, and returned to her bed to lie awake and think of home.

✦

Katalla had grown in the few years since she'd seen it. Modest cabins had replaced some of the white men's tents. Ann wanted to leap from the canoe almost before it hit the beach, but as Grace and Nellie each sat upon one of her legs, she had to reel in her spirit that had gone out in advance of her body. By the time she and George filled their arms with girls and gifts and walked into her parents' home, Ann was beside herself with anticipation. Mother, Father and Little John were busy at the table filleting salmon for drying. Caught up in their industry, they didn't even look up.

"Grace Margret. Nellie. Say 'hello' to your Grandparents and *Kaak,* your uncle," Ann said.

Everyone's eyes turned toward them. Ann's mother looked as though she'd seen a ghost, and then she was on them, embracing with fish-slimed hands. Nellie was overwhelmed and cried.

Over the next few days, Ann found that the very chores she used to dread doing for her mother now seemed like an honor and a privilege. As they worked side by side, Ann confided in her. "Sometimes I just want to come back and live with you. I get so lonely. George leaves me and the girls too much. I got no women friends."

"If he don't hit you, you got a good man and you better take care to show him you happy. He hit?"

"No. He's a gentleman. Only sometimes I think we are nuthin' to him. He'd rather be with his friends."

But her mother only replied firmly, "No complainin' Annie. You wanted him. He's yours now. These girls be your woman friends 'fore you know. Time passes fast. Be happy Annie."

It wasn't just herself she pitied, thought Ann as she watched her children in the arms of their grandparents and jostling with their young uncle. There were no other children on Kayak Island. She watched as Little John and Grace played endlessly like brother and sister. Occasionally, Nellie boldly entered the fray and endured bumps and tumbles. Being home was refreshing even if her mother's advice seemed unsympathetic.

In the evenings her father told stories, some of which even she'd never heard before: chilling stories of Land Otter Men, who were the spirits of the drowned, and the story of the Woman Who Married the Bear. He told stories of their family. During these stories, George was his most steadfast listener. This night he sat puffing on his pipe as the two of them played a game of cribbage on a caribou antler.

"Comes From the Sun," Father said, referring to the ceremonial Copper shield that he had given to George as a wedding gift, "was made by my great-grandfather from big piece of copper he brought back from trade with interior.

"We *still* trade with them up there. Back when Ann just learned to walk. It been cold, cold winter with snow deep. Them Stick Indians come down Copper River from Taral Creek. There was a family with a boy, wasn't much older than Ann. They come to trade with us. The boy, now he's chief Taral Nicoali, he keep coming back to visit and bring us gifts from his own copper." He reached for a tin can on the windowsill and dumped the contents onto the table, old bullets of copper and silver alloy. "These Taral Nicoali give me. You see, them 'Stick Indians', I calls 'em but you call 'em Athabaskans, is rich but they can't eat bullets and copper nuggets so they like to trade with Tlingits for dried seal and things they don't got. Taral Nicoali, still the big *tyone* up there."

On her rickety cot next to the stove Ann tried to stay awake but the sleeping weight of Grace and Nellie against her made her tired. She closed her eyes, listening to the men talk.

"Now the name 'Katalla,'" queried George, "would that be of Tlingit or Eyak origin and what's its meaning?"

"Katalla mean *shining rock*. Eyak give name for the greasy stuff on rocks near here."

"Greasy? What you suppose? Coal? Or some old whale carcass washed ashore in the past?"

"Could be coal, I don't know no story 'bout a whale washin' up near here…" Father's voice trailed off.

Ann awoke when everyone in the house still slept and realized it was Raven's call that had opened her eyes. She lay silently, staring up into the smoky rafters of her family home. Today they had to leave, and as she lay there wishing she could slow time, she remembered her long-ago dream of Raven on the beach. He had told her that George would love her. But what else had he said? She listened to the soft snores of her mother and father as Raven's bell-like call rang out through the still morning air. Suddenly, like the flash of a wing, her youthful dream of Raven on the beach with his words of warning came back to her: *You will become like a raven among gulls. You will cry for your people.* Yes, that must be it, she thought, and her tears spilled at the thought of heading back out to the post.

Then before she knew it, all the children were awake, turning the morning into tumbling, squealing, chaos. George joined in, and soon the children were shrieking as he pinched and tickled. Ann rose and made coffee.

✦

George, his curiosity stimulated by Ann's father's stories, soon rounded up Tom White and a new friend, Michael Davoll, to go explore. It was a good feeling to have his domestic bones stirred, but his wife's expression was dour. She said, "You got a wild glint in your eye."

"You don't seem to trust me, lass. I have a hunch I need to follow. I am doing this for *us*."

"I'm gonna have this baby and you'll miss it."

"No, I'll be back in time," he said, giving her round belly a pat. "Why I'd sooner lose my leg than miss it! I'll bring Mother when I come. The only way I'm wild is in the way I love ya lass." Finally he saw the smile he needed from her. He held her in a long embrace and then strode down the bank to the waiting skiff.

The three men had worked out a plan to comb the backlands of Katalla, starting nearest the village. If their intuitions were right, there could be oil in the area. Armed with guns and shovels and brush hooks, canvas tents, compass and binoculars, they set forth.

All three of them shared a sense of urgency. If there was oil, it was only a matter of time before a trapper or a cannery worker found it. But after a fruitless week in steady rain, they began to doubt. By night they swigged whiskey to dull the pain of their aching muscles as they planned the next day's direction.

It was with a foggy mind the following morning that Tom stumbled into a bog and called out to his buddies to help him. By the time they showed up, Tom had pulled himself free and was waving his gooey boots in the air. "I've found it gents! This is it. It's oil, I swear!"

They sniffed it, poked it, rubbed it with their fingers. George tossed a match into the bog and they backed away, awed, as a flame burst upward. They stood slack-jawed at the beauty of it. They split into three directions with a plan to meet by evening. George went east and was far beyond the sight or the smell of the flame and without a compass when he realized he'd lost track of time and might be turned around. It was raining and the light was flat and fading when he decided it was safer to bed down than wander further in a direction he wasn't sure of.

As he lay under his moldy canvas in the pelting rain, he thought of Ann. How warm and sweet she was to sleep with, and what a mate he had in her. She'd made it possible for him to soar, freed him to travel and explore again as he had when he was younger, though the hardness of the ground told him he wasn't so young any more.

He could be nestled next to her in their cozy bed right now. Yes, he loved her. She radiated beauty and confidence but mostly he loved her for her earthy simplicity. She was a loving mother and he felt grateful to be blessed with the joys of fatherhood. He could hardly wait to give them the news of the oil! Oh, how thrilled Ann would be. But then his thoughts began to drift toward Jack and how often he visited, how much time he spent playing with the children. Did Ann fancy that tramp? How dare he teach *his* Grace to count! He began to think he'd been a fool to stay out so long.

The rain strengthened and thundering gusts spun branches from the trees. George hunkered miserably and at dawn set off through the storm, as disoriented as he'd been the evening before. He imagined he could smell the burning oil and began following his nose, but after some time he noticed he was climbing in steep terrain. How could it be, he thought, a grown man like me, lost! He had enough experience to know not to panic. When the front of the storm blew over, he'd get his bearings and find the Katalla River and follow it back to the village.

He took shelter and waited for another day while the storm pounded. He wondered about Tom and Michael. Were they lost too? Were they looking for him, or back in Katalla making plans to get rich off the oil without him?

Finally, on the third day, soggy, cold and trudging through mud, he found his way back to the fire that still shot into the air as it had when first lit. He was a pathetic sight, wandering into camp, but his friends were as pinned down by the storm as he had been. They were good honest men, they hadn't deserted him.

By next evening they were back in the dimly lit house, telling Ann's parents of their trials and exciting discovery. Ann's father could not share their enthusiasm, but was happy to host them. Mother on the other hand was in nervous fits, waiting for the storm to end. "My bags is ready George. You better be ready too, soon as the wind stops. Annie needs us."

✦

It was the month of *Xoots kúdi*, Bear's Nest moon. George had been gone three weeks, and Ann cursed the storms and her husband. How could he leave her? She knew she could give birth on her own *if* all went well. Although Grace was only three, she could be counted on to care for her sister and run small errands around the house. This was far too private a matter for Ann to ask any of the other island residents for help. No hooch drinkers or cannery workmen were going to help bring her baby into the world.

Two nights later as the glass in the windows rattled and the curtains puffed in and out, Ann's baby came. Ann screamed in anger and pain through the toughest contractions, but when she saw Grace and Nellie's frightened faces, she closed her eyes and focused on opening as her mother had instructed. She sobbed and called out to her. Grace asked if it hurt. She reassured the girls that it didn't hurt more than it was supposed to. Nellie curled up in her dad's chair and dozed but Grace refused to sleep. She lay wide awake next to Ann and was a sweet and silent witness to her brother's arrival.

In spite of her solitude, Ann's joy was profound. The baby boy lay next to her breathing strong sweet breaths and looked with deeply dark eyes into hers. Finally he seemed content with his new surroundings and fell peacefully to sleep. Suddenly the spell that had allowed such joy seemed to evaporate, and she began to cry uncontrollably. He had better have lost a leg, or she'd never forgive him!

✦

"You had that baby all alone? George never got back?"

It was Jack who brought her an extra blanket and took away the soiled sheets. And it was Jack who got the word out to the cannery workers. Soon they began to arrive with offerings of fish stew, apple-cakes, and fried potatoes. Ann was grateful for the gifts and for the opportunity to show off her beautiful son, even if only to the locals. As it turned out, they were surprisingly kind and generous. She had underestimated their goodness.

It was two more days before the white-capped waters of Controller Bay flattened into low swells. Ann found herself constantly watching the sea, and by mid-morning she spotted the far-off boat plowing in the direction of the island. As it drew near she could see it was her mother and George. The girls held hands and danced in a little circle when she told them their Papa was coming.

He came ashore as sheepishly as a whipped dog, and picked Nellie up, but the words he spoke were intended for Ann. "Nellie Edith, I hope you aren't too mad at yer Papa for bein' gone a spell. I love you sooo much but them nasty winds kept me land bound. Were you a good girl fer your mama?"

Nellie replied, "Mama has a new baby." She spoke the words clearly and pointed.

He set Nellie down and came to her, taking her by the shoulders, looking into her eyes. "Good Lord! Where is it? Oh Ann fergive me. In my heart, I thought you would not have given birth yet!"

Ann pulled away and walked past him to her mother who was carrying a bundle from the skiff. "Mother! The girls have a brother! He's beautiful and strong. Come and see him." She grabbed her mother's load and the two of them climbed the path up the bank, leaving George to follow with the girls.

For the next few days, George played the part of the genuinely repentant husband. Before long, she forgave him again, and soon he was telling her of his adventures. "Lass, it's a wee bit early to get too encouraged but I think we just may have stumbled upon some good fortune."

She rocked the baby and listened.

"Your father got me wonderin' about those shining rocks. And just as I suspected, there was oil up there! We walked right into it! If it's seepin' out at the surface, imagine would you what's under the ground! We could be rich by it!" He said, "Considering my son was born at this promising time, I'd like to suggest we name him Petroleum Barrett. Don Petroleum Barrett"

Ann rather liked the idea of being made rich. Maybe they could even move back to the village. But, looking down at the perfect black-haired boy sucking at her breast she said, "You want to name him after *oil?*"

"Aye, I tell ya Annie, I perceive this to be possibly a monumental discovery and I want me son to always know that he came to us at this time."

Ann, caught up in her husband's enthusiasm, decided the situation perhaps did call for a unique name, relented. "Don Petroleum," she said, as she looked down at him. "But I will call him 'Pet.'"

❧

Though Pet was George's "pride 'n joy," George spent less and less time at home. He and his partners were now known up and down the coast as the "Three Greases." The samples came back as high-grade crude oil, and soon they were making schooner trips to San Francisco to meet with various oil companies, swing deals and collect advances.

Still, Ann doubted him. And then there were his children, ever hopeful that he'd have the time to romp with them. They were most enchanted when he played his accordion. They'd dance their little childish jigs around the room. These times with them lightened his heart, and his only regret was that they happened so seldom.

❧

Ann's mother was right. As her family grew, she found that she was less lonely. A second son was born, by the "Great good fortune of God..." as George had proclaimed, when he *"was home!"* They named him Patrick which lovingly became "Patsie."

And now it became clear to her that George was right too. The family would soon be wealthy. Now she began to dream of building a big white house in Katalla, one that she could share with her parents. They'd sent Little John to the boarding school years ago, and she knew they must be lonely. George still came and went and the only thing she wanted more than a new home was to hold and be held by him.

At night, in bed, he'd tell stories of his excursions. As busy as motherhood kept her, she still envied his freedom and craved the colorful accounts, down to the details. She was like a swimmer too long under water, and his words were fresh air. Then he'd leave again, and she would to sink into the mundane routines of her life.

He went away to Sitka, and this time he returned not with a tale of adventure, but with a newly purchased passenger ship. Now everywhere was talk of copper, coal, and oil, and there'd be no turning back the tide of fortune seekers. He said Katalla was going to become a prize destination.

To her great joy, he told her that the first cruise would be a "lark." He would take her and the children down the coast to Yakutat and pay a visit to Little John.

Finally, *she* was going on an adventure with her husband!

"When shall we go? Now?"

"No, mid-July. There's an expedition party coming to Yakutat. The Duke of Abruuzzi, the Italian Alpine Club, a photographer and fifteen climbers, they're all set for an assault on Mount Saint Elias."

Suddenly it seemed less like a family outing than like another of George's schemes. Assault? Her people believed that the Spirit of any mountain must be approached with humility and respect. Even one's voice must be soft in the presence of its snow and ice. She had seen capes of woven hair from goats hunted on that mountain and knew it was not unfamiliar territory to the Tlingit.

✦

On a warm and blustery morning in the moon of '*At Gataa Dísi*, the molting month, they steamed out of Controller Bay, passing between the long, sandy arm of Oklee Spit and the north tip of big Kayak Island and into the unbridled Pacific. The girls played tag on the long deck but Ann kept Pet near her side and Patsie in a shawl on her back.

As they approached the high cliffs of Cape Suckling, she gathered the girls to see the human shapes, explaining that at the beginning of time, Raven had magically sculpted these forms of legs and arms and faces in the rock. They passed the caves where their Papa had found crystals, and pulled into the bay above Seal River where the great Bering Glacier calved towering cliffs of blue-fissured ice into the brackish water. George pulled alongside a floe and chiseled chunks, and the children ran to the galley for sugar. They sprinkled the ice with the sugar, licked it off, reapplied it, and licked some more.

By late afternoon, Ann could see the *Tayeesk'*, Raven's splitting adze, known also as Cape Yakataga. Yakataga was also the original landing place for the survivors set adrift after a great flood. Ann's earliest clan ancestors had their origins there. Thinking of these old stories, she was reminded how grateful she was to be living in modern times, no longer like the *Taat Kwaani*, those People of the Dark.

It was evening by the time they rounded Icy Cape into Icy Bay. There, looming at the head of the bay, was the colossal Mount Saint Elias, a monolith of snow and ice, glowing like a bright orange ember in the low light of late evening. They anchored behind Egg Island, and Ann bedded the children down with the promise of one quick story.

"Looong time ago, Raven got stuck inside the belly of a whale. It's true! You see, Raven was always the curious type. One day while watching a whale come up again and again for air, Raven swirled down from the sky right into the blow hole. It was dark inside the whale so Raven made a fire and lived off the fat of the whale for many days because there was no way out.

"Finally, Raven *really* wants out and starts jumpin' up and down and bangin' from side to side, making the whale have a tummy ache. The whale starts rolling like it's getting' washed up ashore so Raven start prayin' for a sandy beach so that they get a soft landing. And sure enough, they come up on a beach. But finally Raven had to eat the whale's heart so it dies.

"Humans come along and hear singing coming from inside the whale, the words are, 'I wish somebody high class like me cut a place open so I can get out.' Those people want of course to be 'high class' so they come back with a hatchet and cut a hole. Raven flies out sooo fast that the people saw nothing. Then Raven turned into a human and asked around the village if anyone had heard any sounds from that whale washed ashore. When a man said that he heard a song, Raven gasped and said that was real bad news. That meant that the whole village would die if they did not leave now. Then that whole village leave as fast as they can and Raven stayed and ate all of their food they put up for winter. That Trickster always up to mischief!"

The story, like a magic spell, put all four children to sleep, and Ann joined George on the deck, where the two of them surveyed the shoreline of the immense bay. Fires burned along the shore, the camps of berry-pickers and seal-hunters and their families. George was relaxed and happy, and Ann slid next to him and rested her head against his shoulder. "Thank you for bringing me here," she said.

"It's *me,* Luv, that needs to be doing the thankin'. This excursion with the lot of you is good for me soul. Tomorrow let's go to the strawberry grounds up there by the river mouth." Their eyes fell again on Saint Elias, still awash in alpine glow. George said, "If we leave tomorrow afternoon we might see the climbers before they head out."

The next morning, George kept his promise and rowed the family in by skiff to the berry grounds. They filled baskets and soon the children's mouths were rimmed in smears of berry juice. Ann laughed at their ghoulish faces as they rowed back to the steamer, and soon they were setting sail for Yakutat.

By early evening, they had tied alongside the Swede brother's schooner, anchored in Monti Bay. They passed the children over the rails, where the good-natured Swedes jostled and teased them, and Ann and George followed, offering a fat Coho George had caught, and a big bowl of strawberries. They all dined in the schooner's fine galley. The children, using ice chipped from the flows, made and proudly served iced tea to everyone. The Italian boat arrived in the night and George stayed the next day to hob-nob with the crew while Ann and the children set off in the skiff to see her brother at the mission.

A pack of skeletal dogs were scavenging on the beach when she pulled the skiff to shore, and the village was so deserted that even the great lineage houses had padlocks on the entryways. Ann knew the locks were to prevent looting by white men, while the native occupants were away at their summer camps. They walked the beach in front of the clan houses. One, the Wolf Bath House, belonged to related kinsmen from Katalla, who had migrated to Yakutat.

Soon they were beyond the village graveyard, and in sight of a modern building. As Ann approached the mission, she felt her gut tighten, but she towed the children along gaily, disguising her apprehension. She spied her brother holding a plank of wood while the Reverend Henderson tore through it with powerful saw strokes.

"Little John!" Ann blurted out. He'd grown from the little boy she remembered into a lanky ten year old. When the Reverend invited them inside, her brother opened the door like a gentleman.

Inside, Grace was instantly impressed by wallpaper with large pink rose blossoms covering every wall. "Little John, how come she paint sooo many flowers all over her house?"

Mrs. Henderson corrected her, "We would like that you call your uncle 'Jonathan' now that he lives here. It's a more respectable name, don't you agree?" she said with a flash of her teeth.

Grace looked at Ann for clarification. "Mama, what's 'respecticle' mean?"

The Reverend's missus answered, "The word is *respectable* and it means it's more decent and White sounding. It will help your uncle adapt to the good Christian life." Mrs. Henderson brought food to the parlor table but gasped when she saw the children's filthy hands, and ordered Jonathan to take them to the kitchen and scrub them.

Grace, Nellie and Pet followed their uncle obediently and returned scrubbed and glowing. He had run a wet comb through their hair. Ann had to admit that her children had started looking somewhat like little shamans, blown wild by the sea breezes of their boat journey.

After they had been stiffly scrutinized, Ann was anxious to get her brother away. "Little, I mean *Jonathan,* can you show us where you sleep?"

He looked for the nod of approval from Mrs. Henderson and then led the procession around the corner and up a steep flight of polished stairs. Framed photos showed groups of immaculately groomed native children standing in front of the mission boarding house.

"Are you the only one here now?" Ann asked.

"No. These two are my friends" Little John said as they entered the dormitory. The two long rows of bunks on either side of the room were tidy and clean but two of the beds had boys in them. "That one there is Henry and that one there is William," he said, gesturing to lumps under the covers that did not stir. "They's sick. There are some girls too but they're out in the garden. Alls the rest are out at seal camps."

Little John sat on the edge of his bunk and bounced little bounces as Grace, Nellie and Pet joined him, also bouncing until soon they were all in a rowdy tumble. They laughed, tussling and pulling their uncle down in a playful joust that soon had Mrs. Henderson flinging the dormitory door open with a look of absolute disbelief on her face.

"I *do* think visiting time is over! Jonathan, escort your family outdoors now."

Ann was glad to have been evicted, but before leaving she informed the perturbed Mrs. Henderson that she would be taking her brother back to their boat. Little John grabbed up his coat and they all held their heads high as they filed past her.

George was willing to tour the family about. He would not be ready to go home until he heard the outcome of the expedition.

"I swear this time, the summit will be bagged. The northerly approach, that's the sure ticket to the top!"

In the coming days, they explored eastward up Yakutat Bay, into Disenchantment Bay and on up to the head of the Hubbard Glacier. The bay was filled with seals and Ann had a terrible craving for the deep red meat and its rich oil. She convinced George that they could do the work of butchering and rendering the fat if he would just do the job of killing one.

George agreed. The shooting was not that difficult but the surf did not allow him to get a line on it before it sank. Ann and Little John were especially disappointed. They had both been deprived of such a delicacy for too long.

It was Grace who lifted their spirits a few hours later when she pointed out, "Something black. Not moving, over there on top the water."

When Ann looked, she could not believe her eyes. There lay the slain seal, caught on a sandbar as the tide receded. The sandbar was not revealed yet and so it *did* look as though the animal was lying on top of the water.

By the time Ann returned Little John to the mission a few days later, he said that he was happy to be so filled with seal meat but even happier to be filled with good memories. "I suppose they'll have to last me some years."

Ann hoped he was wrong about that. They'd be sailing home that evening, but she allowed the children to stay with him until the last possible minute.

With the sun still high, they churned their way out of Yakutat Bay. Much of the first part of that day, as they followed the shore, Mount Saint Elias was in view and George talked about the men of the expedition and what he had learned from them.

"Not one but *all ten* climbers made the summit. It was so clear they could see Mount Logan, Mount Augusta, Mount Cook, Mount Hubbard and Mount Fairweather! Imagine the brilliance of such a sight, Lass!" He drew an arch in the air towards the majestic snow-capped peaks.

George's enthusiasm was sweet, almost child-like, thought Ann. She loved to see his simple excitement. It was clear she could not keep a man like this from his quests. She watched his bright eyes and knew he could go on talking all night about the expedition but what really appealed to her was the idea of a good sleep. Ever since their wedding night, she had favored sleeping aboard a boat. She liked the gentle rocking and pitching and the magical way the boat pivoted from its anchor-point, providing ever-changing views from the porthole and the sounds of water lapping at the hull. Perhaps, she started to think, she had more than sleep on her mind. Indeed, a deeper desire was calling, a desire to immerse herself in the same rich sensations of her wedding night. How alluring he still was! She took his hand as he rambled on, and slipped it through her unbuttoned dress.

✦

With renewed spirit, Ann returned to the more mundane tasks of the Commercial Company. What with the many transactions taking place on a barter system, the book-keeping could be formidable, but there was no getting around this chore. George was once again pursuing oil matters.

As the children grew, so did their orbit around her. She went from worrying about them being underfoot to worrying about their safety as they struck out on little adventures.

One day the girls took Pet away all afternoon. They came back with their pockets full. Proudly they showed her. Even little Pet, four years old, pulled out a greenish-brown egg.

"Where'd you get these?" She felt sick, not because they looked bad but because of where they must have come from.

Nellie and Grace assured her they had only taken one or two from each nest.

"And where were the nests?"

"Over by the cliffs. On the other side. We didn't break a one of them."

She had never imagined them going to the edge of the steep west side by themselves. She remembered her mother's old story then, and knew what it was for. "You shouldn't *never* go up there without momma! There's an old ugly woman that's got a mustache she's called *Tsoniqua*. She live up there and steals little boys and girls. She puts 'em right into her basket and takes 'em away.

You got lucky this time 'cuz she didn't see you. You hear me? She's *bad!*"

Their eyes went wide and they promised never to go back there. Ann hugged each of them in turn. As she leaned down to hug Pet, she heard a strange peeping noise. Pet heard it too. The sound was coming from the pocket he had not yet emptied. He reached in for an egg and pulled out a freshly hatched little chick. The children shrieked with delight.

She said, "It's a baby raven. Let me see the others." She was relieved to find the rest were gull eggs. By then they were begging her to keep the chick.

"No," she said. "It's going to be too hard to care for. It's going to die."

Nellie, to prove her devotion, ran off to find minnows at the water's edge. Grace lined a wood crate with wool scraps. She put the box near the stove. Pet said that since he had found it, he got to name it. He chose, "Trix" he said, "Cuz Ravens are Tricksters, right momma?"

The children were true to their word. They took shifts feeding their baby everything from bugs to oatmeal. Every half hour in the early days of Trix's life they were loyal to their duties, even keeping the bird's bedding clean. To Ann's amazement the bird survived and thrived. It was a bit disconcerting for her to be sharing a roof with a tame and caged descendant of the Creator. Sometimes instinctively she would find herself asking the bird's advice on family matters, only afterwards remembering it did not have any particular powers.

Then she would sympathize with its life of confinement using one of Colonel George's favorite sayings, "Just remember Trix, we got a good life and we wouldn't trade all the whiskey in Ireland for it. Right?"

Trix would answer a throaty, "RRRUIOT" in the best agreement he could muster.

✦

In *The Sitka Gazette*, George read the story of the Army's persistent attempts to acquire copper rights from the very Chief Nicolai of which Ann's father had told. Chief Nicolai was finally ceding to the government, for a seemingly deficient sum: his entire copper holdings. George knew that this transaction alone would affect Katalla.

Other headlines splashed across the *Gazette* told of gold in the Yukon Territory, and of one engineer's determination to open that country up. He was quoted as saying, "Give me enough snoose and dynamite and I'll build you a road to Hell!" It seemed to George that Alaska was busting wide open. Would it become Hell or would the opportunity for great accomplishments make it all worthwhile? He had a sense of a paradise lost, but also of excitement about being on the leading edge of these discoveries.

His latest scheme was more outlandish than any before. George's years of fighting under Miles and Custer had shown him how powerful men earned respect and credibility. He was confident with his plan and persuaded Tom and Michael to use their speculation monies to buy every seat on an entire train. The hope was to impress all the California big oil men by wining and dining them in style, so that they would continue to back the Katalla oil interests.

The Great Northern departed from San Francisco pulling four first-class sleeper cars and a diner car. George and his partners spared no luxuries in their effort to dazzle the oil men and their associates. They plied them with finest Cuban cigars, Cognac, and provided each with a stack of gold coins to spend, gambling their way north.

By the time the train reached its destination in Seattle, twenty-three spent but merry businessmen parted ways. They may not have remembered precisely what promises they had made or secrets they might have divulged, but none seemed to care. George did learn from their guests that they could expect endless bidding wars, transcontinental and transatlantic negotiating, inspections in the field, scientific studies, reports and laws to work around. But as he and his buddies steamed home to Katalla, rehashing the information, they glowed from the promise of it all.

✦

Pet ran to meet his father on the beach. He had missed him bad. Now that he was seven, he was different from his sisters and from Patsie, who still clung to mama. He wanted to know things. Like, "What makes a gun shoot?" "How did steam make the boat go?" And "Why, Papa, did you help hunt Indians in the cavalry?" And "Since mama is Indian, don't that make me Indian too?" He wanted to know "where hooch came from" and "why the white mens are so many coming by Kayak Island?" He wanted to catch a salmon and hunt a bear. He wanted to be with his Papa!

"For the love 'o God lad, it's like a dam broke in yer brain! So many questions you have! I think the two of us need an outing so I have some time to provide fittin' answers. Being September, it's a right good time for catching a nice Coho. What do you say about spendin' the day on the water tomorrow with yer Papa?"

Pet smiled, spun on his heels and ran back up the hill to tell the news to the rest of the family.

That night he could hardly sleep, but when he did, he dreamed of pulling to the surface a fish the size of a whale that thrashed and nearly capsized the skiff he and Papa were in, and when he suddenly woke, he realized his bed *was* pitching.

He couldn't believe it. He *had* to still be dreaming. But then he heard the cries of his family. In a flash, Pet remembered the story his mama had told him about *Tayee shaanák'w,* an old woman from underneath, holding the Earth up by a pole. Raven would sometimes pull on her and the whole Earth would shake. Surely, Raven was tuggin' hard on her right now! He grabbed the fishing pole he had set by the bed and ran with the others from the crashing, breaking noises of the post.

Outside, the family knotted up and wailed with fear except for Papa. Pet watched him lurch this way and that, securing falling things and checking on the skiff and boat. He hunkered down and closed his eyes. Beyond the sounds of his crying siblings he could hear low rumblings of mountains falling. He pulled his arms tight around his folded legs and trembled.

A few days later, when aftershocks still rolled under their feet, they received more bad news. Grandma and Grandpa, along with Kaak, had not returned from Yakutat where they had gone to visit Little John. Their sail launch was found floating with nobody in it. Pet could not bear to hear his family crying again. He ran to the bed and threw blankets over himself.

When the Reverend came up from Yakutat with Uncle Little John, Pet had to put on a scratchy starched shirt and they all went together to Katalla. He stood amongst the sad gathering. Mama hung from Papa's long overcoat and his siblings sniffled. Pet could only wonder about the bodies of the drowned. Were they water-logged at the bottom of the sea? Was it peaceful in those depths?

*

Even though the 1800s had ended poorly, George still felt in his bones that he would prosper in this new century. He imagined that he could feel the reservoirs of oil through the soles of his feet. It was down there undulating, pushing, searching for escape from its ancient pools. He would be the man to bring it to the surface, he knew it. But *when* it would happen was still a secret, as trapped for now as the oil itself. He and the other "Greases" had finally been given the money and the go ahead to begin construction of a derrick. The paddle boat, *Thlinket,* was busy ferrying supplies up the coast. George and his partners hoped to start actual drilling by year's end.

One thing he knew for certain was that the babies kept com-ing. Ann had just whispered to him that night in bed. She was pregnant again. He lay awake wondering if the baby or the oil would come first. The Post already felt as if it would burst at the seams. What would it be like with a fifth child? If only he could get his oil strike developed and use his riches to get the family into a new larger home in Katalla.

Torrential rains came on. The drilling gear arrived on the beach and sank; they dug for days in mud. George spent his weeks in the oil camp and each Friday he returned home. Pet helped him pull off his mud-caked boots. The house was muggy with kettles of bath water heating on the stove. The children, starting with Grace, and on down through the ranks, took turns protesting loudly as Ann scrubbed them. Patsie always ended this weekly routine with an episode of defiant bellowing.

"Lass can't you quiet the little demons? Some peace is all I need right now!"

"I'm doing my best," Ann huffed, "but if you can do better, then try," and she gave him the washrag and left Patsie lathered and wet.

One thing that brought peace to his home was reading. He had made it his duty to teach Grace and Nellie to read, and lamp oil, siphoned direct from the seeps, made for endless hours of light. He puffed his pipe while Grace read from the paper about the Nome gold rush, her face glowing in its halo of light. More than 20,000 prospectors and other business opportunists had overnight turned one of the most desolate parts of Alaska into a seething, swarming, city of rapacious land grabbers. The hustle-bustle of Katalla paled compared to the Nome "stampede," but the paper was over a year old and that gold rush had come and gone, a flash in the pan. Now many who had gone bust in their quest for gold had found their way to Katalla for yet another shot at riches, or at least at employment.

Grace read on, and he was just starting to sink into a pleasant sleep when suddenly, the most grating, flat notes bellowed from his accordion. It was Pet!

"Why for the love of God lad, must you drag that beast out at such a peaceful moment? Put the damn thing away!" he said.

But when Pet's tears welled up, George felt instant remorse. He drew himself forward in his chair and told Pet to bring him the accordion. At least, he thought, his son seemed an attentive and sincere student. Taking control of the instrument, he soon found he was energized by the jig he played and the joy it brought his family as they danced around him.

◆

It was only five days after Papa and his team struck oil, resulting in a gusher spurting "a tremendous 85 feet into the air" at a rate they estimated to be 1,600 barrels per day, that George Jr. was born. Pet didn't care for the way his Papa referred to his new brother as his "wee namesake." He gushed over him almost as much as his oil strike.

George Jr. was a pain as far as Pet was concerned. He bawled and got no end of attention from his mama and sisters. Sometimes Trix would join in, adding to the cacophony. At these times Pet would tether the leg of his raven friend and together they would escape into the peace of the outdoors where they could do manly tasks to make Papa proud. He split stacks of kindling while Trix hopped around in the woodchips looking for bugs. Or he tucked the bird under his arm and went to go check trap-lines in the woods.

Today Pet looked into his friend's intelligent black eyes. "Someday Trix, you and me are going to see the world. I'll be big and important like Papa, going places and doing things and you'll be with me. Maybe I'll even have my own schooner and you'll be my First Mate!" Pet smiled as Trix bobbed his glossy head.

From up in the forest limbs a large flutter of wings startled both Trix and Pet. It was a flock of ravens coming in to roost. As they landed, they broke into raucous calls. Trix beat his wings and fell from Pet's grip. Pet leapt to put his foot on the tether but missed. Trix was hopping and lifting himself with strokes of his wide wings. Chasing Trix through the woods, Pet was finally able to grab the loose line, but as he did, Trix delivered a sharp peck to his hand. Blood streamed but Pet held tight. The wild birds lifted from the branches and flew. Trix beat his wings hard, trying to join them.

Pet, with his jagged wound, felt confused. Tears spilled from his eyes. He said, "I know it's not your fault. You weren't never meant to live in a cage."

When he got home he announced to his family his plan to set Trix free. Their protests could not sway him. "I'm the one who hatched him so it's me who's his papa and I say he gets set free!" Pet invited them to come to the cliffs the next day to release him.

He spent the night composing an emancipation speech, copying words of President Lincoln he'd found in one of his father's books.

The next day the family followed Pet and Trix to the nesting area near the cliffs. He struck a noble pose and gestured, "I, Don Petroleum Barrett by virtue of the power in me vested, hereby state that Trix is thenceforward and forever *FREE*." Pet felt light-hearted, almost joyful at the sound of his own words.

Trix only stared blankly with his beady black eyes and stayed near them all. He hopped and fluttered along after them as they returned home.

Over time with a new policy of no-feeding and no in-house visits, Trix finally made forays far enough away to meet the other ravens. After that, he only rarely made visits to trees near the Post where he would mimic baby George's cry. The girls and Patsie thought it was the funniest thing they had ever heard but the bird's cries sent shivers up Pet's spine.

✦

It was one of the rare, hot days of summer when George asked Ann and the kids if they would like to go to Katalla to see the progress on the oil works.

Ann felt her heart leap. It had been too long since her last visit to Katalla. With little George on her hip, she scurried to pack a picnic lunch. Boiling eggs, she suddenly felt woozy. God, she thought, I'm pregnant again! She continued to pack but felt some wind go out of her sails as the realization of a sixth child sunk in. Still, she was on the beach and helping to heave the children into the boat at departure time. As they glided smoothly across the still waters of Controller Bay she smiled, remembering herself as a young woman paddling out to the island with the "Love Dope" in her pocket. She was less enthusiastic about *this* mission to visit the oil derrick, but surely it would be good to see how things had advanced. She would never have the new home she longed for if he did not succeed in this oil venture. And she was excited to see Katalla, and to show her children the favorite places of her youth.

As they neared the settlement she felt they were pulling into some other town, not *her* Katalla. Instead of making a beach landing, George came alongside a new pier. This did not seem right.

"Why can't we just go ashore with the boat? We're so far out and there's a lot to carry," she complained.

"That earthquake lifted the entire seabed. It's shallow from here on in. It's not like it was. All the copper, coal and railroad men agree it's a problem. Katalla won't be a viable port unless we build a breakwater. Here," he offered, "I got two strong arms. Give me George."

Ann followed her brood as they merrily trip-tropped along the wooden pier. Where the dock ended, iron tracks began. Ann tried walking on the ties but the spacing made her steps awkward. She was so busy concentrating on walking the rails, that by the time she looked up, she gasped at the sight of town. Instead of tents, now there were sturdy houses. A store and a busy lumber mill stood on each side of a wide main street. She saw a new hotel with a painted sign above the entry that read, "The Northern." She could hardly imagine the need for a hotel in Katalla. But what she found most disturbing was the saloon. Ann recognized a crumpled figure outside the door to be her Auntie Nellie's son. She had an unsettling feeling about just what this new future for Katalla might be. She crouched and shook him gently but could not totally rouse him.

He only mumbled, "Bears in the mountains. Gonna git me some claws. Bear claws."

Ann gave up and went on along the walk. The children were all watching a filthy grubstaker hop around while playing a harmonica.

"Come on all you," she called. Why did she feel so skittish? George *had* been keeping them abreast of Katalla news but seeing it with her own eyes made her spin.

She could not hide her feelings. "George, I want to take the kids to mother and father's cabin. Should we see the derrick before or after?"

George seemed more than willing to walk to her parent's home first. "Come lass, let's go see the ol' place."

Ann was speechless when she saw that the cabin was gone. In its place was what would soon be, George proudly proclaimed, "Your new dream home! *This* is the *real* reason for our trip to Katalla." He stood puffed up and glowing.

How could her childhood home be so thoroughly erased? She began to weep.

"Luv, tell me those are tears of joy?" he said as he held her near.

His need to please her was so sincere, she forgave him in that instant. What could he know about her feelings, her tender memories and ties? He was focused on building *their future* and she loved him for his devotion and enthusiasm. "It's going to be more beautiful than I ever imagined."

The children had no reservations about it. They ran through the skeletal structure, each shrilly claiming their territories.

When George was sure his surprise had delighted them all, it was time for a picnic. Ann knew the beach was the one place that would feel the same. With her back to the new town, she calmed as she watched the children play in the surf. But even the surf rolled differently because of the lifted seafloor. *Nothing* was the same. She found herself wondering if she could really live here again. Soon the children were thoroughly wet and chilled, and as they departed for Kayak Island, she did not look over her shoulder.

✦

When they arrived back at Kayak Island, Pet refused to disembark. "Papa, if you let me go back with you, I could help. I could carry boards, I'd be good at hammerin'." With a roll of his sleeve, he proudly said, "See Papa, look at this muscle." He was pleased to see Papa's eyebrows shoot up and his eyeballs widen.

"I would'a never thought a lad not quite ten could have such manly arms. You look to be qualified. Run and get yer bedding."

Pet exploded out of the boat. He was back in a heartbeat, hugging Ann, and as they pulled away again he sang a happy sea chantey. He watched his mama and baby brother grow small in the distance as he continued to sing.

Way Ho and away we go, travelin' on the water.
The skies are blue and seas are green and our hearts are filled
*   with laughter.*
So Way Ho and away we go to find the fisher's daughter.
Way Ho and away we go, travelin' on the water.

The next day they began work. He was proud to be right there with the board or nail as it was needed.

"Papa? Do us boys get a window in our room?"

His father's eyes twinkled, "Yes, you do Pet, and I'll even let you frame it in today!"

Papa supplied the cut boards and showed how they fit. As Pet nailed the frame, he liked the view he'd have. From *his* window, he looked toward town and pictured himself with his brothers and maybe some new friends running down the street playing. But then again maybe childhood playing was behind him. He felt more grown up after their long day on the job.

When the tools were put away, Papa suggested they go down to the saloon for a bit of supper and a drink. Pet was surprised. "I might be still too young, don't you think?"

Papa ruffled his hair. "Ah, not for a bowl of chowder yer not."

The two washed up in a rain barrel and headed for the new saloon. Pet felt lofty striding in with his father. There was a warm greeting to Papa from the man behind the counter, and then a silence as eyes fell on him.

Papa stood with a hand on his shoulder, "This here would be me eldest son Don Petroleum, but we call him Pet. Don't worry, he won't be hitting the sauce, only cares for a nice bowl of yer fine chowder."

"We have a policy of no service to Indians and that includes half-breeds."

Pet looked up at his Papa. He felt his father's hand clinch his shoulder and turn him around. They walked out the door.

"Pet me lad, that man's no man at all. He's a slitherin' snake and a half-wit. Pay him no mind but I'm going in ever so briefly for a quick shot. Sit out here and I'll bring you some soup."

As Pet sat on the rough planks of the boardwalk, he puzzled over the scowl on the bartender's face. He knew there was something about Indians that white men didn't like, but no one had ever disliked him solely for being Indian.

And there was still the disturbing fact that his father had helped to chase down Indians when he was younger. Pet had never managed to satisfy his curiosity about his father's past. He would not even know this much had he not overheard his Papa talking to Tom White one night when he was supposed to be sleeping. Pet could only make out portions of the muted dialogue. He heard Sitting Bull, and Dull Knife. From what he could understand, it had been his Papa's job to scout out the Sioux renegades trying to come back across the Canadian border, and to hunt down rebel bands that still evaded capture and made trouble for the white settlers.

After that, Pet had tried to get his father to talk about those days, but he always seemed to dodge Pet's questions, responding only with talk about favorite horses or the beauty of the Yellowstone country. He talked about the cantonments full of infantrymen and the heavily loaded steamships that brought supplies. He described buffalo, swollen rivers and starry skies. And even now as Pet sat trying to figure out his feelings, he saw a figure staggering toward him.

"Hey you! It's me, Thomas Mack." He stumbled onto the boardwalk, nearly falling at Pet's feet. "I seen you before. My cousin's kid, I think."

He pulled a bottle of hooch from his coat pocket and swigged. What didn't get into his mouth ran out the edges. He swung the bottle directly out to his side almost knocking Pet's teeth with it. "Here! Sammy boy won't let us in his slooon but we got's our own so we don't care, right?"

Pet was repulsed but had always wanted to know what this notorious liquid was like. He decided to give it a try. His sense of smell warned him that it would taste awful but he was not prepared for the fire it caused in his throat. He coughed and sputtered but didn't want to appear inexperienced, so he forced himself to take another deep draw. This time, he kept a straight expression, then passed the bottle back. Thomas Mack did not respond so Pet kept hold of it, sipping while he waited, enjoying the warm and dizzying effect it had on his tired body.

He was almost asleep against Thomas Mack when Papa finally stepped out.

"For the love of God, Pet!" Papa grabbed his suspenders and yanked him to his feet. "You've been sharing hootch with that degenerate? I leave you for half an hour and you become a drunk? I'm ashamed of you!"

Pet felt oddly unconcerned with his father's stern chastising; he was concentrating more on trying to walk.

"You know that Samuel might just have a point about not allowin' Indians in his saloon. I advise that you cultivate your whiteness and don't go near that hooch again. You hear me lad?"

Stumbling along, trying to keep up with his Papa's angry strides, he slurred "Yes Papa."

The next morning Pet could see that the happy mood they had shared on the construction site was gone. He shoved his hands deep into his pockets, lowered his head. "I know I done wrong yesterday and I'm sorry, Papa."

"That's 'did' wrong." his Papa corrected him.

"I know I did wrong Papa and I promise never to drink that hooch again."

Papa was loading the boat as Pet trailed behind. "Really Papa. Don't ya believe me?"

His father threw Pet's bed roll into the boat and then turned and looked him in the eye. "I forgive ya lad but what's even more at issue is that I cannot protect you from influences of the local riff-raff. It's my mistake, I see now that perhaps you are still a bit young and should be home with mother."

As they crossed the bay back to Kayak Island, his Papa's words rang in his head. Pet hung his head all the way. He dreaded coming home, and even worse was to see them all down on the beach. Mother was bent over mending a sailcloth, while his brothers and sisters clambered on logs. When they pulled ashore, Pet bolted up to the Post.

It was an evening of taunts from Patsie and cruel whisperings between his sisters. The only solution was to steer clear from all of them. He went to the beach in the twilight, and threw rocks long and hard into the slate-gray water. He would have stayed out all night if mama hadn't come with a cup of hot tea. He sipped until it warmed his insides.

Mamma said softly, "Come on now, come to bed. There's plenty of time to become a man in your Papa's eyes but you are *already* my little man."

✦

The brutal storms of fall and winter slowed progress on the new house. But nothing got in the way of the progress the baby made as it grew within Ann's slender frame. It seemed this sixth child would be right on schedule.

By evenings, she sat helping George plan the home's interior. "I'd love a washroom here near the kitchen," she said, pointing to where he had penciled-in "pantry."

She had mulled over her summer visit to Katalla, and kept trying to picture herself settling into a new life there. The coming child seemed to be the tie breaker. No denying, there would be more space in the new home for her growing tribe of children. It also meant they would see more of George and *that* was equally important.

She expected that he might overrule her suggestions as she continued planning the house details, but he only nodded in agreement and replaced his word for hers. Colors, counter heights, closets sizes, storage areas, these decisions he left to her. Soon she was actually cursing the cramped quarters of the trading post as she dreamed of her new Katalla home.

Ann knew her heart was lighter when she started singing the song she had composed about her love for George when she was young. She smiled, remembering her youthful strength and spirit. One night, settling onto the bed with Grace, Nellie, Patsie, and George Jr. pressed in around her, she remembered a story her mother had told her, and began:

"Looong time ago in a village very near to here lived a mother and her son. They were both slaves and were not treated well. They called the boy 'coward' and only fed them moldy dried salmon. The mother decided to take her boy and go away back up into the mountains. They stayed away four years.

"When the boy was 18 years old he had become a strong and good hunter. He starts to have spirit dreams at night. The spirit voice comes to him and tells him to go further back into the mountains and stay. He did not remember his dream when he woke but he did go hunting the next day further in the mountains than he ever was before. There he saw six mountain sheep. He killed them and opened them with his flint knife. He went back down the mountain and went to sleep and had another dream. A spirit voice came again. It said, 'If you see four blue flames in the fire, that is me.' But he also forgot that dream when he woke.

"He followed moose tracks when he walked into the mountains again for four days and again he dreamed of the blue flames and again he forgot. He made a fire, striking his flint four times, each time, no sparks. Then finally sparks fell on his moss and he makes a fire and sees four blue flames shooting up high. He makes a prayer to his ancestors, 'Help me know what this means!' In the morning when he gets up he digs in the ashes where the four flames were and in each place he finds a piece of copper as big as his fist. He's never seen that before but he breaks off some and makes himself an arrowhead and goes and kills a moose with it.

"When he told his mother she said, 'It's time to go back to the village now. You will not be called a coward anymore.' When the boy shows the copper, the chief wants the boy to tell where he found it but the mother says, 'No, first you must say you will call us 'brave' from now on.' The chief agreed and for long after that, every spring when the snows melt the mother and boy still must show the way.

"This is how copper was first found here and it was slaves that found it. Now we know because of what happened to them, that any of us can get respect and have a good life if we work hard for it."

When Ann finished the story she reminded the children that soon the family would be one more, making story time on the bed even more crowded. She let them lay their hands all over her belly. She laughed as they gave shrill exclamations when they felt the baby's jabs through her dress.

Although there were still days with wintery blasts, Ann knew spring was near when the Arctic loons passed over on their way north. It was the Moon of the Green Leaves and she had a hunch that the birth of her baby could be any day. When George brought her aunt Nellie from Katalla to help, Ann prayed she wouldn't need to be with them long. Nellie was grim. She sang endlessly in Tlingit, mournful songs of her drowned husband and her hopelessly alcoholic son.

Ann's prayer seemed to be answered when her pains began the next evening with a gush of water just after she had bedded down the children. She roused auntie from her sleeping cot. This dramatic start would mean a quick birth, no upright pacing.

Nellie opened the window near Ann's bed and the fresh air and the grating croaks of wood frogs calmed her as she settled in to the rhythms of the labor. Soon she lost track of time and was only aware of waves of pain and dreamlike interludes of muted color and sound.

Ann returned to awareness of her surroundings when she heard a sound that filled her with dread. "Auntie, are the children awake? I just heard one of them calling."

The sound came again. She could not deceive herself this time; it was not a child calling for her. It was an owl!

"Auntie close the window. Get George for me. Tell him an owl has called. I need him by my side."

She listened as Nellie went to wake George. "Your wife wants you. She got a scare from owl. You come calm her."

She was relieved to feel him beside her. He took her hand. When he kissed her she softened and sank back into the bed. Soon they were working together, one on each end of a bedsheet, pulling it down hard over her belly. She screamed in protest and he stopped. Nellie tried to reposition the baby. Ann heard again the bellow of her own voice and saw George's shocked expression and then passed from the present into a shadow-realm.

A Tlingit shaman stood nearly naked with his long uncombed tresses. He was bent over a person covered by a blanket. In his hand he shook an Oystercatcher Rattle. The carved human figure that straddled the back of the Oystercatcher was bent in a tortured way. The shaman danced jolting steps around the body, he chanted and grunted and yelled. Dim firelight illuminated his face and the many talismans around his neck. Ann saw long black hair. The body was a woman. Ann saw her children watching from a dark corner of the room. She tried to get their attention but they stayed huddled together. The small finger of the woman's left hand lay revealed from the edge of the blanket. Ann reeled when she saw the Aleut ivory ring that George had given her years ago. She always wore it on her little finger, and there it was on this poor woman's hand.

George responded quickly to Nellie's demands for toweling and hot water, but felt in a daze. For the love of God, he thought, let this be just a bad dream.

She murmured deliriously, "I'm on Raven's back. Raven's back. We're flying."

George watched through his tears as her life flowed onto the bedding. He felt suffocated by his own shallow breaths and the floor seemed to tilt under him. He stumbled for the door and escaped to the beach and waded deep into the cold water, fists swinging wildly, cursing toward the black heavy clouds. This wife of his laying in her own blood, with not a breath from her lips, this could not be so!

He was numb when something warm took his hand. He looked and saw Pet pulling him. George did not care to go. "Leave me Lad!" But his son would not stop yanking on him, so he followed him out of the water and sank next to him on the beach log.

"Oh God lad, we've lost our Ann! What, pray God shall we do?"

✦

Ann lay in state for two days while friends gathered. The Swede brothers made a special run up from Yakutat with Little John.

Pet slumped in a corner. He did not want to look at his mama. Grace and Nellie brushed her hair. "Come see," they said. "Her hair looks like kelp ribbons in a current, she's so beautiful!" They were braver than he. How could they be near her and not cry?

When Little John arrived he acted important, reading scripture and saying that his sister was "in the arms of Jesus." Pet would rather have been left alone but Jonathan enlisted him to help build a coffin. When it was finished, Pet was glad he had helped. Papa was pleased. "You did right handsome work," he said. "You made it worthy of Ann to be laid to rest in."

Papa shuttled mourners from Katalla and brought extra food and whiskey. Two fiddlers took up playing; sad and slow at first, and more fiery as day turned to night. Papa's buddies hung close, sharing a bottle. The whiskey seemed to make Papa happier. Pet wanted to feel happy too. It was easy to take a bottle. No one noticed or cared. He sat on the outdoor steps and drank until he felt fuzzy and was unconcerned when Patsie came out and saw him.

"I thought you told Papa you weren't gonna drink no more?"

Pet gripped the bottle tighter, afraid Patsie would take it, but he only turned and went inside.

When the door opened again, Pet thought he was in trouble for sure. Patsie was bringing Papa out to scold him. But no, it was Grace with Little George on her hip. Nellie followed her and then out came Patsie. They sat all around Pet. Grace hugged him and they all cried as they looked into the sky. Together they saw a star shoot toward the sea.

✦

George's partners had chimed in on his dilemma about what was best for the children now that Ann was gone. Their council created a battle between his heart and mind. Eventually his heart lost. The more he reasoned and rehearsed his arguments, the more confident he was about his proposal to the children.

He announced one evening the need for a family "pow wow." George put a steaming pot of tea on the table and placed a cup at each chair. He watered down baby George's tea and sat him on a stack of his medical books. Looking into their five sets of black eyes was like having five ghost-images of Ann staring back at him. A memory flooded back, the eyes of those Indian mothers years ago, watching to see what their fate would be at the hands of the U.S. Cavalry. He pushed this image from his mind and proceeded, hoping Ann would not roll in her grave at his plan.

"Now me luvs, it's time we had a serious talk about our future. It breaks me heart to see you all without your dear mother, and I want you each to know that I love you as big as Mount Saint Elias and as deep as the ocean and as far out as the horizon, but I can't love you like a mother. I have taken your best interests into consideration, in thinking about your care as well as an education. It has been brought to my attention that a fine Indian school exists in Oregon State by the name of Chemawa. It's for both boys and girls."

The children looked nervously at each other and Grace spoke up. "Papa, are you talking about sending us all away?"

George knew it was inconceivable to them. They had known nothing but this isolated life.

"First let me make clear that even though our family home is almost built in Katalla, it is out of the question for you all to live in that town without a mother. It grows wilder by the day and is no place for children. Nor can you stay alone out here. But at the Indian school you'll get a real education."

The tea that the children had initially been sipping now stood, growing cold in their cups. Only George Junior banged his up and down, saying, "Mo! Mo!"

Nellie reached over and dumped her tea into his cup. "Papa" she said, "You mean we would *live* there? And when would we get to see you?" Her eyes were welling up.

George, wanting to prevent the talk from breaking down, tried to sound bright and optimistic. They could come home for visits as they got a little older, and might also enjoy staying at the school for summer employment.

"You've never had the chance to make your own money now have you?"

Patsie's eyes lit up slightly at that thought but Pet still glowered from his end of the table. He said, "Where's Oregon?"

"Now *that's* precisely one reason school will be good for you. I've been neglectful of teaching you geography and that's not right. This will be your chance to get a white man's education that will serve you for your entire life." He said, "I would like you all to go with good brave hearts into this next part of your lives because we have no other choice but to make it good. Grace however, you'll not go to Chemawa. I have wired me brother in St. Paul to see about you going to live with him and his family. They are fine people with a successful livery business. They'll raise you like a lady."

The children set to howling and yipping like a pack of wild abandoned wolf pups. George heard each of their concerns in turn. It was a pitiful and painful process but it gradually imprinted on the children's dewy young minds that their lives were soon to be changed, with or without their consent.

Through the days that followed, George accepted the glumness of his children as natural and unavoidable. Their sorrow tore at him, yet he saw no better solution. God save me soul, he thought, if I'm doing wrong by them. And he meant it.

◆

Pet could barely remember the agonizing last days before leaving Alaska now as he stood on the bow of the steamship with the angular outlines of Seattle slowly coming into view. Papa pointed out the landmarks as they drew closer. Wharfs jutted out like greedy fingers beckoning them.

Nellie wondered if Seattle stores might sell silk hair ribbons. Papa figured it was likely, and when he promised the girls each a half a "fathom" of a color of their choosing, they squealed with glee.

Pet was wishing he could be made happy that easily when he noticed a huge ship bristling with guns. The name *USS Oregon* was on its steep, steel hull. "What's that Papa?" Pet asked.

"That's a battleship lad. It's heading into the naval shipyard. Aye, the *USS Oregon,* she's a famous vessel."

Pet was transfixed by the war ship, the way (even from its distance at the mouth of the bay) it dwarfed other vessels near it. He had no idea something so mighty and powerful existed. He imagined how small he would feel aboard it, but could also imagine the power he would wield if he could man the guns.

Soon the steamship docked and Pet and his siblings took their first unsteady steps down the clamorous pier. Pet saw decrepit shanties along the waterfront. Indian boys in rags threw rocks into the water. The city scene behind the shacks did not seem to belong, or was it the other way around? He stepped faster to catch up.

City folk, all dressed in black with black umbrellas, pushed by, and a train blew its whistle as it screeched past the tall brick buildings. Little George, who'd been sleeping in Papa's arms, screamed and cried. Papa was trying to sooth him when he had to yank Nellie from the path of a man on a bicycle. They crowded into a carriage and then it seemed to Pet as if they were flying. He tried to read the many signs as they flashed by. He saw the telegraph office, and an Alaskan outfitter store called *Cooper and Levy.* He read another sign that he did not understand. "Papa. What's 'Nickelodeon'?

Papa explained that it was a place to see "moving picture shows" and that if there was time he would take the lot of them to see it with their own eyes.

The carriage stopped in front of the *Rainier Grand Hotel.* Papa signed in and then prodded to keep everyone moving. The carpet was like walking on moss and the chandeliers in the lobby threw rainbows all around. But the best were the beds in their room that Grace proclaimed to be "the softest, cleanest, prettiest beds ever!" They lost no time jumping wildly on them.

Papa looked relieved to have arrived. "I'm glad you're havin' fun but just don't break anything! I'm going to share a drink with my friends and associates."

No one missed him as pillows flew. Even Pet laughed as he clobbered Patsie. By the time Papa came back, Pet was the only one still awake. He heard muffled sobs. Was that coming from his Papa? He lifted his head slightly and saw him sitting in a leather chair, looking out the window. He rested his head again, but could not sleep.

After the business of telegraphing the Indian School and buying train tickets, Papa kept his word to the girls and bought them each silk ribbons. Then he treated them all to the Nickelodeon. The film was called the *Great Train Robbery*. Pet was thrilled at the close-up of the outlaw shooting his gun directly at the audience, but embarrassingly, his sisters screamed and George Junior began to cry, and it became such a disturbance that they all had to leave. Pet was disappointed.

It was only the rhythmic swaying of the train as it trundled along that finally allowed Pet the deep, peaceful sleep he'd been missing for so long. By the time they arrived at Chemawa, there was so much commotion and excitement that it took him time to realize what was happening.

Chemawa had its own train stop. They could see the school's large buildings just up the hill. A contingent met them as they disembarked. Some older students came as porters but Pet would not relinquish his accordion to them.

The Superintendent, Mr. Wadsworth, welcomed them, and they were all shown to their dormitories and were then free to explore. They followed Papa as he sauntered about the campus, nodding with satisfaction at the classrooms, the blacksmith shop, shoe making shop, wagon making shop, tailoring room, the kitchen and the dining hall with its rows of tables.

They poked their heads into a dark chapel and Nellie asked, "What is this room for?"

Papa explained that it was a place for praying. He said, "Me and your mama always called out our prayers into the winds or under the moon or over the spirits of the raging sea. We were alike in that way, the good earth was our chapel. But…" he continued, "in the interest of making you kids acceptable in the eyes of Chemawa here, I gave the answer I knew they'd like to hear. I told them the family's faith was Catholic."

Pet rather liked the idea of calling out his prayers to the wind. He said, "Since Grace will be in Minnesota and papa will be in Alaska and we're in Oregon, we could all be listenin' for each other's prayers whenever the wind blows."

Patsie stated matter-of-factly that he would prefer to write letters. Grace hugged Pet. Tears ran down her round brown cheeks. She said, "I'll be listening for your words on the winds if you listen for mine."

When Nellie saw her sister's tears she joined the hug and cried too. Soon Papa had dropped to his knees and the whole family embraced in front of the chapel door.

In the morning Papa carried Little George to the train stop and gave him up only at the last minute, handing him over to Nellie as he and Grace boarded the train for Minnesota. Pet waved half-heartedly as he watched them, their hands pressed to the window. Then they were gone.

✦

Just as Pet feared, Patsie was an exemplary student at Chemawa. He smiled politely and said his "Yes Madam's" and "Yes Sir's," with respect. He wrote long letters home to Papa once a week and also read and studied hard. He had no problem making chums with other boys and even volunteered on the cleaning duties in the dormitory. When Pet was near his brother, people would look right past him or worse, they'd scowl and their eyes would then fall on Patsie and shine.

Pet found it easier to be alone. His mind often drifted back to Kayak Island. He'd see his mama doing chores and singing. He thought of Trix and imagined how his bird must have felt like he did now, at least until he'd been set free. Pet wanted free. He was not alone in his misery. He saw that other children who came, and did not speak English, cried a lot. They got whacked and scolded if they spoke their Indian language. Pet was glad he didn't grow up speaking Tlingit.

The next best thing to being back home was when he got to see and play with Nellie and baby George. Pet almost didn't recognize Nellie the first time because all her long hair had been cut short. She was still red-eyed from that, and saying she should've given Grace her ribbon because it was no good to her now. When Pet told her she was still pretty, "even as pretty as mama," she smiled again.

The next, *next* best thing to being back home was when he was allowed to play his accordion in the school band. The heart that Pet was unable to put into studies and rule-abiding, he saved for his accordion playing. Monthly, the school held a dance in the gym. He became keen on the idea of winning the attention of girls and took pride that *his* playing made the girls dance. How he fared in math classes or in the shoe-making shop or in geography seemed of little importance compared to playing music. This was at least one thing *he* had over Patsie.

With Pet's new interest in girls, he thought less and less of home. And when he and Patsie discovered the opportunity for summer employment, they chose to stay in Oregon rather than returning to Alaska with Nellie and little George. They spent the apple-picking season working for a local grower outside of Salem. The rolling hills of the orchard were a pleasant escape from the regimented life of boarding school. Pet did not care to compete, but Patsie was always challenging him, racing to top-off his picker first. The problem was that Pet would lose concentration on the race when reaching the top of his ladder. From up there he could see a great distance over the billowy tree tops as the orchard spread out around him. Pileated woodpeckers, with their flamboyant red crests, flitted from tree top to tree top, pecking holes in the shiniest apples. Swallows swooped and dove over a nearby pond and an occasional redtail hawk careened between the trees. At this elevation, cool, early-autumn breezes rustled the leaves and made him think of Kayak Island. He could almost smell the sweet, salty wafts of kelp and eelgrass, and thought of his time spent poking around in the island tide pools. But then his mind would stray to girls and he reminded himself there was certainly no promise of girlfriends on the island. Even with these distractions, Pet managed to pick only slightly under Patsie's daily average. The orchard owner smiled as he handed them each almost seven dollars. He said "266 boxes of apples was damn near as good as any two full-grown men could do," and told them he would gladly hire them next season. Pet was proud and happy to have his first, very own spending money.

✦

More years of school followed, and summer work picking apples, cherries, and hops. Nellie warned Pet that Katalla had changed since they left, but his first return was a shock. Katalla was practically a ghost town!

The town, Papa explained, had boomed and busted in practically the blink of an eye. A few winters of deep snowfall; fierce, pounding hurricane-force winds; combined with *more* earthquakes and tidal waves had brought their hopeful town to its knees. They could never build a breakwater along such a vulnerable and violent coast. And with no safe moorage, all interests quickly shifted to the rival town, Cordova. It was a shame.

Along with the bust of the town, Papa's oil dreams also went by the wayside. But in spite of it all, he seemed content to stay. His home was completed, smartly furnished and heated by an oil stove.

Pet was not as comforted by the new house as he imagined he would be. A woman, whom Papa introduced as his "housemaid" Laura, seemed a little too easy and familiar. It was good though, to catch up with Grace. She was nineteen now, and wanted to come home, and Papa was not putting up much of a fight. He practically glowed as he looked at her. He doted on young George, and pampered Nellie, and praised Patsie endlessly on the good reports he'd earned from Chemawa. He went on and on about how much he'd enjoyed his correspondence. Even though Pet knew he deserved no praises, it did not seem fair that he was made to feel like a shadow in his father's house. When he brought out his accordion to play, Papa told him that Laura could not tolerate the loud bellows.

The last weeks of their summer vacation, Pet tagged along as Patsie tried to persuade other children to come with them to Chemawa. The Superintendent had hinted there would be favors for those students who recruited the most enrollees. Patsie's eyes had nearly gleamed as he had given out application forms for them to take home on their summer vacations.

Pet tried to reason with his brother. "Patsie, are the favors you'll win from Wasdworth really worth making kids leave their families?"

Patsie only shrugged, "It's boring here in the sticks. These kids will thank us someday. You'll see."

In the final days before the steamer came to take them south, Pet made off with a silver pocket flask filled with whiskey. He sat on the beach enjoying the fiery liquid. Little Kayak Island shimmered in the sea's reflective light, giving it an otherworldly appearance. Did he once live a life there with his mother? The place looked hopelessly distant now. Why could he not just move forward as Patsie seemed to do so effortlessly?

A raven flew overhead with the buzzing beat of wings that were missing a flight feather or two. This could be an old raven. Pet thought of Trix and looked up, but if it were Trix, he was mute and gave no hint of recognition. By the time the flask was empty, Pet was on his back, staring into the sky's blue depths. He felt better now, held as he was, in the embrace of the warm sands.

He fell asleep and dreamed of shooting guns from the deck of a battleship. Sailors took commands from him. He seemed important and in control of a dangerous situation. Explosions and choking black smoke then twisted the dream into a nightmare. Pet realized that the ship was sinking into leaden waters. He was forced to swim. He woke to find his little brother George standing over him, laughing.

"You was kickin' and coughing!" he said. Then noticing the flask, "You shouldn't be drinking Papa's whiskey. I'm gonna tell."

Pet picked up a handful of pebbles and threw them at George. "Scram! You good-for-nuthin'."

When his little brother left him to his peace, he tried to recapture the images of his dream. What was it? He then remembered the battleship and its explosions and the memory sent a shiver of excitement up his spine. Maybe it *is* too quiet here in Katalla, he thought as he got to his wobbly feet.

♦

When Patsie was seventeen, the doctors removed a growth and surrounding infection in his throat. They claimed he was "as good as new." And he did continue to be of good spirit, and a dedicated student, but he never recovered his health as promised.

Pet was always the troublemaker, the one caught kissing girls behind the blacksmith shop, the one draining wine bottles, the one who dropped out of school. He was a drifter, kicking around the streets of Seattle playing for occasional weddings when word came of his brother's death.

Why, Pet wondered, of anyone in the family, why Patsie? Why not him?

After that last visit to Katalla, he'd rarely punished himself by returning. But now it was his duty to return.

The loss was unbearable for his father. As the eldest son, Pet knew he didn't measure up, he was a worthless misfit in his family. The best he could offer was a tender rendition of "Danny Boy" on his accordion for the funeral. He didn't linger in Katalla.

It seemed almost a lucky turn of events to Pet when Woodrow Wilson declared war on the Germans a month later. The next day, he joined a throng of 50,000 people gathered in the streets of Seattle to watch the "Preparedness Parade." The Naval Militia, hundreds strong, led the parade, looking brave, dignified and purposeful, and he knew in that instant that he'd enlist.

Boarding school life had accustomed him to discipline and the rigors of Navy life. The difference was that this time he was here by choice. For the first time he felt a draw to something greater than himself, to rid the world of evil, to be a hero!

Shipboard maneuvers had him coming and going from the Bremerton Navy Shipyard. He developed a habit of stopping in at a soda fountain near the main gate. There, a sparkly-eyed, fair-skinned, curiously bold girl served up sundaes, cones and shakes in almost choreographed, graceful movements.

"Why is it you look like you're havin' so much fun?" Pet teased. "Don't you know there's a world war going on?"

On tippy-toe and stretching her small body across the ice-cream bins and counter, she handed Pet his single-scoop vanilla cone. "Nobody's shooting at *me!*" she said.

Her attitude was perky. Her breasts were perky. He liked this girl. "What's your name, sunshine?" he asked, as she leaned down into the barrel and rolled up a perfect ball of chocolate ice cream. He was transfixed by her deep and mysterious cleavage.

She straightened, placed the ice cream on a cone, and proceeded to lick. "Well, you see my mama named me *Irene* after a Greek goddess of Peace, and maybe that's why it's not my inclination to think much about this war, but I figure I'm doing my part just serving sweets to you brave servicemen."

Pet, emboldened by her forward manner, congratulated her for her "selfless acts" and asked her to a dance on the coming weekend. To his delight, she said she was "crazy about dancing," and agreed.

Pet brought along his accordion in case there was a chance to join the band. He walked jauntily along with his pretty date at his arm. He liked the way heads turned when they walked into the dance hall. They sat at a table in a quiet corner and ordered drinks. She talked a lot, but that was all right with him. Everything she said intrigued him. She was a musician too, she said, or anyway she played ukulele. She'd played and sung for private parties and on the local radio station before she got the soda fountain job. She'd also grown up in Salem, and left home at sixteen. She didn't look much older than that now.

"Odd we didn't see each other," she said. "Salem's a small town. Where did you live?"

Pet glanced away and mumbled, "Chemawa."

Irene squinted and looked quizzically at him. "Oh! I took you for a Spaniard!" She lifted her glass and toasted, "Here's to you, my handsome *Indian* friend."

Pet was relieved she did not seem disappointed. In fact, with the music just striking up, he wasn't sure but thought he heard her say something about their meeting being "destiny." Pet was indeed taken by this little firecracker of a female. He had never met a girl quite like her before. After a few beers, he felt loosened up enough to ask to join the band. They were playing all the favorites, "Pack up Your Troubles" and "Keep the Home Fires Burning." He knew them well.

He saw Irene tapping her toes and turning away requests from other men. He was happy to end the set and dance the rest of the night with her. Holding her near, he smelled her sweet perfume. He pushed at her hip and pulled at her waist as they glided around the floor. He held her close. The rhythms of the music moved through his body like water and pulsed against hers. He felt wild and weak in the same moment.

When the music ended for the night, Irene did the leading. Pet gathered their belongings and stumbled after her into the parking lot. When he set down his accordion case, she stepped up onto it and he thought he'd be mighty mad if anyone else did that. But he moved close to her and held her by the waist as she draped her delicate hands on his shoulders.

She said, "Are you really the gentle, kind soul you look to be?"

He picked her up and gave her a spin. "Invite me to your place and I'll show you."

Pet had never known such deep joy. To physically love this perfect woman was indeed a wondrous gift. Her buoyancy aroused him. He spent as many nights with her as he was able. Yet he felt he'd barely begun to indulge in the pleasures of knowing her when he learned he'd be shipping out.

As the time drew near, he could see Irene's brave façade fade. No one could forget how many millions had already perished. He told her that now the Americans were in, the end might be near, but inwardly, he couldn't deny the threats. Torpedoes and bombs still caused death and mayhem. Naval ships, in spite of their might, were still sitting ducks. On the night before his deployment, she began to sob on his shoulder. On his accordion, he played her "Send Me Away With a Smile."

He didn't want their last night of lovemaking to end, and hoped her memory of his embrace would keep her faithful while he was gone. He talked about what their lives would be like when he returned. They'd marry, he promised, and have babies, and especially they would *dance*!

✦

Irene stood on the dock flourishing a pink embroidered hanky as the Navy freighter, the *USS West Apaum* pulled away. She wasn't sure that she could really spot "Seaman Don Barrett," as he now was called. There were *so many* men on deck in their navy blues, all waving at someone they loved. But she had showed him the color of her handkerchief, so she knew he could see her. She brandished it again exuberantly as she bounced on her toes, taking some comfort in knowing he wouldn't go off to Europe immediately. First the ship would head for Chile to take on a cargo of guano for bomb making. Then it would make its way through the Panama Canal and off-load the nitrates on the East Coast before heading across the Atlantic. She was thankful for every minute of time stalled before Don's ship entered the fray.

✦

Eventually he did see action in Europe. Irene kept his letters in her lingerie drawer and read them almost every night after returning from the soda fountain. He mocked the French who he said arrogantly claimed to possess "élan," which was supposed to be a special quality of spirit that would help them overcome the Germans. But it was the Americans who were really driving the enemy to defeat. He also grumbled about American troops being called "doughboys." It seemed to insinuate that they were soft and unconditioned. "We may not be as crusty as those louse-ridden Europeans but if we were to withdraw our 700 naval ships, they'd sorely feel the loss of our contribution." He always ended his letters with loving words for his "Goddess Irene," and promised to be in her arms by the year's end.

When she wrote back, she dabbed her letters to him with Jasmine perfume and expressed, in flowery prose, the depth of her love for him. But she could also not help mentioning the startling battle taking place around her, with the Spanish Influenza.

> *We who are working in the public must ALL wear gauze masks and there are signs everywhere telling us 'No Dancing, No Spitting and No Gathering,' the worst of all of course being 'No Dancing.' My sister and I miss going out for the weekend dances. But I don't mind complying because all around me, people are dropping over. Seattle has already lost 1,500 people this spring. Wouldn't it be ironic if you were to come home from the war and find that I had perished from the flu? That's an awful thing to say, I'm sorry! Don't worry; I'm taking all of the suggested precautions to be sure I'm still here when you return. They say they have vaccinated 10,000 naval shipyard workers against the flu, which should also reduce the infection rate around here. Anyhow, I'm being a good girl and staying away from sailors!*
>
> *Adoringly,*
> *Your Goddess Irene*

Irene kept her word about staying away from sailors. But her sister Helen often visited from Salem; they were each other's favorite companions. One day they were out together when a touring car pulled up to the curb. Two dashing young men wearing goggles and scarves boldly invited them for a spin. They introduced themselves as brothers, Erick and Carl.

"Oh, come on," Helen said. "Why don't we?" It sounded like a thrill to Irene. The sisters jumped into the back seat and the fellows drove them to Seattle. They went to Woodland Park and then on to Alki Beach. While walking along in the sand behind the brothers, Helen whispered to Irene that she was going to "make a move" on the driver. Irene knew her younger sister was frivolous, but this seemed overly impulsive. Still, she was having fun and agreed to stick with Helen on her mission when the brothers offered to extend the date to dinner and dancing. Before the evening was over, as the sisters powdered their noses, Helen told Irene that she and Erick were going to be married.

"Married! When?"

"Tomorrow."

"Tomorrow! That's crazy! Why you don't know the first thing about him!"

"I do!"

"Well, what's his last name?"

"I don't know and I don't care. I just know he's the one for me."

Irene threw her hands up. She knew Helen's hardheadedness. "Okay, his last name could be Satan for all I care. Just don't let him take you far away!"

Irene was happy to learn that the newlyweds were staying put and it seemed Helen had even convinced Erick to rent a house on the same block as hers. Irene was dazzled by the romance of it all and could hardly wait for Don's return so that they too could marry.

Finally the eternally long wait for her absent lover was over. On the 11th day of the 11th month at the 11th hour, the Germans petitioned for an armistice. The news of the cease fire had Irene, Helen and Erick out celebrating wildly in the streets with thousands of others. They threw caution to the wind. Flu epidemic be damned! There were no masks in sight as throngs of people hugged, laughed, cried and sang. The war was over, Don would be coming home!

On the day of his return, Irene put crisp linen sheets on the bed, curled her hair and baked a cake. The cake slumped when she took out of the oven so she frosted it with grey icing and made a miniature licorice periscope that she stuck in the top. She giggled at her finished creation: a sinking German sub!

And then she was at the docks, running to him. His face lit up and he dropped his duffle. He lifted her high and she nestled her face into his warm neck. He smelled of aftershave. His sailor cap fell to the dock and his black hair gleamed in the sun. It was trimmed neat and brushed like a wave over his crown. She planted lipstick smudges on his cheeks and then tugged him toward the taxi she had waiting.

Irene could not help clinging to her returned war hero like a medal of honor pinned to his lapel. Not that he had earned any decorations himself, but the fact he'd returned unharmed to her was worth fanfare. She accompanied him into the dimly-lit, smoky depths of bars where the vets boisterously retold their experiences and drank to less fortunate comrades. She felt somewhat privileged to be with the rowdy and robust men in their inner sanctum. She smoked and tossed back shots of whiskey with the best of them. Other girlfriends and wives also joined in with their men and some would stay late, dancing limply as one by one the musicians packed up and went home. By the time only a slumped harmonica player or a tired guitarist provided the last imperfect chords, Irene and Don were, without exception, still dancing and the last to leave. For a time, these celebrations were exciting for Irene. Don and the other men adored her. But eventually the novelty wore thin. She realized that, as much as they seemed to enjoy her presence, they also seemed to not miss her when she was gone. The gleam of Don's "heroism" was losing its luster. Enough was enough. It was time to move on to other important things in life.

Since Don was still not ready for the shift, Irene decided to begin without him. She didn't mind her low-rent bungalow and happily shared it with him but she decided it could use some embellishing. The shipyard was hiring thousands of civilian workers and the pay was better than the soda fountain. Irene took a new job as file clerk and spent her extra earnings on paint and curtains and a new refrigerator. She did her best to lure Don home with his favorite dinners of salmon or steak and also arranged dinners and outings with Helen and Erick. She did not care for the look of pity she often received from her sister when Don would not show up as planned. Irene made excuses. Eventually, she ran out of plausible ones and her tears and frustration spilled out.

"How can he choose those bar rats over me? He promised he'd be here." She dabbed her eyes. "After our dad ran off and left mom, I promised myself I'd only ever love a man that loved me equal. I'm pretty sure he loves me a lot but he's got himself pretty tight with his seaman buddies. I guess that's to be expected."

Helen wrapped her arms around Irene. "Give him time. He may not be a homebody like my Erick, but he's sweet. I'll be here for you any time you need me in the meanwhile."

As if to prove he was aware of the suffering he caused by being out late too many nights, Don would rally and swear off going to the bar. During one of these times he went right out and got a custodial job at the shipyard. For a while, he sprang out of bed each morning as if he'd heard reveille. He'd come home with a twinkle in his eyes, and nibble at her neck and croon in her ear, "I've been dancing all day with my broom and I've got some new moves to show you." Then he'd spin her around until she'd land pinned to the floor or bed or table in his loving embrace.

But whenever Irene, still glowing from a sexual romp, was moved to mention marriage, Don's mood would change.

Unlike Helen's quick courtship and wedding, it took a year of hinting and then six months of a swelling womb for Irene to convince Don that marriage could not be put off any longer. She decided on a simple ceremony performed by the Justice of the Peace. When her mother came from Oregon, she was disturbed by Irene's condition, but Helen only told her, "Mother, she may be pregnant out of wedlock but you are onto your third husband, so let her be!"

Then she turned to Irene and gently patted her tummy. "I may have set a record getting Erick to the altar but it looks like you'll beat me to the diaper changing!"

Pregnancy worked like a drug coursing through Irene. She had never felt so light and joyful. She glowed like a harvest moon. Maybe she was a foolish optimist. She knew Don was far from perfect, but she could not keep herself from loving him.

Sometimes when she watched him from a distance going about his day, she admired an essence about him that was pure, a boy-like quality, tender and vulnerable. But she hoped he was a man as well, and would step up to his new responsibilities.

Becoming a mother meant quitting her job. Don stuck to his part-time custodial work and they settled in as man and wife and soon their baby boy was born. Irene could see that Don was proud and pleased, especially with the name she chose: Don Petroleum Barrett II. But when she suggested he write to his father in Katalla to give him the news, his eyes glazed. His voice, when he spoke, was flat. "My sisters might care to know," he said, "but my father's disowned me and I guess it's well that he has. I really only wish my dear mother could know."

She knew that when she saw this look that the whiskey bottle would soon come out. Irene had a soft spot for her husband's blue side. She never doubted his goodness; it was his very sadness, she decided, that gave evidence of his depth. She saw value in this trait. The other men at the bar she knew seemed crude, and far less capable of emotion, but that was not the case with her Don. Still, she hid the bottle. And still she wondered about his despair. Was it the war? What had he seen? Perhaps there were things he hadn't told her. Sometimes she could head off a storm by shoving his accordion into his arms and begging him to play a song. If he started a slow and somber, she'd cajole him to play something happy so she could sing. In turn, her singing would liven him up. She'd sing and dance, and flip her skirt high, until soon they were both smiling and laughing.

When Irene could get Helen to watch the baby, she made it her mission to get Don out dancing. She fell in love with him over and over again on the dance floor. He was light on his feet and moved her around like a leaf on the wind. She felt beautiful and delicate as she responded to his grace and direction. At these times she swore to herself she would follow her man absolutely anywhere he cared to lead her.

Almost without fail though, as the evenings wore on, her dreams dissolved. Whiskey cut in like a hussy and stole him each time, turning him into a clumsy, stumbling fool. He'd hang on people and sob, or worse, he'd want to kiss all the women, oblivious to their disgust. Embarrassed, Irene would be the one, in the wee hours, to get him standing and then shoulder his weight for the walk home.

At least for solace she had her baby Don. He was a quiet, contented being. She pampered him with attention and sweet lullabies. She had no complaints about her duty to raise him well. But in the quiet of the night when he was sleeping and Don was out, she couldn't help but compare her life with Helen's. Helen wasn't waiting up for *her* husband. She didn't have to drag him home and sober him up so that he could get off to work the next day. Erick was responsible, kind and gentlemanly. He worked and brought in enough so that Helen could now and then buy a new dress or shoes or magazines. Irene was happy for her sister, and it was not beneath her to accept these items as hand-me-downs when Helen generously passed them along. Still, it didn't seem fair that Don was so much more a piece of work than Erick. Then too, she was a little envious of Helen and her friends' unrestrained night lives. But then she'd tiptoe to where little Don slept blissfully, and knew that she had something better.

✦

Soon they had a second son. She and Don were delighted. They both agreed on Homer for his first name and Don gave him Patrick for a middle name. But everyone just called him Buddy, because it was easy for little Don to pronounce. Irene was busier than ever trying to make ends meet and feed her boys. Although she still felt blessed to be a mother of such adorable sons, she never could have guessed how much work it was. Maybe, she thought, if Don even had the smallest abilities to lend a hand, she'd have some free time for herself.

Don rose to the occasion one afternoon when Irene cried from pure boredom, "Please, get me out of here! Take us to the carnival. It'll be fun and I don't want to go without you."

He must have seen her desperate look, because he made not the least attempt to back out. He even seemed up for the family outing. "You get the boys ready and I'll rig the pram with a board so little Don can ride sitting above Buddy."

Irene felt almost bursting with pride as Don rolled his sons along and she locked her elbow with his. A warm summer breeze lifted her hair away from her face. She closed her eyes as rays hit them and pretended she was blind but being led by a man she trusted utterly. Her sister's handed-down shoes were so big, she had to allow herself to see again, to keep from tripping, but she thought she could actually have found her way there blind, just by the thick smell of cotton candy and caramel apples on the air.

Little Don pulled tufts of the sticky candy from the paper cone as Don Sr. took shots at bright yellow ducks. "Lookit son, your Papa got another." He took aim with the rifle and shot again. "And another!" He let little Don choose the stuffed animal and then handed it to Irene with a kiss. In spite of the blaring music, flashing lights and the shouts of roustabouts, Buddy slept. Irene convinced Don to keep the pram bobbing while she rode the merry-go-round with Don Jr. Finally, little Don could not stay awake any longer, so Irene laid him next to his brother. It was late by the time they wove their way through the crowds toward the exit, where Irene spotted a small tent with a sign that read: *Madame Sonja's Fortune Telling.*

"Oh! Please?" Irene pleaded, "This one last thing! I've never had my fortune read before."

Don gave her his last coins. "Ask her when we'll get rich."

Irene really could not conceal the dread that she brought back out from her visit with Madame Sonja, but she clutched her stuffed animal tight as they made their way home. She deflected Don's curiosity by talking about their beautiful boys, and only divulged the news that they weren't to be rich any time soon.

✦

The Barrett brothers were inseparable mischief-makers. Double trouble! As soon as brother Don could coax a laugh out of Buddy or get him to follow on hands and knees, he would orchestrate their dual misdeeds, taking advantage of Buddy's innocence. Once Irene found little Don smiling angelically while watching Buddy rub potting soil into the fabric of a couch Helen had just given her.

Little Don protested the spanking he received. "How come Buddy only got's a hard hand-washin' and no spankin'?"

"You! You, Don Petroleum Junior, encouraged him! So don't play innocent with me!"

Irene had to be on her toes with these two. Mischief seemed to be the theme of their brotherhood. But they also gave her so much joy. Their little escapades were to be expected; she was equipped to deal with them. It was Don's drinking and lackluster work ethic that really worried her. Not only was it part-time work, but he often called in "sick" after drinking binges.

Still, she refused to let her spirit be broken. It was not always bad, she told herself. Don loved and cared for her the best he could, even if his "best" was coming home *after* the bars were closed. Irene could always count on Helen for fun. The two of them arranged outings to learn to dance the Charleston. Helen and Erick now had a baby boy named Eddie. Sometimes they could get their husbands to go with them to the dance hall, where they tucked the sleeping children in blankets under the benches and danced the night away.

On most nights, though, he stayed away from home. While he was elbowed-up to the bar, Don seemed oblivious to any neglect or wrong-doing. Irene knew where to find him, but usually she just waited for him to stumble in. She shrank under the covers when she heard his blundering steps. When the bedroom door opened, she'd smell the wretched stink of smoke and beer. He seemed to hone in on her like a dizzy bee seeking a flower and then he'd land clumsily on top of her. She did not fear his fists. He was not a physically violent man. But his foul, smothering kisses and unwanted passion enraged her. She could not reason with him to get off of her and let her sleep. He would push himself against her in a drunken attempt to make love and then seem perplexed and dismayed when she yelled and shoved him off. In frustration, he'd break lamps and plates or anything he could lift. On nights like these, she fled with her boys to Helen and Erick's house. Irene could count on him to knock on the door, sobered up and looking sheepish. If she was not of a mind to go with him, she would see the hurt in his eyes and know he would be off again to the bar to nurse the pain of rejection.

Irene remembered her simple carefree life before Don. Now when she looked in the mirror she could hardly see a trace of her earlier self. It had only been seven years but they were seven years that stole her innocence and etched worry lines into her brow. Surely she had been the lighthearted girl who once sang on the radio and for private parties. But where had that girl gone? Now, between the bickering and dashed hopes of her marriage, if she *could* sing at all, she imagined she would sound like a soprano holding the last exalted, tragic note of an opera, her voice growing thin and brittle like ice. She wondered how long she could sustain.

Ultimately it came down to her love of life. How could she squander this one chance for her and her sons to live a beautiful life? Weren't their days too precious to waste? She could not reason with Don that for the sake of his sons he should come home sober, or that he should stop drinking away their little income, or that he should take the boys fishing or play ball with them. No suggestions or threats had an effect on halting or slowing his slide. He seemed in the grip of a dark force.

The only option for their salvation was to leave. She coached herself to be strong. She packed their belongings and left the damaged, sweet man she knew she would always love. They moved in with Helen and Erick. She did not reconsider even when he brought her gifts of reconciliation or pounded on the door in the night sobbing and pleading. She did not give in when she dreamed of his dark, beautiful body making love to her. She did not give in to his promises to sober up. Keeping her heart amply armored was her only defense from falling victim again to his hurting soul.

Irene was not worried for Don and Buddy, who did not see their father often anyway. For them, moving in with their cousin was not shameful; it was unparalleled opportunity for endless play. Irene went back to work as a file clerk at the shipyard and was relieved to be able to contribute to rent and food.

One night, when Helen and Erick were away, Don knocked on the door. He wanted to see his boys. Irene wasn't sure of his motives, but decided his intentions were good when he settled onto the couch with them. He gave Buddy a set of miniature cowboys and Indians and gave Don a long, glossy, black raven feather. From the kitchen she listened as he told the boys the story of how Raven brought Light to the world. This story, he explained, was one his mother had often told him. Irene heard her boys' laughter when he told them about himself as a young boy, hatching the baby raven in his pocket and raising it as a pet. She nearly cut her finger with the kitchen knife as tears filled her eyes.

Irene let herself imagine for a moment that Don was the ideal husband and father. She looked at the warm scene of him with his sons nestled against him. She imagined them soon all sitting down to her meal with happy conversation. She was resisting the urge to invite him when she heard the familiar, her *real* Don, now saying he needed to go meet with his buddies. The boys had tangled their legs across him but he stood and brushed himself off as if brushing off all traces of parenthood. He patted their heads and shot one heartrending glance her way. When he turned and left, it was like seeing his ghost pass through the door. Only his sad vapor stayed behind.

Not long after this visit, Irene heard that Don had left Bremerton, taking only his accordion, and gone north to Alaska.

How perfect is the innocence and vigor of childhood, Irene thought. She marveled at the fact that the boys didn't seem to mind that their father was now completely gone. They also didn't notice her wallet was empty or her heart was broken. They didn't complain about the repetitive dinners of cabbage-onion soup. All she had to tell them was, "It'll put hair on your chest!" and they would gobble it up every day. And they were willing to believe her tears were from all that onion dicing.

✦

By the time Don was ten and Buddy seven and a half, not only was Irene struggling, the stock market had crashed and people everywhere were losing jobs. Helen and Erick toiled to put food on the table for Eddie and their new twins, Roberta and Robert. Irene could not stand burdening them any further. Nor could she be a good mother without a home. The money she made was not enough for all of them. She sat together with her boys on the stoop and explained the hard economic times, and that harder times were coming. "Like an ominous cloud," she said, and saw her boys glance up to the clear blue sky.

She said, "The two of you will have to be each other's strength. When I find better work, we can be together again. But until then I'll have to leave you with the good people of the orphanage. Do you understand?"

"No, I don't understand" Don Jr. complained, "What orphanage? Where? Can Eddie come? Where will you be?"

Buddy chimed in, "What's a 'orph-nage'?"

But when the brothers saw Irene's tears this time, they understood them. Don and Buddy quieted themselves and wrapped their arms around her.

They made their best with the last days all together at Helen's. Irene made dinners with meat and also served-up strawberry sundaes the night before they left Bremerton.

✦

It made Irene almost sick with guilt to have to place her sons in an orphanage. From Bremerton she'd called the Ryther House, a children's charity home, and arranged for the boys to live there. But it wasn't until she and the boys arrived and saw the home that they gaped. Irene looked up and down the street, thinking they must have the wrong address. The house they stood in front of most certainly could not be the orphanage.

Don spoke up. "Mama! This is huge like a castle! Is *this* gonna be where we live?"

Irene took a boy by each hand and playfully marched them up the walkway. "Come my little prince charmings, the Queen of Ryther House awaits her royal visitors!" The boys laughed at her clowning and marched with her.

The headmistress who greeted them did not look like a queen, but she was old and feisty and *did* possess an air of authority. Her name was Ollie, and she told Irene that for 50 years she'd made it her work to take in orphans and unwed mothers. Irene could not doubt her. Her muscles were sinewy and her movement quick for someone so aged. She was a woman driven by a mission.

Ollie looked at her two new charges. "You know you're lucky. I've mothered over three thousand children in my time and I've refused no child, but never has there been so many needy children as right now. After your two boys, we are at absolute full capacity."

Mansion or institution, it was still painful to leave Don and Buddy. As Irene stood with them on the wide veranda, she put on her cheeriest face, "Now just think of this as a little adventure. Pretend you are princes of your own kingdom and know that until I find a job I'll be in Bremerton with Helen. And then I'll work as hard as I can to get you back with me." She looked at each boy. "Will you make me proud and be happy, princes?"

Irene breathed a sigh of relief to see her boys smile. She vowed to herself that she would *not* by any means allow herself to sink to the level of the despondent souls standing in the soup lines or living in the miserable shanties of Hooverville. She would get a job and find a room for let. Her boys would not stay here long!

Irene supposed the classified ads were read by more eyes than there were stars in the sky, yet she felt hopeful as she stood in the long queue outside the glistening white Smith Tower building. Her feet were blistered from a month of chasing down elusive possibilities. Today she hoped to get hired as a cleaning lady. As she craned her neck to look up to the spire at the top of the building, she felt almost dizzy. The very fact that this building was the fourth tallest in the whole world gave her a glimmer of hope. There surely would be need of a lot of cleaning.

She struck up a conversation with a rail-thin woman in line behind her. Her name was Lil and she lived in Hooverville with her brother, an out-of-work lumber mill yardman. Irene pitied Lil for having to live in the shanty town. But she herself had found nothing but rat-infested tenements where dirty bums slept in the doorways.

"Is it awful there?" Irene could not help asking. "I mean, do people get robbed and roughed-up?"

Lil's reply was matter-of-fact, "Well I *do* live with my brother and no, it's more civilized than you may think. Why, we have poker-playing nights and fiddle sessions and we sure don't have to throw no money away on rent! It's got its charms."

As the line worked its way into the lobby, Irene immediately felt insecure about the mere possibility of being responsible for maintaining the gleam and luster surrounding her. The very floor she stood on was a mirror-like polished black onyx. Everything glittered. When she realized how small and out of her element she felt, she gave herself a lecture about how her "bright spirit would fit nicely into a place like this" and reminded herself to hold her head high. Lil wished her luck as the elevator door closed.

Irene entered the basement office where a staid man in a starched shirt sat in a cloud of his own cigarette smoke. He looked bored, and Irene decided he'd probably heard enough hard-luck stories. She decided her best tactic was to be sharp and perhaps a little flirtatious. She sat tall and crossed her bare legs. She twinkled like dew on a spider web.

When the elevator door opened onto the lobby, there stood Lil waiting to go down. Irene hugged her excitedly. "I got the job! But he says there are 540 offices here and they need an army of us. So good luck to you too!"

No amount of positive thoughts, however, could get Irene into a flat. She simply couldn't afford a decent place. When she came from Helen's for her first day at the Smith Tower her heart jumped for joy to see Lil among them. Irene decided it was time to swallow her pride and ask Lil if she could live with her in Hooverville.

Lil's eyes brightened at the idea of having Irene as a roommate. "It's not how the Vanderbilts live but yer welcome to share my bed. Eugene has a cot in the front. He won't mind."

Irene was no Catholic but she mentally made the sign of the cross as she followed Lil through the labyrinth of hovels to her new home. Though it had no amenities but for a rain barrel and basin, she was relieved to see that it was spacious and stout with a tin roof and two rooms, thanks to Eugene's time at the lumberyard. Neighboring shacks looked flimsy by comparison. Three shacks shared a privy. Hooverville was close enough that Lil and Irene could walk to the Smith Tower, and they enjoyed this time to talk. Eugene was a sad-eyed man with a gentle, undemanding nature. They made for perfect housemates. The three sometimes went out for an evening drink and danced, though long hours of strenuous work left both women in need of sleep. Irene often had nightmares of not being able to find her boys. She would wake and stare at the ceiling, wondering if she ever could save enough money to get them back.

✦

Don had no inkling of what to expect from an orphanage. He only knew he would no longer see his cousins and this fact alone made him glum. As he grudgingly unpacked his few belongings, he came across the rumpled raven feather his father had given him. He smoothed it until its blue-black iridescence caught the light, then held the feather out and began to soar in circles, pretending to fly. He liked the small fluttering the feather made as he dipped and dove around the dormitory. He thought of his father and wondered where he had gone. If only he could fly like a raven, he could maybe spot him from the air. He tucked the feather carefully back into the cloth pocket of his suitcase. It was the only thing his father had ever given him.

Don and Buddy saw their Mamma only on some weekends when she rode the trolleys to the Ryther House. On one visit she brought Don some old flight magazines with articles about the aviator Charles Lindbergh.

The magazine articles and his father's raven feather had Don dreaming about flight, day and night. Sometimes in his sleep he saw himself leaping into the air and simply staying effortlessly aloft. In these dreams he flew above the treetops and over landscapes, their power and beauty only marred sometimes by the anxious feeling that this flight was in a futile search for his father.

One day, bringing home the weekly donation of stale bread from the bakery, he spotted two old wooden crates in an alley. Using the boxes to contain the bread was a good idea but as he and Buddy walked home, Don hatched a grander plan. He would build an airplane!

As one of the older boys at the orphanage, he had no problem orchestrating the construction crew. Ollie gave permission as long as the boys picked up after themselves. Don knew he might have been overstepping when he told some of his crew to take a loose siding board from the back of the tool shed, but the plane needed wings. They capped the forward crate with an enamel mixing bowl for a nosecone. Buddy helped to paint a swastika on it after his brother told him that it was an important "good luck" emblem for aviators. They nailed a small propeller to the nosecone. With a light flick, it twirled nicely. They used two battered pram wheels for the front landing gear and a rusty pulley wheel for the tail drag, and lashed the two crates together with slats removed so the pilot's legs could go through. They tapered the aft crate into a tail and finished it off with fins. By week's end, the airplane was complete. Don congratulated the team and announced that Buddy would be the test pilot. The kids looked at Buddy with envy, but Buddy looked at the flimsy aircraft with trepidation.

"We'll have the maiden flight tomorrow after morning chores," Don announced. "Everyone meet here. We'll need all hands to transfer the plane to the top of the knob."

There was a lot of excitement as everybody dispersed. Don spent the rest of that evening fashioning a crude leather pilot's helmet from a tattered discarded coat. He repeatedly jammed it onto Buddy's head in an attempt to get a perfect fit. The finished helmet was complete with ear flaps. He liked it so much that he decided he'd want it back after Buddy's flight.

At the agreed-on time, sixteen of them gathered. They took turns tugging and lifting it through and around obstacles on their way to "the knob," nothing more than a high patch of ground with a pitch of open "runway" that abruptly ended in an embankment and then a sidewalk. Don thought it was perfect for lift-off, and told his brother he would rather be the test pilot, but he was too big. Buddy was small for an eight year old and therefore the "lucky one."

With cheers and encouragement all around, Buddy wedged himself into the plane. Don pulled the helmet over Buddy's ears and with a slap on the back, the ground crew got the rattle-trap rolling until they could not keep up with it any longer. They all stood and watched, with gathering understanding, the fatal flaw of the intended mission. The plane took an immediate nose dive at the embankment and crashed onto the sidewalk below.

Don could only pray as he ran with the others, to hear a cry or any reassurance that his brother was not dead. They arrived to find Buddy whimpering in the wreckage with one arm bent in an odd way. But what a relief to see him alive!

When news of the accident got back to the staff, Don knew he'd catch hell. He was to blame for everything, including the missing items they'd find on the wrecked plane. He was ready for the whipping when it came his way, and knew, too, that Buddy's broken arm hurt worse. More curious, though, were the words coming from the woman doling out the punishment. With each smack of the rod she uttered "you dirty little *siwash*." Don had never heard that word before. He repeated it under his breath so he wouldn't forget it.

When Don's mother came, he asked her, "What does '*siwash*' mean?"

She told him it was an unkind word for Indian. Her eyes looked on fire so he thought he was about to get a second whipping but instead she said, "How dare her! I've got no other place for you to go, or I wouldn't leave you." She was crying when she hugged them goodbye.

That night, Don tossed the word *siwash* over and over in his mind. He thought about his father. The Raven story his Papa had told him was an Indian story. Don felt an upwelling of pride at his new awareness of having Indian blood. He knew his Papa lived in Alaska and pledged that someday he would find him.

✦

Irene was not able to save money as fast as she had hoped. Her days passed one after the other, shining surfaces of Alaskan marble and scrubbing floors of corridors that stretched endlessly before her like a road to Hell. But the Hell was that there *was no end*: banisters, bathrooms, stairs and elevators led her to nowhere, every day.

Bent and glowering over her pail, Irene was thinking she could not take one more inch of her perpetual polishing or one more thrust of her mad-making mop, when she heard a scream. She turned and saw Helen slipping on the wet floor as she ran to try to surprise her. She was on her way into ungraceful splits in her tight dress. Irene squealed with delight and dashed to help her back to her feet.

Helen said, "I did that on purpose! It's a new dance move. No but seriously, I came to whisk you away to a dance marathon. I've got a car. We can go as soon as you're off work."

This visit could not have come at a better moment. She avoided taking Helen back to the shanty by washing up in an office bathroom and brushing out her hair. Then they were off!

The sisters caught up on each other's lives as Helen drove to Tacoma, where the marathon contestants had already been dancing for five days straight. It was a Friday night so there would be live music. The hall was already packed with spectators. They settled into seats with their popcorn and a good view of the musicians.

Irene was attracted to men who made music. She secretly hoped to be noticed by a handsome horn player or drummer, perhaps. She would really rather concentrate on *anything* other than the dehumanizing, demoralizing show on the dance floor. Helen on the other hand seemed mesmerized by the charades of the MC and the plight of each contestant as they vied for the prize money.

In between bits of conversation with Helen and the distractions of the circus act on the dance floor, Irene struck up a conversation with a large and animated woman sitting next to her. Her name was Hester. Somehow, Irene felt uncommonly comfortable with her and more or less divulged her whole life story through the course of the evening. It was as if they had known each other a lifetime. She told Hester about the heartbreak of having to put her boys in the orphanage and of their father's incurable drinking and about living in the shanty town while hardly making enough to eat.

Hester, offering Irene a cigarette, related her own hard luck stories but confessed that "at least farm life allowed for my family not to go hungry." She now lived and worked in Seattle but told Irene about her family's farm in Monroe, and how her mother had divorced her alcoholic father, divided the land and moved onto her half where she, with her second husband and *his* two children, were now living.

"And come to think of it," she continued, "seems mother was sayin' just recently they could use another field hand or two. Are your boys good workers? You might consider farmin' 'em out. The country air would be healthy and their meals would be nourishing."

It had never occurred to Irene to get the boys in with a private family. The more she thought, the more it seemed like a logical solution. It would not be convenient for her to have them so far away, but it wouldn't matter if she could have more peace of mind about how they were treated. By the end of the evening, her mind was made up. She would contact Nettie, Hester's mother.

✦

Don rode in the back seat with his head out the window. He had his leather flight helmet on. He liked the way the wind felt against his face. He pretended to be on a dangerous mission, piloting from the open cockpit of a biplane, banking just in time to miss oncoming aircraft. He shot now and then, "rat-a-tat-tat" from his imaginary gun.

The dirty city air had given way to the sweet pungent smells of pastureland. Cows became the enemy target and quite a number of them went down in fiery balls of flame. It wasn't until they made the turn onto the long rutted road of Nettie's farm that he pulled himself back into the present. A sprightly Shepherd greeted their car, barking and bounding all the way up to the farmhouse.

"Now don't think for a minute that I'll be leaving you boys here if I sense the least little thing amiss about these people," Mama said in her most convincing tone.

As they rolled to a stop, the inside of the car grew silent. A dead, desiccated raven hung by its feet from a pole in the field near a stand of dying corn. Aside from the dog the only other living thing was a flock of hens pecking around a squeaking, rusty windmill.

They were looking at each other nervously when the screen door flew open and out of the house lumbered a large, disheveled woman, smiling and waving warmly. Her hands and apron were covered with flour and as she tried to sweep wisps of hair from her eyes, she smudged flour on her face.

Before any of them had time to respond, she was at the car and offering her hand to mama. "So you must be Irene," she said, glancing in the back, "and these young men must be my new boarders? Come! I have a supper of biscuits and chicken gravy ready to serve."

She led Don up to the porch and handed him an iron rod and told him to bang it around inside the triangle that hung there. He had no idea why he was being asked to make that racket but apparently it was not racket enough because she held his hand and assisted him in clanging it much louder.

"Now *that'll* bring the others in from the field," she said.

While they waited for the fieldworkers, Nettie brought them each a glass of fresh cow's milk and pointed out the nearest features: the hand pump, the fruit orchard, the pig pen and rows of raspberries neatly tied and arching over.

A threesome appeared, coming through the field gate, a lanky black-haired boy, a pigeon-toed, mop-headed girl and an older man. Introductions were made all around. When mama called his brother "Homer," Buddy looked at Don with raised eyebrows. She put her hand on Don's shoulder and said, "This here is Don, named after his Papa. So you can call him 'Junior' if you like."

Don learned that George was the lanky boy's name (named after *his* papa but was in no way wanting to be called 'Junior'). George Sr. preferred the more formal, "Mr. Fahrenkopf." The girl's name was Mary. She shyly peered out from her curls and then ran off to wash her hands.

They took their places at the dining table. Nettie smiled kindly as she brought in platters of food. It looked as though mama was right about her. She was warm and jovial. Mr. Fahrenkopf, however, did not give a comforting feeling. He sat rigid and ate methodically, only answering in grumbles. Don could see he made mama nervous. She could only stutter when he addressed her. When he turned his attention to him and Buddy, Don knew he'd have to handle the old man's stern questioning unflappably. His questions were prying, flat and calculating. Don would not show the weakness Mr. Fahrenkopf was looking for. Why should he tell him the truth about how much he weighed or how many hours he thought he could hold up to hoe work, especially when he'd never even done hoeing! Small lies did not seem inappropriate.

Don was proud of his brother too for holding up to the scrutiny. Buddy was bright and polite. The two of them had encouraged each other beforehand. They agreed they were ready for something new. Luckily, it seemed, they had been persuasive enough because by the end of the meal, Mr. Fahrenkopf scooted back his chair and said they could move in immediately if they liked, but it was time for him and his kids to head back out to the field. Don noticed how dutifully George and his sister got up to follow their father, even though Mary trailed behind. She whispered something in her mother's ear and then ran to catch up with her brother.

Everyone pushed aside their plates and stepped out onto the porch. Mama called out a loud and cheery "Thank you!" to Mr. Fahrenkopf. Don looked out at his new brother walking away. He waved, hoping George would acknowledge him, but instead Mary saw him and waved back.

She was cute like Orphan Annie, thought Don. It might be fun to have a sister.

"Colonel"
George Barrett Sr.
later in his life

My grandfather, Don
"Pet" Sr. with his sister
Nellie, later in their
Indian school days.

..... Now I want you
to leave Chemawa
on the evening train
on th 12th day of June
as the Steam Boat leaves
for Katalla on the 15th of
June.

When you get in
Seattle I want you to
go and stay at the
Rainier Grand Hotel as
that is where all my
old friends stay.

I will give you a
letter of Introduction
to Mr Cunningham who
is there most of the
time and I do not
want you to act bashful
but Be a good Boy and
talk up to everybody that
talks to you straighten
up and act like a
white Boy and dont
forget to be a gentleman.
Keep yourself nice
and Clean Be shure
your Clothes are all

Page one of a letter from Colonel George in Katalla telling his son how to conduct himself as he returns to the village for a summer visit.

213

when you get there.
Be a good Boy until
We see you.

When you are
nearing Katalla
clean your self
up nice as all the
people here would
like to see you looking
nice and if you dont
they'll laugh at you.
We will be on to
the Boat to meet
you

Your Loving Father
Geo T Barrett

Page two of same letter.

Patsie's letter back to the headmaster of the Indian school with regards to not having luck recruiting new students from the village.

TO OFFICER SENDING TELEGRAM.

1. Keep copy on this form for your files.
2. Mail confirmation to addressees indicating that purpose by check mark in this circle. ○
3. Mail copy to your Supervising Field Office, if any.

MEMORANDUM COPY
OF OFFICIAL TELEGRAM

WILL NOT be accepted if presented by Telegraph Company attached to bill for tolls, in lieu of original message.

213

Receiver's No.— Time Filed— Paid _____ Word _____ Government rate—Toll, $ _____

Sent by—

(Name of sender) Telegraph Co. Salem, Oregon, Sept. 1, 1916.

To Patrick Barrett From

Katalla, Alaska via Cordova Hall Superintendent

Will pay your transportation to Chemawa as escort if you bring eight pupils or more. See Bessie McGuire, David White, John Lawton, Leslie Bremner, Susie Bremner, Pearl Durkee, Patrolena Barrett, Ben Durkee and others. Pupils under fourteen pay their own fare. Transportation your order placed Katalla. Railroad representative meet you Seattle.

Reproduced at the National Archives and Records Administration – Pacific Alaska Region (Seattle)

DEPARTMENT OF THE INTERIOR
UNITED STATES INDIAN SERVICE
SALEM INDIAN TRAINING SCHOOL   **213**
CHEMAWA, OREGON

Katalla, Alas. Sept. 3, 1916.

18 collect. nite.

Hall, Superintendent.

Have seen all expupils and others. None desire enrolling.

Patrick Barrett.

Letter sent by Pet to the Chemawa headmaster from a special conference he was attending.

DEPARTMENT OF THE INTERIOR
UNITED STATES INDIAN SERVICE

Lawrence, Kansas. June 25, 1914.

Mr. H. E. Wadsworth, Supt.,
    Chemawa, Oregon.
Dear Mr. Wadsworth:

We had a grand trip, and the conference done me a lot of good, and especially the Indian Conference, which was held their. We discussed the religious and moral problems of the Indian, which resulted, that the Indians need a Christian training, and that it must come thru the Indian himself. There were twenty-seven Indians and six missionaries present. This conference is expected to be an annual event there, and they expect that the different tribs of the United States will be represented there hereafter.

*Wedding photo of my grandfather Don Petroleum Barrett Sr.
with my grandma Irene, pregnant with my dad.*

Paddling into Port Simpson

I HAD SPENT A WEEK paddling in Alaskan waters but was leaving it behind after my hours-long paddle across Dixon Entrance. Now the vast coast of British Columbia stretched out ahead of me for hundreds of miles. Through these long, wet miles to come, I knew I would continue to ruminate on the generations before me who had passed along their love of Alaska and desire for adventure, and to be inspired by their vision and empowered by their courage. As a boy in an orphanage, my Dad had dreamed of flying. After the war he'd had to stretch his teacher's salary to provide for six kids, but he still managed to manifest that dream. Now I, his fifth child, had sprouted my own kind of wings and felt emboldened by his spirit to "fly" onward. However, as I paddled into Port Simpson, I had nothing more lofty in mind than a piece of pie, a cup of coffee, and a hot shower.

Fresh from a shower on a fish-buyer's barge, I walked along the dusty roads of the village. Trucks drove past in seeming circles. Although there was talk of a road coming over from Prince Rupert, the only real way to leave this town was by plane or boat. Sadly, no pie or coffee was to be found here. I settled for bananas,

Reese's Peanut Butter Cups and a popsicle, none of which I ordinarily cared much for. However, after nothing but fish and rice for days, I was desperate for variety.

I kicked on down the road trying to savor my popsicle. When I got back to my kayak, a boat full of men at the dock were so impressed with my endeavor that they gave me two fresh-cooked crabs. Little acts of kindness like this were always bolstering my faith in people. I left Port Simpson and by the time I had paddled out to Burnt Cliff Island, I was exhausted and ready for the delicacy of a crab feast.

From where I camped, I could see the point of land called Tree Bluff. I studied my charts. The psychic's second prediction warned that I would have a "blocked passage" at or near this area. Looking at her notes again, I thought to myself, that's ridiculous. The point of land jutted right into the open sea. She'd gone so far as to say that I "might have to even get out and carry my boat." Well, I thought, Laurie's certainly missed the mark on this call.

I fell asleep and woke the next morning surrounded by mudflats. An extreme low tide had left me no choice but to drag my boat a long distance and when I *was* finally able to paddle again, I realized that the same low tide had exposed a very long sand-spit off of Tree Bluff, "blocking" my intended route again. Paddling far out of my way, I was finally back on my planned course with a renewed respect for psychic powers.

Rounding Point Ryan, I wished for a nice nor'wester. Soon the tide began to flood and the wind picked up, allowing me to put up my little sail. I scooted through the channel past Metlakatla. When the wind died, I took up paddling again. I was somewhat confused about when and where I would see Prince Rupert until I shot through a little narrows into a big inlet. There was the town but it was so far away; the buildings were so tiny! I would have to summon my strength for this last stretch. After six hours on the water, I was aching to be ashore. Suddenly, much to my delight, the west wind came direct at my back—a little shove by my Spirit guides?—enabling me to set sail again. Away I flew, making what I imagined was a grand entrance into town, sailing right up to the marina.

I was exhausted and disoriented and found myself in the middle of a hustle-bustle town. Before even stepping out of my kayak I was besieged by three young ruffians, full of questions, asking to paddle my boat and use my fishing rod. It dawned on me that it was going to be no simple matter to just leave my boat and attend to my many needs, the most important of which was a cold beer!

There was a phone on the dock right above the float my kayak was tied to, so I called Gregg and Raven from there. They were amazed to hear from me already. Gregg said they were in the middle of a scorching heat wave and he was having to draw down the pond to keep the garden and greenhouse watered. The berries were all coming ripe at once and the chickens were ready for slaughter. Remembering how much work and devotion it takes to live the "simple" life gave me a different perspective on my six hour day of paddling. This was hard work, but at least it was a vacation from all of that.

At the Post Office I picked up a parcel that I had mailed to myself from Lopez. Ugh! I was just starting to have room in my kayak so that re-packing each day wasn't such a challenge. Now I had a whole new box of supplies and was not too enthused about jamming it all in. It had been hard, from home, to gauge what my daily progress would be. I had overestimated how long it would take to get to Prince Rupert.

I found a tiny room in a backpacker's hotel, the Pioneer, for only $10, and the bed was oh-so-comfy. There was a nice bathroom down the hall, and a tub. I left my package in the room and trotted back to the waterfront to see if my kayak was still there. It rested peacefully, securely tied to the dock.

From a comfortable pub with an outdoor deck looking right down on my boat, I could finally relax and enjoy a beer and meal cooked by someone else. Afterwards I felt a bit woozy but more confident that things would all work out.

✦

I had planned to leave my kayak in Prince Rupert and take a small diversion by ferry out to the Queen Charlotte Islands.

When I'd first started talking about my dream of a solo paddle, Oscar, a Lopez elder, said, "I know a woman who did that almost 60 years ago." This had sparked my interest. Who was she? Was she still alive? Where did she live? Oscar remembered only that her name was Betty, and that she was the sister of Bill Lowman of Anacortes. With Bill's help I'd been able to talk long distance to Betty Lowman-Carey in the Queen Charlotte Islands, and she had invited me to visit on my journey.

The next morning, I arranged to leave my kayak at the Yacht Club for two days, and caught *The Queen of Prince Rupert* across the opalescent waters of Hecate Strait, enjoying the dazzling sun from the aft deck. Betty and her husband Neil were waiting to meet me. It seemed coincidental that she and I were almost exactly the same height, 5′ 3″, and with very similar hazel eyes. She was more than twice my age with completely white hair, but otherwise she was spritely, nimble and bright. For years they'd lived a hundred miles away on the wild outer coast at Puffin Cove, but they'd recently retired to Sandspit, another short ferry ride away.

We arrived at a home surrounded by a wild but oddly organized profusion. From their decades of life on the west side, they had collected all manner of flotsam and jetsam and then transported that entire collection to their current home, from the tiniest plastic toy to immense iron wreckage. They seemed to have brought home every bottle, ball, doll and life ring they had ever seen. Mountains of buoys, hard hats, shoes, net, rope, Japanese glass balls in every conceivable size, whale jaw-bones and skeletons. Every color, kind and shape of rock, shell and pebble. All of their treasures were neatly categorized and displayed on every wall, fence, door, out-building, cubby, corner and crevice of their property, the piles all ordered and labeled and identified by signs reading, for example, "Japanese hard hats."

The inside of their home was its own adventure-in-discovery, from its salvaged brick floors, to stone walls, a large stone fireplace and right on up to the rafters with every available perch or platform filled to overflowing with more beach treasures. An

immense library was somehow jammed between all of these salvaged riches.

This was a tight husband-wife team who shared a deep and
mutual love, won by a lifetime of adventuring together. My first
day with them passed quickly as they entertained me with stories of the Queen Charlottes, Canada, Alaska, Coastal Natives and
World War Two. They graciously allowed each other equal time
in the telling of their life experiences. In addition to their keen
interests in the world around them, they were funny and generous. They wined and dined me and drove me to see the sights and
to meet their friends.

Of most interest to me was the dug-out canoe Betty had
accomplished her solo paddles in. Actually she hadn't paddled—
after fitting it with a seat and rowlocks, she had rowed the canoe.
She told me the boat had quite a story of its own.

When Betty was a girl in Anacortes (the same time and place
where my mom was born and raised) the canoe had drifted into
the American half of the Juan de Fuca Strait. A U.S. Coast Guard
cutter brought it into the cannery dock owned by Betty's father.
At the time, neither white nor native fishermen could identify its
ownership. After a year of sitting unclaimed, Betty's father gave it
to her as a birthday gift.

It was in this native-made 14-foot craft fashioned for the open
ocean that Betty, at the age of twenty, escaped Anacortes during
the Depression. It had taken her 62 days to reach Ketchikan.
Twenty-six years later she'd repeated the journey in reverse, in 46
days. She explained that in the days of her coastal expedition, very
little food was needed because she could dine with lighthouse
attendants or at the numerous canneries. Also in those days more
mission boats worked in and out of the settlements. All of these
were considered places of refuge along the shores, so she had
been able to abandon the heavy canvas tent she'd started out with.

I asked if they might bring the canoe out from storage. Neil
seemed reluctant at first but then happily agreed. Once it was out
on the lawn I could see they were proud to lay eyes on it again.
In the sixty years since it floated into Betty's life, the precious
relic had been lovingly cared for. In recent times it had been

reconditioned with glossy red paint and the addition of ribs and gunwales had changed it from a paddling canoe to a rowboat, but the lines and integrity of the antique dug-out still suggested a story all its own, created by the hands of a native canoe carver. Betty said that she'd eventually learned who the original owner was when by chance she met a grandmother from Vancouver Island's west-coast village of Clo-oose, who had lost it. It had been scaled to and made for use by a woman.

❖

Although I'd enjoyed my detour, I came back wondering whether I had squandered good paddling weather. The clouds were coming in. I spent the morning a bit overwhelmed, reorganizing and shuffling gear to make room for my new provisions. Finally I was off. My right arm complained about the sudden transition from leisure to work, but after a few miles, I was back in the rhythm.

I paddled the Inverness Passage and by late afternoon I'd found a deserted boatshed on the back side of DeHorsley Island. By then, a hard rain was falling, so I was glad for the dry (if untidy) space, and for the luck of a small wood-burning stove on which to cook my dinner. The boatshed framed a monochromatic watery scene like a movie, and I ate and took it in. The deep quick emerald waters of the channel shot by my stationary perch. Rain blurred the forested hillside across the channel. Salmon broke the surface of the water here and there. It was hypnotic, and after eighteen miles of paddling that day, I was ready for a sound sleep.

I set out early the next morning into a thick damp day. The current was with me, and migrating salmon jumped all around as they headed toward their spawning grounds up the Skeena. I knew they wouldn't bite at this stage of their single-minded journey, but I figured I might try to snag one. I wasn't proud, just craving protein and thought it was worth a try, but it was to no avail.

I needed to cross a small span of about two miles but clouds obscured my destination, so I decided to stay on a compass course of 100 degrees, south-by-southwest, until I could see the hilly range I was headed for and then turn more southerly. Soon a wind lent its strength and pushed me the twenty-four miles to Baker Inlet.

The inlet was so serene it looked more like an alpine lake. There were no beaches, but a nice floating boat dock seemed like a good place to make camp. I did not have a free-standing tent and so I would just have to throw a tarp over me if it rained, and it did. A crab boat came into the inlet toward dusk as I huddled under my tarp. This boat sent a bit of a chill up my spine. I viewed it with suspicion. The psychic's third prediction for "trouble" came in this area and she had certainly proved herself. But it seemed to pose no threat as it anchored out, and I was too tired to stay awake. My evening passed without incident.

The next day was July fourth, and it was a happy Independence Day for me, if a bit too ambitious. I paddled all day with no help from the wind, from Baker to Lowe Inlet, bucking a pretty heavy current the last part of the day. To give myself a break, I went ashore on a miserable rocky beach. I had only been there about fifteen minutes when suddenly one of the huge, skyscraping cruise ships appeared without warning. Its engines must have been fathoms below the water level, because its approach was silent. The scene of this mammoth vessel in the confines of narrow Grenville Channel was surreal! I decided it was, in fact, so bizarre that it was worth dashing down from the grassy bank to my kayak to grab my camera for a shot. Luckily I was at my kayak's side because the cruise ship passed quickly and I had not anticipated the size of the wake behind it. The ship displaced so much water in the narrows that with very little warning, I was suddenly desperately trying to save my kayak from destruction. One huge rolling wave after another smashed it against the rocky beach while I did everything I could to lessen the impact. At one point my paddle fell under the boat, which continued to slam down on top of it as the reverberation of the waves continued. My arms were strained by the time the waves finally eased, but I had managed to save my boat and paddle from damage. Nothing broken, no gash in my hull, just a cockpit full of water. Not that the captain of the cruise ship could have done anything differently, but I was unnerved by the disruption. I left and finished out my day's paddle after about eleven hours on the water.

My camp was down the impossibly long Lowe Inlet, or it *seemed* so very long but my fatigue no doubt magnified the distance. The only place to pull out was on marshy ground at the far end of the inlet. I couldn't make a fire. Instead I used my little gas stove for the first time on my paddle. After my meal, drained of energy, I crawled into my soggy sleeping bag and slept like a rock, or at least like a very tired kayaker.

For my tenth paddling day I made fifteen miles, anxious to emerge from the close grip of the Grenville Channel. I made camp on a minimal but comfortable beach just as the sun triumphed in a day-long skirmish with rain clouds. This was a rejuvenating break. I bathed, dried out gear and clothing, and studied my chart. Although there were qualities of the steep-sided Grenville Channel that were enchanting, I was ready for something different. I decided that I would really rather stay away from its twin, the Princess Royal Channel, choosing instead a wilder course. I would paddle Wale Channel on Gil Island's east coast and onward to Camano Sound. A more exposed route would have more action and life. Because I was accustomed to paddling the wilds of the Brooks Peninsula of northwest Vancouver Island, I felt confident that this choice would suit me better.

✦

The next morning I paddled out of Grenville into the enormous intersection of Wright Sound. Waterways converged here from many points. I was immediately confused. Across the wide span of water were dim landforms in all directions. Many of the hills and islands were cloud-covered, making it difficult to determine my path. No problem, I thought, because it was here at this very location that Laurie MacQuary predicted I would have an "Angel Guide." In my opinion, I had my Spirit guides all along the way, but since Laurie's prophetic insights usually involved physical objects or obstacles, I began looking for an Angel Guide in the flesh. As I sat bobbing in my boat, trying to puzzle out the scene, I saw a far-off fishing boat churning across the broad expanse of Wright Sound, heading in my direction. Oh! There's my "Angel." Right on cue! It would be reassuring to have a person on the boat positively identify Gil Island/Whale Channel. When the boat was getting close to me it began to veer off in a different direction. I was perplexed. This guy was supposed to be my "Guide." I waved my arms, but in open water a kayak can look like nothing more than a speck. Either he hadn't heard that he was supposed to be my guide or he just couldn't see me. Either way it was up to me, with perhaps a slight nudge by an ancestor, to make the decision. Finally I did and all was well.

I had never really learned how to properly use a compass for setting courses. I did it all by line of sight. I would generally spot a destination and note the direction in degrees on my compass. If I should lose my line of sight along the way then I would follow the compass heading I had noted. Thick cloud cover from the get-go could make my method less than ideal.

Also less conventional was my aversion to wearing a life jacket. So far, I had not worn my flotation vest once. It sat on the aft deck of my boat held by bungee lines. I did however use my spray skirt to keep white water out of my lap. As I headed out once again into more open waters with a headwind, I continued with this same routine. Because of my habit of leaving camp very early in the mornings, I generally set off into calm waters. The winds always started later and would usually pick up in strength over the course of the day. The way the weather, currents, swells, and waves built by increments allowed me to grow gradually accustomed to conditions that I figured would scare the hell out of any family member if they were to witness me battling swells and white caps, as I often did for some hours of any given day. It's the sort of slowly heating water syndrome that eventually cooks the happy and unconcerned frog. I was not oblivious to the harsh conditions, I was just moving along with them. I felt as though I was engaged in a long slow dance with the Earth herself, a dance marathon to be sure but there was a good degree of grace involved as well.

I was chased by white-capped waves as I closed in on my seventeen mile paddle that day and landed my boat at my new "home" for the night, a home blessed with its very own waterfall spilling out onto the beach. I was a happy camper, getting to wash my hair and clothing. Perpetually craving protein, I tried to fish but could only seem to jig-up sea cucumbers. I figured they were probably someone's delicacy but I threw them back and settled for reconstituted dry beans and rice, which, as it turned out, tasted fabulous. After a long paddle day, probably shoe leather would taste like a gourmet treat. As I snuggled down in my bed, I heard the distant rumble of thunder. I was asleep when the storm crashed in, followed by a terrific little thundershower. I poked my head out of the tent. It was 10:30 P.M. and there, like a Technicolor dream, was a tangerine-cast thunderhead scuttling right up Whale Channel toward me. In front of and behind this solitary cloud was blue sky. It marched right on by as if it were some kind of parade float accompanied by thundering bass drums, passing solely for my entertainment. Attached to the entourage like a banner was its own flashy tangerine rainbow!

The next day was brilliant and warm. I was forced to devise yet another use of my roll of duct tape when I fashioned some alpine-style sunglass deflectors. I was glad that glare off the water was actually a "problem." The Aleut who share the same coastal area of my Tlingit forbearers had devised long-billed wooden visors to wear as they paddled their skin kayaks. Hours of paddling in bright sun while hunting for prey *or* searching for a camp can be blinding. My duct tape helped to cut out the light that bounced up through the edges of the frames. The retro-fitted sunglasses, though not as stylish as an Aleut visor, made me feel pretty ingenious.

At midday, I touched in on the shore of Princess Royal Island at an abandoned, boarded-up First Nations fish camp. Thirteen or more small wooden houses lined the beach. Each dwelling had its own outdoor kitchen and smokehouse. It seemed idyllic. I imagined that this small village, on its pristine shore surrounded by primal forests, was not unlike my great grandmother's village of Katalla, and was now as devoid of life as Katalla had been for close to a century. I could almost hear the ghost-like laughter of children running on the beach and smell the aroma of smoking salmon. I would have been ready to end my paddle and live here forever more, *if* I could have talked my family and friends into joining me.

Not long after the fish camp, I met a boisterous kingfisher who told me to start fishing. I obeyed, following it to where it was fishing, and pulled up many black bass, keeping the two biggest. I then struggled on against a stiff headwind, in search of a place called Surf Inlet.

The shoreline was rugged and inhospitable and a dense fog blew in, obliterating the sun. Through the wind and fog, I continued to pass headland after headland of sheer rock walls, searching for any place to pull out, but there was nothing. I'd already paddled twenty miles that day and I was worn out, but I had no choice but to continue, looking into every nook and cranny along the way. With about twenty feet of visibility and the wind still blowing, suddenly out of the milky whiteness, I paddled right into a calm, harmonious environment. The scene slowly revealed itself through the haze. A tranquil, soft white-sand beach lay before me, like a mirage. I could not believe it! In the ten miles since I had left the fish camp, there had not been even the most minimal place I could bring my boat ashore, and now this! It was 6:30, and although the sun would have been shining onto my beach, the fog was still too thick for it to penetrate. Still, I was elated to the point of tears to have found such a magical spot to rest my weary body.

I fried my bass fillets with garlic and curry powder in lots of olive oil, and ate them along with my usual black beans and rice. The beach was covered in animal tracks, and ravens and eagles flew through the woods above me.

I considered staying at this lovely camp for an extra day, but thoughts of making some sort of contact with Gregg got me off the beach bright and early. It had been seven days since my last phone call, so I decided to keep my eyes open for some boater to request a marine operator call.

I sent my paddle blades through liquid that looked and felt like mercury; thick, shiny and resistant, not thin like water. My arms ached from yesterday's strenuous journey, and a headwind added to the challenge. I hoped it wouldn't be a long day. My first wish came true when a live-aboard boat came along. The owners were retired Canadians with no particular destination or agenda, so they were more than happy to offer me the use of their radio. When we realized we were in a "dead zone" for reception, they told me to tie my kayak to their yacht, and they made me tea and a sandwich as we cruised out into Laredo Channel. At last I was able to patch a call through to Gregg and Raven, which really buoyed my spirits. My kind hosts took me back to where I had first run into them and bade me farewell. Once again I gave thanks for the kindness of strangers.

I was back now to the dilemma of finding a camp, when I came on a small tugboat towing a powerboat down the channel at a slower pace than I was paddling. The power boat occasionally took off on its own independent missions, zipping ahead, disappearing and re-appearing from inlets. The driver then motored up to me and struck up a friendly conversation. I told him I was looking for a decent beach to camp. He did not know of any but offered to jet down some of the inlets and report back to me if he found a beach.

He returned and confirmed my belief that there was nothing. I was at least happy that I had not wasted my energy looking. Later I found an extremely minimal site squeezed against a fringe of dense underbrush. But with a 20.5′ high tide due, I was reluctant to settle in until I knew I would not be flooded. Meanwhile, I dug butter clams and discovered bountiful bottom fish. I kept one red snapper and one greenling. The seafood, along with nourishing clam nectar, was my total dinner.

I slept without the tide running me out of my tent and continued my paddle down Laredo Channel the next morning. To my delight, I now had a northwest wind and was able to sail. Sailing was not necessarily less strenuous than paddling; it required an isometric grip on my paddle which caused my arms to ache and my clenched hands to seize. The wind and vigorous waves threw my stern around so that I continually had to paddle brace and adjust the rudder to keep from capsizing. I'd planned to head for a peninsula on Swindle Island, further to the west, but I was pumped with adrenaline and enjoying the rowdy joy-ride, even as it took me away from my goal. After four hours of this, I could feel my strength and vigilance began to fail and I was looking seriously for a place to rest.

I found shelter in a little island group and rested until I had enough strength to resume my search for a camp. As I paddled on, the wind became even stronger. For a while, it had been nice hitching a ride with it, but it was time to go the direction of *my* choosing, not the way of the wind. I saw a group of kayakers, way off in the distance, just going out of sight into Meyers Passage. Meyers Passage hooks back into the south end of Princess Royal Channel. That must have been where they were headed. I was still being pushed around by the wind. It forced me into a boulder-strewn cove. Each rounded rock was nearly as big as a VW Bug. I clambered out onto one and had lunch. From here I could make out a thin strip of what looked to be a sand beach across the other side of Kitasu Bay on the Swindle Island peninsula. It was barely visible and rolling waves would challenge me every inch of the way so I could only hope I was not wrong about finding a good camp there. With renewed inspiration, I summoned my powers to paddle into the big wind. To get there I quartered the waves and turned straight into every seventh wave. The effort paid off when I discovered there was in fact a long beach and it was indeed a welcome sight. After eighteen miles of hard paddling, I surfed straight into a landing.

✦

Here my tent became my moon lodge. A persistent hard rain gave me more reason to stay undercover. I was not surprised by my clockwork-like female functions. The only complaint I've ever had about my body's precise and reliable reproductive ability is that, if anything, I was too damn fertile!

My mothering instincts had come on early. I gave birth to my daughter Summer Moon when I was nineteen and Cody Marlin was born twenty-two months later. They were both born in a hospital but I was the first and only woman in my immediate family, including my mother, to breastfeed. I had no role models or friends with babies. I was a pioneer, at least in the world I knew. When Cody was born I demanded to have him in my hospital room with me, which the staff granted, but they were in a quandary about what to do to "protect" the infant when visitors came. Should everyone scrub and don gowns and masks? This was a new concept for them: a mother that wanted to keep her child at her side!

My second son Raven was born at home, and, knowing he would be fatherless, I'd invited many friends to the birth so that he would know from the moment he emerged that he was surrounded by a tribe of people who would love and protect him in lieu of a father. To that end I passed him, minutes-old, around the room to all twenty-four family members and friends who were at the birth.

Due to the healthy and fecund ways my body served me, I knew I was as close to an earthly goddess as any woman could hope to be, albeit not particularly in the voluptuous sense. However, as I lay bleeding in my tent with lashing rains and tired muscles, I felt more like a rag doll than a goddess!

❉

In spite of my womanly circumstances and a continuing downpour, I cast off the following morning in hope of finding Higgins Passage. As soon as I rounded the headland peninsula of Swindle, I met fierce winds blasting straight up Laredo sound. Every stroke felt as though I were pushing through an invisible force field of resistance. I thought to myself, *this* is what I asked for by taking the outer route! Not only that, but the perspective of my map for this area might as well have been drawn-up from the distance of the moon! I paddled on in confusion. Where my charts gave the impression of a smooth, uncomplicated coastline, in truth it was about as convoluted and shaggy as a dog with its hackles raised. Why hadn't I just spent the money to buy charts that actually covered this coast in detail? I consoled myself with the idea that once I paddled into Higgins Passage at the north end of Price Island, things would get easier.

Desperate to find the passage, I ducked in and out of this ragged edge searching, but instead found only countless dead-ends of jagged-rock crannies and coves. Though my muscles burned, I had no choice but to return each time into the fury of the wind and ever-increasing seas. Each time I forced myself back out I became weaker. Mesmerized by the relentless conditions, I fell into an exhausted trance, to the point that I no longer felt my own fear or exhaustion.

It wasn't until I somehow left my body and viewed myself from a short distance, slightly above and in front of the kayak that the reality of my true peril sank in. Here I was, hair plastered back by the wind and pelting rain and surrounded by hurling whitecaps. My eyes were glazed and my paddle strokes almost completely ineffective. This out-of-body experience revealed to me my stupefied state and imminent danger, causing me to snap out of the hypnosis. I *had to* find a camp! I came ashore on a depressingly rocky outcropping. The waves crashed onto it. Sharp rocks would be my bed at this site. The high tide, due at midnight, would be 22.4´ and I wasn't sure if this pitiful perch would keep me from the tormenting waters, but I was too exhausted to worry. This bed of nails was my best and only choice, and I was so tired that I slept peacefully.

The next day was my 16th paddling day and I woke to no improvement in the weather. My search for Higgins Passage was the cause of yesterday's torture, and now I worried that the challenging winds, waves, and currents were preventing me from making more than the most incremental headway.

I paddled on. At last I saw a fishing boat and asked where Higgins Passage was. He pointed in the direction I was paddling and said, "It's around the next big point," which was the end of the island and all the way up its eastern shore to the top. In other words, full circle from where I started. Could it be true? It's not always easy to judge just when a coastline will end when you are paddling close in. As I continued on, I came to the southern end of Price and paddled around it. Finally, I realized what I'd done. I had probably paddled over twenty miles the first day while I searched for the passage, when in fact it should have been an eight-mile paddle. I was embarrassed. A *real* kayaker would never have become so confused! But also I knew that the extreme conditions and lack of a good chart had distorted all sense of time and distance.

Now as I paddled north (!), I prayed for a good campsite and water. The age-old adage of "water, water everywhere but not a drop to drink" applied to me at this point. I was still dazed by my circuitous route, but happy to be on the lee side of Price. My prayer was answered when, after about eighteen miles from my morning camp, I found a cove with a large creek. I knew the tent site would be marginal because high tide would be a whopping 23´.

At my new home by the creek, I bathed and washed a few items and filled my water jugs directly from the stream. I had no filtration or need of it; all the water I encountered was pure and sweet. As I built a big fire to dry by, I caught a whiff of pee near my gear and I knew it wasn't mine. I looked toward the woods, wondering what bear pee smelled like. Seeing nothing suspicious, I took to studying my charts and revised my paddle plan from this new location. I crammed my tent into a thicket near the river. Was it high enough? I wondered as I fell off into a deep sleep.

At 12:30 A.M. I awoke to a gush of blood and a surge of water, as the big tide washed in under my tent. I flew into action, throwing all of my bedding and gear up further into the bushes and dismantling the tent. Next, I walked on beach logs to check on my kayak. I shone the beam of my flashlight across what had been a large dry bay, now filled to the brim with seawater. My kayak sat precariously atop a very large drift log far across this span of water, preparing to drift away without me. In fact my paddle, life vest and sail were already floating free. This situation called for Super Woman! Instead of disrobing and changing into a costume, I just disrobed. I then swam to a floating log and, straddling it, I used my hands to paddle across the bay. I got hold of my boat and gear and tied them to my log and paddled my log back to the other side. There was no beach left anywhere, so I tied my bowline to a tree and lay down on a huge boulder to try to sleep through what was left of the night. I actually managed some shut-eye but was awakened by a splish-splashing sound. Before I opened my eyes I imagined it was a salmon going up the stream, but when I looked it was a large, beautiful wolf walking in the creek only twenty feet away. Now I understood the scent of urine near my gear. The wolf must have marked his territory when I hadn't noticed.

I was glad I had rescued all of my important gear in the night. I was tired but ready for something different. My new plan of action this morning from *this* side of Price would be to paddle straight across Milbank Sound to Seaforth Channel, and from there onward to Bella Bella.

◆

On a rough day, Milbank Sound, open to the great Pacific, could have been an impossible ten-mile crossing. But if my ancestors were testing me on the outer coast by giving me what I asked for with the wildness, here, they were giving me a needed break. It took me three and a half hours to reach the opposite shore where I was delighted to find the Ivory Island Lighthouse, not marked on my chart. A kind woman, Cheryl, "manned" this outpost along with her husband, and let me borrow their telephone to call home. Gregg didn't answer, and I had to leave a message on the machine to let them know I was "doing well." It wasn't until I hung up that I realized how shaken I still was, and how badly I needed to decompress. Luckily, Cheryl was there to offer a sympathetic ear.

Since I had just blundered onto Ivory Island, not even knowing of its existence, I was pleasantly surprised to find it inhabited. I was not the only visitor, in fact. An interesting fellow by the name of Stewart Marshal had also been visiting for the past five days. I'd read about Stewart in a book by Kenneth Brower, *The*

Starship and the Canoe, in which he helped build baidarkas with
George Dyson and then adventured in them along the coast back
in the seventies. Now, more than ten years later, here he was,
living and traveling aboard a mammoth 22′ x 36″ beam kayak,
crafted from laminated cedar strips and fitted with running lights,
solar panels, a Plexiglas window in the floor and a mast for sail.
In his large cargo hatches he kept a pressure canner, jars, and art
supplies. For months each year, he not only slept in this boat, but
cooked, ate, and sketched scenes that he would later turn into
watercolors.

I spent the afternoon digging steamer clams, and Stewart collected turban snails, and that evening the two of us joined Chris,
the assistant lighthouse keeper, who treated us to some of his
homebrew, along with fresh-baked bread. All in all, it was a heav-
enly banquet after the monotony of beans and rice!

I slept peacefully that night in a pristine white boat shed and
Stewart slept in his boat so that he would be ready to paddle
at the 3:00 A.M. high tide. When I awoke, he was still there in
his boat in the bay. He had lost the backrest to his seat and was
waiting for light of day to find it. While he searched the beach
I got packed and was ready to go by the time he found it. It
was the first warm sunny day and I was happy to be on my
way. Stewart paddled his immense kayak and showed me the
way to Fisher Point, not far from Ivory Island. On the island
were old decaying mortuary totem poles. They were carved,
Stewart said, in memory of seven natives, perhaps children, who
had drowned in a boat accident. The tallest pole still showed its
features quite clearly. It looked like a female figure, both haunting and curvaceously sensual in its dignified stance on that
small, wooded isle. Judging its age by the deteriorated condition, I guessed it could have been there since the turn of the
century. With only a seven-inch core of wood at the totem's
base, I doubted that she would stand for too many more years.
She was a beauty.

While we were on the water, we shared a lunch of coffee,
spring salmon and leftover clams, all cooked right inside Stewart's
boat. After our meal we said our good-byes and parted, Stewart
heading off to Shearwater, and I to Bella Bella.

At Bella Bella, I planned to call my son Cody. This would be my second attempt, but I knew it would be hard to catch up with a young man so devoted to pursuing his career. I admired his ambition.

I had been single since Cody was a year old. As he grew older, visits to his father had taught him some good skills I could never have offered: electrical wiring, mechanics and construction, and now my boy had grown into a strong, handsome young man who wanted to make a positive mark in the world. After graduation he'd enrolled at a firemen's academy in Bend, Oregon, and had already had one harrowing experience in the line of duty, during a Bend wildfire, when he had fought a blaze as it engulfed a rural driveway. He and another fireman had arrived with the fire truck to save a house but had quickly been surrounded by flames. As the one fireman drove the engine frantically down the driveway, Cody had stood atop the truck with the hose and engaged in a life or death battle with the blaze as they made their getaway. I'd been both proud and horrified to realize that there was no stage in a child's life when a mother can stop praying for his safety.

Once again my call didn't reach him. I bought baked goods from a native woman and camped.

The next morning, crossing Burke Channel, I stopped and was raising my camera to photograph a scene down that body of water, when there in my viewfinder I saw three swimming deer quite near me. I marveled at how nature's creatures adapt to survive and move with such grace through their environments. They looked as though they were enjoying their swim on to new foraging ground.

From there, I paddled into Namu, the town where the infamous first-time capture of a Killer Whale occurred. "Namu" the Killer Whale was sent to Seattle for human entertainment and died about a year later. I remembered the sad story of his family pod following along for over 150 miles as he was dragged slowly south. How cold-hearted humans can be!

Thankfully, my own experience in this town was good! I'd been dreaming for too long of a hot shower and pie á la mode, and was happy to find both of those, and also to receive a fabulous frozen King salmon from a kind fisherman. I used this stop to fill my water jugs and call Gregg again. One final luxury was a splurge on a six-pack of beer. With the hot weather I was now experiencing, these would be a treasured treat.

I paddled on. Early in the day I passed by a fishing boat with a Croatian crew, one of whom tossed me an orange, but by the end of the day I was battling waves and chop that had developed into more than I cared to handle. At last, I spied a wonderful little river inlet with a sweet sand beach. It looked like a perfect camp. I changed course, turning my boat to run with the waves. Even doing this, I was barely able to keep my boat under control as I was hurtled wildly in the direction of the rocky shore. Being so singly focused on preventing myself from capsizing, I had not even seen a fishing boat anchored to my portside. It took all of my skill and attention to maneuver my kayak around to the leeside of the vessel. The crew all came on deck and invited me aboard. The boat was the *Tracy Lee,* a gillnetter from Vancouver. The skipper was another friendly Croatian. The crew gave me coffee and hospitably offered to let me stay aboard for the night. I was fairly certain they only had the noblest of intentions, but explained that my destination was very near. I only needed to wait for the waters to calm. After about an hour I was able to re-board my kayak and paddle to camp. I wished them well in their gillnet opening the next morning.

I chilled my beer in the seawater, lit a fire, and put half of the gutted salmon on the fire. The other half I set on a log in the middle of the beach while I tossed the guts in the water and rinsed my hands. With my cool beer now in hand, I walked back up to grab the other fillet and it was gone. I looked up to see an eagle whistling overhead. I sat in the hot sand, sipping my beer, supposing that it was actually perfect that the rascally raptor got what it did, since in truth it was near gluttony to eat the whole remaining fillet. Somehow, I managed!

My aim was to get a good night's sleep in preparation for the twenty miles I hoped to make the next day on down to Penrose Island. High tide would be at 5:00 A.M. and that would be a good time to leave. The evening was warm and clear so I decided not to set up my tent, and lay down in the fine sand, prepared for an exceptional slumber. But the sand that had baked all day in the sun now radiated the stored heat back through me. I was sweating and the mosquitoes and gnats relentlessly fed on me. I lay awake so long that when I finally did sleep, I overslept my planned departure time.

Strong tail winds finally cleared my groggy head and also allowed me to sail from the Addenbroke lighthouse, three quarters of the route. Eventually, as the waves coming from behind grew bigger and bigger, I began to feel smaller and smaller, and I surrendered my sail and paddled the remaining distance to splendid Penrose Island.

Someone somewhere on my journey had told me to stop here, and it was better than I'd imagined. Blinding white shell beaches, unlike any I had seen, fell off below the bay, illuminating the water. It looked as tropical as any South Pacific shore. This could not be the maritime Northwest! Where were the young and muscular Polynesian guys to help me ashore? The bright sun supported my tropical fantasy, but the reality was that I did have to schlep my own gear, as usual! I spent the last part of my day lazing out of the wind in the hot sun.

I thought that evening about my mother. She would love this island. I have nothing but praise for this amazing woman. She has always been my friend. She would drop anything to come to the aid of any one of her children. There were six of us and each about as different in personality and appearance as we could be. It did not matter in the least to her. She loved us all, and though we never had much money, she did her best to feed and clothe us. She made most of our school clothes and outfits for special occasions. When we went car camping with the whole gang, she would home-can cases of food that sat top-heavy on our car roof rack, making the whole car lean as we rounded corners. Her reasoning for the pre-made meals was so that she could actually enjoy the camping experience too without having to cook the whole time. She was always fun-loving and would happily engage in any adventure. We hiked and camped and paddled around Lopez. She came to dances, wild parties, attended more serious ceremonies, and was always open and non-judgmental. And to her credit, she could then turn around and fly off with one of my sisters to pull slot machine handles in Vegas. She was capable of much diversity. She raised us all in a simple and loving way, free of guilt-trips and pressures. From neither parent did I learn the slightest prejudices. All humans were equal in their eyes. My parents were living proof that people don't need a church to be moral and principled.

As my dad had gone off looking for his father, my mom also searched for her real mother, Hilda. I remember as a small child (sitting in the back seat of the car), an air of intensity as she drove around the Olympic Peninsula searching for clues about her Makah Indian mother. The leads all ended up at dead ends and she finally gave up, but I knew her mother's disappearance was a source of sorrow for her.

And then amazingly one day, when I was about thirteen and my oldest sister was 23, my mom's real mother, Hilda Mae, showed up. We were all joyful and in disbelief. It looked like we were finally going to learn about her life. My mom had not seen her since the 1920's, when she was about four years old. It had been forty years. Hilda, as we learned, suffered greatly from the pain and humiliation of being forced to leave my mom and uncle and then endured the further tragedy of losing her third child in a car accident. She had suffered from addictions and wandered to California where she sang in nightclubs.

It was here that truly the first good thing came into her life. Joe Losavio fell in love with Hilda. He adored her. In the 35 years they were together, she had never told him of her "shameful" past. As time went on, her health began to slip and she became more tormented. Joe had begged her to tell him about her life, thinking that if she could overcome her demons, perhaps her health would be restored. He could only imagine that maybe she had killed someone. Finally in a therapy session that Joe arranged for her, the story came out about her children, Mary and George. Joe made immediate plans and insisted that they drive north to look for her long-lost children. It was not hard for them to track down my mom's maiden name, Fahrenkopf, in western Washington.

My uncle George, my mom and everyone were in tears at this miraculous reunion. Hilda discovered that her two children had each had six children. Many of her twelve grandchildren now hovered around her. We could not believe our eyes. She and my mother were like carbon copies of each other. We all compared and laughed about our similar genetic features. Thinking that we would finally have the chance, now that Hilda was in our lives, to learn the broken pieces of our family history, we were shocked and saddened to hear that she died less than a year later at her home in California. As sad as that was, we were all, no one more than my mom and my uncle, thankful that she'd finally revealed herself.

✦

I was up at 4:00 A.M. The sky was still moonlit. I made a fire for tea and pancakes and was gone by 5:30. Gale-force winds were forecast, and once away from Penrose I would be laid open to the full wilds of the sea. For the next few days, the Queen Charlotte Sound and the Pacific beyond would be all there was to be seen to the west. To be prudent, early morning departures were a must. I paddled hard to Kelp Head where it was wild with huge rolling sea swells, but I was relieved that there were no breakers. After making it around to the south side I decided the conditions looked good enough to go for Cape Caution, about eight miles further. From there, I paddled toward Blunden Bay on the cape.

As I made my careful approach to the bay through large swells and increasing winds, grey whales spouted like geysers all around me and their immense bodies rolled at the surface. I could hardly appreciate the grandeur of the scene because with every stroke I was concentrating with all my power on riding the roller-coaster waves without mishap. Even though I knew whales were all around me I could not concern myself with the possibility that one could surface right under me.

At last, I surfed into a long sandy beach. Fresh wolf tracks were everywhere. Though I was unlikely to hear them above the pounding surf, I hoped I'd have a chance to see them.

I lay on the beach that evening and watched the whales spout. While the hypnotizing, pounding surf pulsed in my tired body, I thought of the shadowy stories of my mother's ancestors, some of whose origins were from down the coast in Washington. They had hunted whales from canoes not much bigger than my kayak. With soft sands under me, rhythmic surf and whale breath blowing in from the bay, I felt enveloped by my mother's ancestor spirits, and pulled to another shore in another time.

My mom and dad before children.

My older sisters. Port Townsend, WA.

Me, my dad and brother. The airport days. Port Townsend, WA.

Early car camping.

My dad as school teacher in Port Townsend, WA.

Totem near Ivory Island, B.C.

A shell beach beckons.

Crossing to Kelp Head, B.C.

At Memkumlis in the Village Island Group. B.C.

My Mother

THE ACT OF POSSESSION

In the most Holy Trinity, Father, Son and Holy Ghost,
Three persons and one true God, the first Maker and
Creator of all things, and without whom nothing good
can be done, commenced or preserved and because the
good beginnings of anything must be in and by God, it
is therefore advisable to commence it for His glory and
honor. In His most holy name be it known to all those
to whom the present testimonial, instrument or letter
of possession comes, that today, Sunday, August 1, 1792...
The said commander and a greater part of the seamen
having been disembarked took ashore a cross which they
adored on their knees and everybody in a loud voice
devotedly proclaimed that in the name of His
Majesty, the King Don Carlos IV, our master (of which
may the Lord our Master, guard for many years with
increase of greater estates and kingdoms for the service
of the Lord and the prosperity of his vassals and of those
very powerful lords, his heirs and successors in the times
to come) the commander of this sloop, by virtue of the
order and instructions that the said most excellent senor
Viceroy of New Spain has given him in the royal name,
was taking and took possession of this country...
...for the sowing of the Holy Evangel among these

barbarous nations who up to the present have turned away
from the true knowledge and doctrine, to guard them and
free them from the devices of the devil and their
blindness in which they exist so their souls may be saved.

> —From the Spanish "Act of Possession."
> Translation of the log of the sloop Princessa Real
> shortly after she anchored in the harbor of Neah Bay.

IN THE YEARS BEFORE THERE WERE YEARS, times were
measured by suns, moons and migrations. The tides, currents
and shattering waves of the great Pacific, then as now, ripped,
tore and gnawed at the fanged maw of Juan de Fuca Strait. In
this domain so fresh and new, the mighty mythological beings of
Thunderbird and Whale still battled for supremacy. Humankind
was new as well. Their relation to the place was like that of a
helpless infant at the breast of a ferocious beast-of-a-mother.
They hung tight and were made strong by this struggle.

The Pacific pinned the *Qʷidičča?a·tx̌* (People of the Cape) with
her lashing waters and madding winds to the arrow of rugged
rock now known as Cape Flattery. They were backed by a fringe
of nearly impenetrable forest. A wall of snow-peaked mountains
looming beyond the forests made their bondage to the coastal
Motherland complete. As wild as the ocean was, the people had
little choice but to let it be their cradle and eventually to conceive
of an inconceivable feat: that of setting out in canoes hewn by
stone tools to hunt, kill and take nourishment from the mightiest
mammals on Earth. They were and still are the Makah.

One hundred and fifteen years before my great-grandmother
Emma Bell's birth in 1890, the first *babaɬid*—floating house
people—ceremoniously claimed this land for the King of Spain.
They were quickly dispatched by Makah warriors. The warriors
had no idea who they were or what their intentions may have
been, they knew only they were strangers who did not belong in
their territory.

Seventeen years later, the Spanish came again, and many others followed, determined to occupy. Missionaries brought religion, traders brought alcohol, hunters decimated the whale populations, and Indian agents renamed their new charges with mocking humor, recording them on their rolls as Abe Lincoln, Mary Washington, Florence Nightingale, or Minnehaha.

By 1890, the winds and waters of Neah Bay were as wild as they had ever been, but what remained of the Makah and their village was a far more tamed and tempered outpost.

✦

Emma Bell was almost eleven in the summer of 1900. As she had never known a different time, this was, to her, a *good* time to be alive. The grumblings of the older people were lost on her. She was happy to attend the Government School in the village, where she was learning to read and sew and getting to eat "Boston man's" food, though as much as school suited her, summertime was still the best!

What could be better about her life? She wondered as she lazily walked down the beach, arm in arm with her cousin Mae. Her long calico dress billowed in the warm wind and her flyaway braids blew across her eyes. They had been up all night for the big potlatch giveaway on Tatoosh Island and had just returned by canoe to the beach at Neah Bay. Emma could feel the good cheer in the village; even the old people's spirits were high as they returned. The Diti·daʔa·t̆x̆ or "King George" tribe as her people called them, had come over twenty miles in many canoes, across the Straits from their village on the outside of Vancouver Island. She and Mae had sat up together, transfixed through the all-night ceremony. Now, in the light of day, the pounding drum rhythms and lilting melodies of songs still reverberated in her head. She felt her footsteps were instructed by those now ghost-like beats her body had absorbed through the long night. Mae must have felt the same, for they stepped along in unison.

"Mae, let's go spend our two cents at Young Doctor's store," Emma suggested.

They altered their course and went inside the big plank house with its crudely hand-painted sign reading, "STORE." Before Emma's eyes had quite adjusted to the dim interior, Young Doctor was walking in his crippled gait to greet them.

He said, "Bet you got some mad money to spend. I seen you girls scrambling last night with all them other kids after them pennies got thrown up. How many-ju-git?" Emma opened her hand to reveal two shiny pennies. "Oh I had to jab my elbow into Willie Mac and I had three but Mae here only got one so I give her one of mine so we can git some candy."

Young Doctor stepped aside so the girls could survey their choices from his neat rows of hard candies and gum set up on shelves in the corner of his house. After some agonizing decisions, they paid and thanked him and stepped back out into the bright day.

Emma saw her mother wrapped in a shawl, walking near the shore with Papa and her sister Ida. They were taking their time visiting with others on the beach. It made her happy to see them together and relaxed.

She sat next to Mae outside Young Doctor's, savoring the candy and sharing licks with her. When other kids came to spend their pennies, the boys got rowdy and Emma rolled her eyes. "Come on Mae, let's get away from these stupid boys! The drums is startin' up. Let's go watch the gamblin'."

Emma grabbed Mae's arm and they ambled to the far end of the beach. The drumming and singing grew louder and more animated as they came near. Many of the potlatch guests and hosts were now here watching or playing *Slahe·l*, the bone game.

"All them things they just got last night, now they're just throwing 'em away! I wouldn't never do that," Emma said to Mae.

The two opposing teams were sitting in rows along the beach facing each other. The cousins' old grandparents sat together, straight-backed among the players. The girls stood behind them surveying the wagered items on a mat between the teams. Emma saw a hand mirror with a matching hairbrush. She tried to whisper to her grandma to try to win the set. The grandparents turned and gave her a stern look. They did not like being bothered. She realized she'd broken their concentration. No doubt their team was counting on her grandparents' experience to help divine the unmarked bone in their opponent's hands. The counter sticks that had stood in the sand like a proud fence in front of their team were slowly being forfeited to the opposing team. Right when Emma thought her blunder had caused them bad luck, they started winning the counter sticks back. Emma's Papa stood near and he'd often show her with a hand signal which gambler's hand *he* thought held the unmarked bone. She was impressed by how often he was right and wished he were playing.

When he slipped off, Emma followed to where he sat with her mama and sister. "This can go on all night! Can Mae and me use a blanket?"

When mama handed her the blanket, a bottle of whiskey fell from it. Her father quickly snatched it up. Emma tried not to show her disappointment. As she dragged the blanket off, she glanced back at her family huddled together. They still looked happy but then, the bottle was more than half full. She wished it had broken when it fell.

When she returned to Mae, they wrapped up and sat in the sand at a distance. The bright fire burning between the two rows of gamblers threw strange shadows and the fever-pitched drumming and chanting that was meant to confuse the gamblers also rattled them. When she saw her mother struggling down the beach toward home and Papa pushing and cursing her, it became even harder to concentrate.

"Which hand do *you* think it's in?" Mae asked repeatedly.

"I don't have no idea!" Emma usually had to admit. She kept flashing on images of her Papa, angry and wild, chasing mama through the shadows of their house. She stayed pressed against Mae until they each started to nod off.

At last they rose and set away for home. Emma felt like she was wading through waist-deep water as she drew near. She would rather go anyplace else, she thought. But she said goodbye to Mae and they parted ways at the junction of the paths. It was quiet as she pushed on the cedar plank door. Perhaps things hadn't gone poorly as she'd imagined. The door met resistance. She pushed harder and heard a moan.

"Papa! Wake up. I can't get in." There was no response, so she pushed until she could wedge herself through the narrow opening and step over him. She looked at him crumpled there, dirty and smelling of vomit. The house was dark and still. Her sister, mother, uncle and his family were all sleeping. A few embers still glowed in the cooking fire on the floor. Emma stirred them, and by the light of the flame, she looked around and noticed overturned cooking pots and a broken chair. She may not have been much good at guessing in the gambling game but she'd certainly guessed right about her father.

In the morning she rose and brought back the day's water from the creek, then sat near her younger sister Ida and looked across the smoky fire at her mother, Lucy. She had her head scarf pulled close around her face, attempting to hide a swollen eye.

"I hate what that whiskey makes Papa do!" Emma said boldly.

She knew it was none of her business, and disrespectful to comment on her mother's suffering, but she had to say it this time.

Ida raised her eyebrows, but mother only tipped her head closer to the steamy pot and said softly, "Least he's out fishin' and that'll bring us some dollars so we can't complain."

It was a fact that Emma's Papa somehow was always able to rise from his disastrous state and set out in his canoe for a day's catch that he could sell for three or four dollars. During the "dry" times when there was no successful smuggling of rum or whisky, things were calmer in the house; there was no hitting, throwing and cursing. In these good times, in addition to fishing, Papa carved model canoes with miniature paddles complete with tiny coiled ropes and bail scoop. Every couple of months he would send them off with the steamer *Libby* to Port Townsend. Papa never saw the shop in the town that sold his carvings, but eventually the cash came back to the family. This money often started his cycle of drinking anew.

Fortunately, the women had their own ways to get through the hard times. Each year they traveled thirty miles to the shores of *ḳaʔuk* (or "Lake Ozette" as the whites knew it), where they collected grasses and cattail reeds to weave into baskets for tourists and mats for their own uses. Emma was always excited to be a part of the chattering group of mothers and daughters who set off.

This time they came back to find the village abuzz with talk: Agent Virginia was out to catch the rum runners who had supplied the alcohol during the potlatch festivities. Emma's mood quickly turned dark when she heard that her Papa was being threatened with jail if he did not supply names. Over the next few days, Papa did the honorable thing by not talking. At last, Agent Virginia and three Indian police privates came to lead him away. Emma and her sister watched him go down the beach in his ragged pants and bare feet. But at least he held his head high as he went with them out to the Bahada Point jail.

Papa loved the white man's whiskey but he hated the white man's food, so mama set aside rations of dried halibut or salmon from their scant reserves and Emma delivered them. This is how she got to know the Agent Peter Virginia.

"Just call me Pierre," he told her.

This day she had also brought her Papa's crooked knife and a piece of cedar driftwood.

"Here Papa, this will keep your hands busy."

But before she could push the carving tool between the bars, Agent Virginia snatched it away. "No no, my dear, this weapon I cannot permit!"

"Say Peter, my girl here's jus givin' me supthin' to do. You let her give it and I'll carve you a model Indian canoe. What-a-ya say?" Papa's hands hung placid through the cell bars.

"Papa's harmless as a fly," Emma lied as she remembered her mother's swollen eye. "But you decide and here's the cedar too. Don't go throwin' it into the stove." She set it down, gave her father a small shrug and followed Pierre into his office.

Emma wanted to resent this fresh-faced man. He had shamed them, dragging her Papa off to jail. He had no right to be here. But she had to admit that she enjoyed his stories, and he seemed to have many for someone who looked so young. She felt almost as captive as her father when Pierre launched into tales of his years as an Indian agent in Canada. He spoke in a thick French accent, telling her of the Indians in Alberta and their herds of beautiful horses.

His admiration for them made her feel a little jealous. "I bet them Bloods couldn't paddle a canoe and chase down a whale!" she said.

"Well I must admit, Makah maybe are the wildest, bravest humans I ever saw. But oh, this climate! It's more than I can bear. I swear not even a horse can live here."

He had arrived the winter before and obviously had his weaknesses. He hated the cold and rain but he did seem to relish his position. Now, as he reclined at a desk cluttered with files, he seemed to want her to understand the mission he was charged with: to hold the Makah to the treaty laws and "That includes prohibition of alcohol. I only do my job."

His stories made her look at him in a different light. Now she could see they were not that different. "Well, I hate that Papa's in jail but I don't like the booze neither. If I could make him stop I would, but I can't, so I guess I'm glad you're here. But least let him carve. It'll make him happy."

✦

Word had it that both Agent Morse and Pierre had received finely-carved model canoes and that may have been why Papa only spent one month behind bars instead of three. The day in late summer when he was freed, Emma went to Washburn's to buy store food, special for his return. While she was paying, Ida came in and whispered in her ear, "I seen Papa pull a bottle from his tackle box! He musta hid it there. I'm not goin' back to the house!"

Emma returned the items and then sat on the beach gathering courage. She felt deflated and weak like she'd been kicked. And this day was supposed to be so good: not only was Papa out of jail but it was also the day of a big whale hunt. Why was he ruining everything again?

When Emma walked in her heart sank at the sight of him. "Papa, there's the whale hunt today. Don'tchya want to see the send-off?"

She tried to coax the bottle from him, but it was too late, he held tightly and it sloshed as it flailed above his head. "Leeeve me lone! Gonna cel-brate my freeedom. Jus leeve me lone!" He staggered from the house.

When he was stinking of booze that bad, she dared not follow him. But when she did see him again, she panicked. There he was, passed out next to his canoe right in the middle of the beach! She dashed to his empty bottle, filled it with sand, and threw it as far into the bay as she could.

The men preparing for the hunt walked past them like they were invisible. She knew they were "big men," and her Papa's condition only proved his unworthiness. But Agent Morse and Pierre would soon be on the beach with everyone to see the whaling canoes go off, and they would *not* ignore his drunkenness.

When Ida came, they worked together to get Papa into a sitting position with his back against his canoe. Emma crossed his legs in front of him and Ida tucked his tackle box under one elbow. Ida went to get the pot of fish head soup, and their mother brought his drum. She sat against one side of their unconscious father while Ida and Emma snuggled into his other side.

Soon the ceremony began. All the families drummed and sang as the men carried the massive canoe to the water's edge, and loaded the smaller support canoes with harpoons, seal-skin floats, fathoms of cedar withe line and buckets of fresh water. Emma knew that sometimes whales pulled men far out to sea and some hunters never did return. She knew this was a joyous moment to honor their men's bravery, while inwardly they also feared for their survival. The singing and drumming became even louder as the fleet launched and paddled powerfully off toward the horizon.

When Emma saw Pierre walking down the beach she waved at him as she leaned into her father's shoulder to keep him upright. She was relieved when he waved and walked on by.

By the time Papa did wake up Emma noticed his shame. He pulled his knit cap down low, lit a cigarette with shaky hands and asked, "How long I been sleepin'? How longs the boats been out huntin'?" He drew a puff. "Was I bad? I bet them Big men laughed at me."

"No Papa, everyone just thought you was havin' a nice picnic with your family." Emma pointed to the empty soup pot, and his drum on the blanket. She picked up his drum. "Papa, can you teach me a potlatch song?"

He nodded, snuffed his smoke in the sand and played his drum softly for her. She laid her head against him.

At dusk, a message canoe arrived to announce the success of the hunters. A Humpback Whale had heard their prayers and offered herself without mishap! People set to building a fire on the beach. Soon Emma saw the silhouette of the canoes and men against the sheen of the moonlit sea. The waters were uncommonly serene as the flotilla struggled towards shore tugging the colossal body. Moonlight glinted off her black leathery back. The victory song of the harpooner coming across the expanse of the water sent chills up her spine. Emma ran back to her house to tell the others.

Mother brought her cattail mats to wrap their family's portion of meat and blubber. She joined Emma and every other soul in Neah Bay on the beach. The hunters came very near but then waited almost two more hours for the high tide. Men waded out and pulled ropes ashore. Emma was proud when even her father, joining with all the able-bodied men and boys, pulled on the mountainous carcass to deliver it as high as possible onto the beach.

This day was even better than the Potlatch days, Emma thought, as she watched her Papa along with other tribal men. It was clear that Mamma felt the same. As they sat on the beach

Mamma spoke spiritedly to her and Ida, telling of the days before so many *babaŧid,* when their men could bring in so many whales that women really had to work. One season they had 30,000 gallons of whale oil. Much, so much they could sell it to ships and trade it!

After the whale was staked to the sands of the beach, it was time for tribute rituals. Emma watched with fascination. She had been too young to remember the last time a whale was on this beach. It seemed correct and good to honor the spirit of this mighty being that had come to her people. The hunters climbed atop the whale's body and placed Eagle feathers and white down along her back. They began a slow tempo song. Emma tried to sing along.

> *I have come to see your village*
> *Will you throw oil on the fire?*
> *If it's good*
> *I will come again.*

When the butchering began, the head harpooner received the prime cut from the "saddle" of the whale's back. Each of the other principal hunters received their cuts in succession and on down through the ranks of the tribe.

By dawn the carcass lay with its enormous rib bones jutting skyward. Emma's family still had not received their strip of meat and blubber but Emma watched her Papa sit with a row of men against a beach log hitting drums and singing the song of the whale, strong and proud. Even if they should be the very last family to get their portion, thought Emma, the sight of her father singing filled her with joy.

◆

More than Ida or their cousin Mae, Emma was excited when it was time to head back to school. Younger children cried if they were coming for the first time. They did not want to be apart from their families. Emma felt a little gnawing guilt. Why was she so happy to attend? Maybe it was because Papa had fallen ill after the whale hunt and now coughed night and day. And too, Mamma always seemed sad and overworked. At school the teacher, though stern, was fair and predictable. Emma liked school so much, in fact, she decided one day she would be a teacher.

Emma took advantage of the fact that tribal status was not as important at school. She could create her own good standing if she performed well. She learned crocheting, knitting and sewing faster than many of the students, and excelled at writing. The teacher, Mrs. Muller, must have taken a shine to her because she gave her the coveted position nearest the wood stove. Emma noticed her cousin was quiet and somber, often staring absent-mindedly toward the walls. She could understand how Mrs. Muller's cold and formal manners were difficult for Mae, who was used to the warmth and affection of their grandparents. Emma knew that if *she* had her father's kindhearted old parents in *her* home, she too wouldn't want to leave.

Weeks of torrential rains pounded on the cedar shake roof of the school house. The boys had the chore of keeping the fire going. Emma was glad the girls got to learn "Boston man's" cooking. Their "lessons" were always the afternoon meals. She helped to prepare big pots of beans. On special occasions they got to add salt-pork, which made her stomach grumble with anticipation.

The old school had burned to the ground last winter, and Emma liked the new school better. It had bright new timbers and a pretty window that looked across the village to the Straits. Still, it was poorly lit and drafty too. Oil lamps extended the shorter winter days, and during the dim light before they were released, Mrs. Muller taught them music.

Because the piano had burned and there were no other musical instruments, they only sang. Mrs. Muller favored Christmas songs. They sang: "O Holy Night," "O Come All Ye Faithful," "Hark the Herald Angels Sing." She said, "I want you all to know what the true holiday is for, and that's the celebration of the baby Jesus."

Mrs. Muller had always made a point of saying that potlatches were evil, but she seemed to have no problem with encouraging them to make and give Christmas gifts.

Emma said to her sister as she crocheted a scarf from salvaged yarn, "I guess it's good because it has something to do with Jesus. And besides Papa can really use this since he's been coughin' so much." Ida gave a small nod.

By the time Mrs. Muller released them for the Christmas holiday, Emma and the others each had their handmade gifts to bring home to their families.

For two days, snow flurries swirled from the black skies to melt on the beach of Neah Bay. Emma should have been happy for the winter break but her home was dark and dreary with sickness. Papa lay on his sleeping platform in the last agonized stages of tuberculosis. Though she knew he had been sick for weeks, his decline seemed especially fast in the past few days. He looked withered and gray.

Emma sat near the cooking fire and watched snowflakes make their dreamy journey down through the smoke hole high in the rafters only to sizzle away on hot rocks near the flames. "Jingle Bells" kept surfacing in her mind and she wanted to sing the happy song, but her father's constant coughing reminded her that this was not the time or place. Emma and Ida were glad to relieve their mother and auntie who had been nursing him day and night since he had stopped eating. He winced from chest pain and sweats soaked his threadbare shirt. Emma noticed that, though her Papa surely suffered, he also emanated a certain comforting peace. She sat next to him and softly sang "Hark the Herald" and when she got to the part, "...peace on earth and mercy mild, God and sinners reconciled," she wondered if her father was reconciled with God like Mrs. Muller had said everyone must be before they die. She held his hand, wondering how many fish it had carried to their house. He had never hit *her* with his hand. It was now so limp that she had a hard time imagining it could ever have curled into the fist that hurt mama and broke things. Emma decided she was going to remember Papa's hands carving and bringing home fish.

When Papa died, he was not carried out through the smoke hole as was the old custom and he was not put to rest up in the

tree limbs of the forest as was also the old way. He was buried
in the village graveyard in a simple box. All from Emma's house
and Mae's house came to the graveyard. They joined together,
standing over the dirty gaping hole, in surroundings that were
otherwise pristinely blanketed in snow. Emma, who'd thought
the snow would never stick, now could not help but interpret
the beauty, stillness and purity of the day as a sign that her Papa
was in fact a sinner reconciled with God. Her grandparents sang
a mourning song as Papa was lowered. They continued to sing it
for days after.

The grandparents' sadness drew Emma to them. She spent as
much time as she could with her cousin Mae so she could be
close. She asked questions and listened to their stories. To Emma,
they appeared ancient. The deep web of lines on their faces, she
imagined, must each have a beginning and an end, and every one
of those lines would lead to a story from their past. All Emma and
Mae had to do was ask, and the stories unfurled. The old folks
seemed to remember the days of their youth as clear as sunshine.

Over the next few days around the fire, sometimes until late
into the evening, the old people shared what they remembered.
Emma learned how some of their family members survived
smallpox that brought the population of Neah Bay down from
thousands to only a few hundred. Grandpa told of the survivors'
struggles and misery.

The cousins listened dutifully as once again they were reminded
that they were not of a noble past; in fact, they were descendants
of slaves from raids on Vancouver coastal villages, five generations
earlier. Through subsequent brave or honorable deeds, their families had climbed to become commoners in the tribe.

Grandpa recalled his younger days when there were 30
whaling canoes and the men also hunted sea otter for the white
traders, who, he said, never seemed to get enough. They often
paid for the pelts in poor-quality whiskey. Emma heard the pride
in grandpa's voice when he said he had never acquired a taste
for whiskey. He made it clear that he did not think *all* the white
men of those early days were worthless. He told about a man
known to the Makah as *čařik*, "painter." The whites called him,

"Mr. Swan." The Makah gave him his name because he always sketched and painted images of them. Emma learned that he had lived at Neah Bay for many years and was the first teacher. Her father had been one of his first students. Grandpa shook his head slowly and finished by explaining that, because he always needed his son's help fishing, her father did not go to school long enough to learn to read.

The story of her Papa made Emma teary. Grandma must have noticed. She handed Emma a comb and asked her to braid her hair. While Emma gently ran the comb through her long salt-and-pepper hair, the old woman told the girls of the famous Makah man named "Circus Joe" who had performed with the Barnum's Circus. She said he had become quite a professional showman. When he returned to the tribe he would startle them all at Potlatch time by swallowing glass and long knives and breathing large flames of fire from his mouth. She laughed when she remembered what a foul mood the tribal shamans would get into after witnessing Circus Joe's feats. She said that *they* were the ones who usually enjoyed all the attention, impressing their tribal kin with gruesome acts of sorcery and trickery. After being audience to Circus Joe, however, the shaman would sulk with envy that *they* were incapable of such impressive magic.

The days Emma spent with her grandparents helped to lift her spirits but when it was time for school to resume, she could not believe her ears when mother said she did not want her to return.

"Mama! You mean not for a week or more 'til yer not so sad?"

"No," Mama said. "You're a big girl now and it's time you learn basket makin' to sell to the whites. We have no money with Papa gone. Ida can go one more year and then it's over for her too. Don't talk no more 'bout it."

◆

This abruptly marked the end of the small joys and easy pleasures of childhood for Emma. For the next year she lived vicariously through Ida's accounts until Ida's school days also ended. Mrs. Muller used every form of threat, but to no avail. The family's need was too great. Even Agent Morse recognized the hardship the family faced, and did not demand their attendance.

Emma dreaded a life that simply followed the same tired path as her mother's. Now, with her hopes of becoming a teacher surely dashed, she tried to find some new direction. She found work cleaning for white families. She wove lidded baskets with whale and thunderbird motifs to sell. The years bled each into the next, punctuated by nothing remarkable. When her moon cycles came, she cried at the sight of her own blood. Her rounding breasts only reminded her that her life was plodding forward with no promise.

Pierre had come to terms with reservation life and stayed on as deputy. He even decided he rather liked the challenge of these feisty and proud people. He tried to imagine their population at its peak of two to five thousand before the Spaniards had come. The Makah defiantly fought them off after they had built a fort with six gun stations on Baada Point. Now the only clue he could see that the Spanish had ever occupied were shards of bricks from their bakery ovens.

He currently presided over fewer than 700 natives, and of them, only the Makah and Ozette could actually claim Neah Bay as ancestral land. Also on the reserve were the Quileute and Ho tribes. The unnatural situation caused endless friction. And in general he saw they had little love for submission and were not above disobedience. To keep the fragile peace, he had to be on his toes.

Perhaps an unconscious seed of desire had been planted when she was a girl visiting her father in jail, but in the years since that event Emma Bell had matured into a creature of graceful beauty. This seemed to have happened overnight. Now, Pierre found himself tailoring his excursions around the reservation so he might cross her path as she walked to her house-cleaning jobs. He would be on the beach on the days she paddled her baskets out to the steamboat. She didn't seem to wonder why he was there to give her a hand as she pulled her canoe ashore.

More and more his mind was consumed with her. He dreamt of her soft doe-brown eyes, of touching the satin-like smoothness of her skin. With every year, that seed of desire grew. At last, when she was sixteen, he decided to pursue her in earnest.

His first chance came when Mrs. Muller's daughter Gertie needed to visit a podiatrist in Port Townsend. She had grown out of her old foot brace, and Mrs. Muller couldn't leave her teaching duties. Pierre volunteered to take the girl, and Mrs. Muller relented, on the condition that he brought a chaperone.

Pierre could see already that he had scored a hit with Emma. Her eyes danced when he invited her. She had never gone further than the network of footpaths around Neah Bay. And by waterways, probably she'd never traveled further than Tatoosh and Ozette.

Within the first hour of casting off from Neah Bay, a squall drove them all from the deck down into the galley. The captain and crew had their hands full maneuvering the boat down the Strait of Juan de Fuca. Following swells rolled the *Bellingham* back and forth like a drunk staggering down an alley. Emma had brought basket-making grasses to teach Gertie, and as the ship rolled, she concentrated on guiding the tangled mess in Gertie's untrained fingers. Pierre sat next to them, corralling cups of coffee as they tried to slide across the table with each big swell. Every so often he pushed Emma's cup toward her and reminded her to drink. He took a deck of cards from his pocket and offered to teach her Crazy Eights, but Emma was so dedicated to her weaving instruction that she barely acknowledged him.

When Gertie became seasick and had to lie down on the bench, Pierre did not offer to get up as Emma scooted over to make room for her. He continued shuffling the cards as if he did not notice, all the while nearly overcome by the sweetness of her scent. He dealt her a hand that she picked up and attempted to fan out. Pierre reached over and twisted her hand of cards gently away from his line of vision.

"You mustn't let me see, Emma."

A sudden lurch of the boat dumped her directly into his lap and sent her cards onto the floor. Pierre's reflex was to grab and rescue her in mid-topple but he was overcome by the less noble impulse of wanting to keep hold of her.

"Pierre! Let me go," she said in a frightened whisper.

He eased up but did not completely relinquish her. He pleaded, "Emma, don't be frightened, *ma cherie*. Please listen. You may think that I am crazy but I have fallen in love with you!"

He was a bit embarrassed by his unplanned confession. He could see the uncertainty and surprise in her wide eyes. What, though, did he expect? How could she ever believe that a white man could want her? Her eyes glazed and she appeared about to cry. He saw that she was waiting to know what his next move would be and he wondered himself. He released her.

"I am very sorry. Please forgive me. But you are beautiful to me. I may have some years more but I *am* debonair, no? Just take some time and consider." He reached out and touched her cheek softly.

Emma glanced down at Gertie, who had fallen to sleep. When she looked back up at him she asked in a quiet voice, "Do you want to kiss me? I've never kissed a man before so I might not do it good."

Again Pierre congratulated himself. She could not be absolutely naive, growing up in a one room house, but knowing and doing were different. He leaned toward her and pressed his lips to hers. She shuddered as he drew her close. He moved from her lips to her neck and was so lost in pleasure that he was taken aback when she pushed him away.

Yet he understood, and moved to sit across from her. He put his elbows on the table and stared adoringly into her shy eyes. "I will not press. No, I will wait for you to come on your own terms. Just know I will treasure you like the first flower of spring. It was nice, no?"

Emma, looking flushed and somewhat bewildered, said softly, "I think so."

Pierre stayed true to his word and did not pursue. But he did show the girls around the sights of Port Townsend.

"They remind me of a mouse maze the boys built in school." Emma said of the brick buildings they walked by.

"Don't worry. I will not let you get lost!" he teased her. "Come, I want to show you something beautiful." He led the girls along to a new fountain in the center of town, and watched as Emma walked speechless around the bronze statue of a nude woman.

"Lookit!" Gertie squealed, "The cute fat little babies and dolphins!" While Gertie played her fingers through the jets of water squirting from the mouths of the bronze dolphins, and touched the metallic toes of the cherubs, Pierre moved close to Emma and nodded toward the statue. "She is very beautiful, no? But also *you* would be very beautiful if I could see so much of you."

◆

Pierre had arranged for the three of them to stay at a boarding house. Emma and Gertie's small room overlooked the main street. From her window Emma saw Pierre saunter down the sidewalk and into a saloon. He had a confident, upright way of moving. She wondered about him as she showed Gertie string stories. By criss-crossing a big loop of string between the fingers of her hands, she created geometric patterns, while telling the stories of each pattern as they transformed into different shapes. Emma had done these since she was a child and could almost perform them blindfolded. Gertie didn't seem to notice her preoccupation. Emma kept her eye on the street below in hopes of catching another glimpse of Pierre. She tried to imagine herself standing before him as naked as the statue.

By the end of their stay in Port Townsend, Gertie had her new foot brace and Emma had a beautiful sky blue dress with mother-of-pearl buttons. Pierre had chosen it at the local mercantile. No one had ever bought her anything new before. Now she found herself obsessed with the desire for another kiss from Pierre. She would wait for the boat ride home and only if Gertie was sleeping.

Emma bundled the new dress together with the money she'd made from selling her baskets, and a picture postcard of Port Townsend. She carried it tight to her chest as they boarded the *Bellingham* the next evening. After all passengers and cargo were on, the whistle blew and the steamer began its run to Neah Bay.

This time the weather was calm and clear. Emma, Pierre and Gertie stood on deck with the other passengers. A pod of Orca whales spouted and rolled, and Emma took in the deep primal scent of the whale's breath, released on the high plumes of mist. The *Bellingham* reduced speed to keep pace with the playful pod. She watched with delight when the sleek, massive mammals propelled themselves into the air, revealing their satin-white undersides and saddles. It seemed impossible that such immense creatures could become airborne. Better yet was the impact when they slammed back into the emerald waters. They were so close that Gertie was splashed and was about to cry from the shock, but Pierre told her she'd just had a "baptism by The Wild," and she laughed instead.

It was night when they arrived in Port Angeles. They watched as the passengers disembarked, and the crew unloaded barrels of whiskey. When one barrel fell from the dock into the bay, Pierre, without hesitation, dove into the dark icy water and saved it. Emma admired his heroics and the captain did too. He rewarded "Deputy Pierre Virginia" with dry clothing and a tall glass of his own private reserve.

It would be another five hour run along the coast from Port Townsend to Neah Bay. Emma resumed her weaving, and Pierre left and came back with enticing news for Gertie. "Our Captain wants to know if you would like to help him steer?"

Gertie's eyes lit up and she ran off to try her hand at navigation. Pierre cupped Emma's face gently with his hands. "A kiss? For that pretty dress?"

Now Emma was unsure how prepared she was.

The dress was beautiful and a kiss seemed like a small price to pay. She did not say a word but lifted her face towards his whiskey-tainted breath. He pressed her against the cabin wall. His tongue slipped between her lips. His hands slid down and lifted her. This was much more than a kiss, thought Emma, but she did not protest. She closed her eyes and released herself to him.

She thought of a dream she'd had many times where she floated under the sea on the back of a large black whale. In her dream she lay close to the whale and held its dorsal fin as it undulated. Now Pierre seemed like that sea creature. But when he tore a button off her dress she opened her eyes in disbelief. Her breasts were exposed. She tried to push him away. His apologies and look of regret were instantly forgivable. Anyway, she really did not want him to stop.

Emma followed him as he led her to the aft deck. Under the moonlit sky he pulled her dress from her shoulders, his mouth moving along her skin as the dress inched down. It dawned on Emma that she was soon to be as naked as the bronze statue and it didn't seem crazy now. She let him lay her on the thick coils of rope behind stacks of crates.

As much as she had been a willing participant, when the fury of the moment passed, she felt like she'd been knocked to the ground by a powerful wave, spun around in its turbulent waters and washed up on a beach. Her dress hung at her waist. After Pierre rolled away from her, she felt jittery and exposed.

Pierre gazed contentedly at the softly lit night sky. Emma could not understand her own tears. Were they happiness, fear, or humiliation?

He noticed she was upset. "Are you not happy, *ma cherie?*"

Emma tugged the dress up to her shoulders. "Please go get my new blue dress in the bundle on the bench, I'm throwing this one overboard!"

When he returned with the parcel, she changed and tossed her old dress into the sea. He turned and looked at her and his eyes got the same dreamy look as when he talked about horses. He moved to brush away her tears.

By the end of their journey, he was standing with his arm wrapped warmly around her, planning to paddle with her around Cape Flattery. She liked the idea but knew she needed time to break the news to her family. They walked out onto the aft deck with shoulders touching. The Olympic Mountains stood bathed in moonlight. Nearing Neah Bay, the moon slipped behind the clouds, and the bay was dark but for the bobbing lights of lanterns borne on canoes coming out to bring them ashore.

✦

Emma knew her family would be awake and looking forward to the stories of her adventure. When she entered and saw them hunkered around a dim fire, it flashed in her mind that this dark life would be a thing of the past, now that Pierre was her man. She felt nearly regal in her fine new dress, and saw that they were also impressed. She told them of sleeping in the white sheets of the hotel and of the tall brick buildings and the bronze statue of the woman and about the steamboat trip. The most exciting news she saved for last, explaining that Pierre had bought her the dress and that he was interested in her. This news was met with a mix of bewilderment and silence. To break the awkward moment, Emma gave Ida the picture post-card. After such heady tales of adventure, the card seemed trivial. Ida accepted the gift, but pouted off to bed. Soon even her aunt and uncle yawned and went to lie down, leaving her alone with Mamma.

Mamma looked upset. "Your Papa can't say nuthin' but you know you dishonor him when you sleeps with the same *babatid* that puts him in jail."

Although Emma had not divulged the detail of lying with Pierre, somehow Mamma knew. Emma suggested as gently as she could that Papa was a drunk and that Pierre had only been doing his job.

Now Lucy's stare was unnerving. "I got sumpthin' to say that I never say before." She edged nearer the fire. "Long time go when I was young and pretty like you now, I got to know a young white fella, Henry Bell, he was goin' from here by supply boat down the coast to Queets. I went with him to work in a cannery there. Henry, he's your Papa. He only want me for his pleasure and when he saw there was a baby growin' he told me 'go back to Neah Bay.' He want no more of me! Them whites you can't trust. You be better to look here at Makah men, they don't leaves the womin."

Emma sat in disbelief at her mother's confession. She had never suspected that her Papa wasn't her father. "What about Ida?" she asked.

"She also Bell's girl. I went back next canning season, left you with mother. I was young and not too smart. Came home with nuther baby growin in me. I keep the name Bell for me and you girls cuz it the only good thing about that white man. Later when you was still small I git together with Jimmy and he bring you up like his own."

Emma's thoughts drifted off down the coast trying to picture some white man living not that far away who was her real father. Her eyes filled and she dropped her head. Her words were muffled. "Mamma, you think now by telling me this I will not love Pierre? He says he loves me. He is not like other white men. Did you love my father?"

"Alls I'm sayin' iz you might think he love you but his words mean nuthin' jus like Henry. He'll be nuthin' in yer life right when you really need him. No, can not trust them white men! I thought I was real in love with Henry but he never want to be no family man and never came to ever meet his girls. I was happy when I heard his boat broke up on the rocks out on the cape. They never found his body."

Emma's head spun. In the course of one short conversation, she learned of a father, a white man she had never known, and then just as quickly discovered she didn't have him. Still she wondered. What was he like? Had he been a whiskey drinker like Papa? Who else knew about him? Had he been rich?

"Mamma, that was *your* life and I'm sad about that but Pierre is a better man. You'll see." She got up and brushed the ash and dust from her dress and walked out the door.

The clouds had rolled off over the sea to the west. She took the familiar path to the beach. Broken clamshells reflected faint starlight, guiding her feet. When she reached the silent and comforting sands she lay down and closed her eyes. Cradled by the solid earth, she felt less like she was about to topple. The news her mother had related, as well as the near aching in her body for Pierre, made her dizzy. It didn't seem possible to be sad and joyful at once, but she was.

When Emma opened her eyes, she was startled to see the Northern Lights pulsing, eerie, green and shimmering. Curtains of glowing color shifted and undulated across the northern skyline. They looked playful and alive. Her body seemed connected to the magic of the night show. Her skin tingled. This certainly was not a coincidence, that she should walk out late into the night and see this. It must be a *sign*, the Spirit world was directly communicating with her. Yes! It had to be! She found herself laughing aloud at her own good fortune.

The following day, emboldened by the positive omen, Emma ran to Pierre's arms. She was reassured by his eagerness to hold her. It had not been a dream. He wanted her! There was one bothersome thing, however, about Pierre's behavior that took her some time to notice. She tested him to see if it was just her imagination. If she held his hand on the Indian side of town he seemed happy and calm, but if he was near whites, he'd drop her hand and act aloof. It seemed odd to her but it was easy enough to resolve. She did not need to go out in the village with him if it made him uncomfortable. She was content to hide away with Pierre and have him all to herself.

When news came by wire that President Roosevelt's Great White Fleet would be parading by at midnight, none wanted to miss the spectacle. That night, many from the village walked out to rocky Koitiah Point. Emma had the idea to climb up into the wide, gnarled branches of a fir tree leaning out toward the water. Pierre was happy with this vantage point and Emma snuggled near him as they waited. The night was overcast and very dark. From their perch in the branches, Pierre was first to see the approaching armada. He whistled and shouted, alerting a few Makah boys who then climbed neighboring trees for a better view.

Emma heard excited gasps and chattering from those gathered below. She too was caught by the splendor coming into view—sixteen brilliantly lit battleships steaming single file into the Juan de Fuca Strait, cutting a long line of light through an otherwise jet black darkness that could have as easily been sky or sea.

No ships she had ever seen compared to these. If they were warships, how big the world must be! She thought of her own tribesmen, the battles they used to fight down the coast; they had even brought home their victims' heads. She wondered what sort of mayhem these steel ships were capable of inflicting, and upon whom?

Emma was still starry-eyed the next day when Ida stopped by. As they sat on the doorstep, Emma only wanted to talk about Pierre. Finally, when she described how romantic it was to be up in the branches and watching the battleships go by, Ida yawned.

"What's wrong Ida?"

"Why is it we never see the two of you around? Is he shamed to be with you? Or, maybe you jus think you're better than us now with your white man. Anyhow, I've heard enough!" She got up and walked away.

Emma wanted to be mad at her sister but how could *she* know what being in love was like? She ran after her sister and caught her arm.

"Sorry Ida! Come back and I'll make us some tea. I've missed you."

As Emma made tea, Pierre invited Ida to come along on the excursion they had planned, a paddle to the outside, around the cape.

Emma was reluctant to share their time and was about to say so when Pierre went on. "I think you will be very good company and I was going to surprise but now I say I want to take your sister out to the 'Wedding Rock' to marry her, *if* she will have me." He patted the pocket of his wool vest and said, "I have a ring so maybe you will come to be our witness? We will have a little ceremony!"

Emma wondered if she heard correctly. A wedding? She felt vindicated. Ida couldn't doubt his love now!

Ida asked, "But will it be *real* with no preacher or nuthin'?"

"It will be *real* in my heart and I think for your sister too, no?"
He looked at Emma.

How could she say anything but "Yes!" to this beautiful man?
She had to admit she was attracted to his impulsive behavior
and he seemed to bring out her recklessness as well. Of course,
she would miss not having her mother or other family members
for her wedding, but since her mother's confession, Emma felt
truly happy only with Pierre. And oh how happy she would be
to prove to her mother that true love was indeed possible with a
white man.

The next day, they loaded their canoe with blankets, kettles
and enough food for three days and shoved off on their ten-
mile paddle. By early afternoon they rounded Cape Flattery.
Sea waters crashed against the towering rock headland, even
though the day was calm. It was clear to Emma that she was
the most competent of the three. She studied the sea and sky
and kept them a distance from shore to avoid the breaking
swells, noticing how little Pierre seemed to know about paddling, and how often he stopped to take in the wildness of the
coast. As they rounded cape, he pointed to the fractured rock of
the cliff wall, commenting that the rock seemed held together
by the very roots of the forests that teetered out from the edge
above their heads. He exclaimed often on the "brilliance and
sweet beauty" of the day and how the rise and fall of each swell
was like the breath of the sea. She loved his romantic way with
words. She could be content doing *all* the paddling if he would
just keep talking. Still, as they paddled by Fuca Pillar, she gently teased, "If you could only talk *and* paddle at the same time,
we'd make it to camp before dark! Besides, I thought you hated
this country."

"*Oui,* but I have learned to endure all for these days of August.
And could *anything* be more breathtaking?" Pierre gestured to the
looming monolith. Emma craned back to see the tip.

"Is this not fantastic? Such beauty!"

Ida said, "Long time ago young men would climb here, always
trying to out-do each other. They'd mark their highest point by

carving their family totem into the rock. Finally, one young man got the highest ever and made his mark, a two-headed bear, but he had climbed so high that he could not get back down. He called for help but his friends couldn't help him."

Emma interjected, "The dark spirits of the rock, held him captive!"

Pierre, with true curiosity, gazed up to the lonely perch. "What happened?"

"He died by starvation. Now it is forbidden for anyone to climb. But it's said that his spirit protects the Makah by sending warnings to the shamans."

"Well, let me know if he warns you of anything!" Pierre laughed.

Emma noticed Pierre dig his paddle in more forcefully as they continued along the craggy and surf-worn headland. Alluring caves appeared but they kept their distance, not wanting to be sucked in by the tide. As the coastline dropped, Emma suggested they go ashore to camp. "This is *hača·wa·t*, old village site; used to be a summer camp for our Ozette cousins down the coast. I don't think they use it no more." No one objected, and they paddled in.

Emma and Ida gathered firewood, glad to move their legs after the long paddle. Pierre brought out food and dipped water from the creek into a kettle. By early evening a pot of cabbage, potatoes and rutabagas bubbled over a fire. Ida flavored it with flakes of dried salmon, and the three savored the stew as the sun set.

Emma made a private bed for her and Pierre but Ida objected. She was afraid of bears, she said, even though there was no bear sign anywhere. But Pierre said that Ida could sleep on his other side. "Don't worry, I will protect you young ladies from any beast as long as you stay close to me, *oui*?" Emma rolled her eyes as Ida trotted over and threw her bedding next to theirs. Then for hours she lay awake, excited for her wedding day.

Over morning coffee they made plans to continue paddling along the beach to the petroglyph rocks. As children, she and Ida had seen the old carvings a few times, and easily found them again. They pulled the boat carefully onto the stony beach they remembered, and walked right to the jumble of large boulders. One of the etchings were of human-shaped faces, with odd shapes hovering over their heads. Perhaps once these faces had looked silently out to sea from this rocky point but now the boulder seemed to have tumbled. The figures stared upwards. Emma shivered. Pierre used his finger to trace the grooves in the stone and asked, "Are these the Wedding Rocks?"

"There are many others here. They're all the 'Wedding Rocks.'"

"What are these shapes over the faces? What do they try to say?"

Emma didn't know, but Ida boldly suggested, "They've got somthin' to do with women. That's plain to see!"

Pierre looked impressed. "Yes, I think you are right!"

Emma cocked her head and reassessed the familiar etchings and admitted to herself that although out-sized and misplaced, parts of the etching were indeed shaped like the most private part of the female! She tugged at her sister's arm and they moved on to another boulder with deeply carved lines of a Spanish schooner. Emma looked out to the ocean and imagined what her ancestors must have felt, to spy the billowing white sails approaching.

Then Pierre announced it was time for their ceremony. They followed him back to his favorite petroglyph. "Emma. Come stand. I give you the ring and come Ida, you are the witness."

Pierre seemed playful yet genuine as he held her hand. His sparkling eyes made her giggle. She couldn't believe her good fortune. He spoke with sincerity, and when he said, "With this ring I thee wed," he lifted her hand and slid the ring on.

Emma was so dazed that she momentarily forgot. "Oh, I have something for you too." She pulled from her pocket a bear tooth pendant carved like a wolf. "This used to be Papa's." She placed it around Pierre's neck and hugged him. "With this necklace, I wed thee!"

There was an awkward silence before Ida chimed in that they needed to kiss. Emma was glad her sister remembered, because that was the best part of all.

Emma stumbled on the rocky beach as they walked back to their canoe. She was so distracted by her gold wedding band that everything else seemed to fade around her. She walked behind, with her sister, while Pierre strode out.

Ida whispered, "I don't think it's real, Emma."

"It might be narrow but look at it shine. I know it's gold."

"No! Not the ring, I mean the *ceremony*. Remember? Mrs. Muller always said only a church wedding was correct. But it *was* romantic!"

Emma agreed and that was good enough for her. She would hear no more of it.

Together, they looked for firewood. At the water's edge, Emma stood looking at the calm sea. "Mamma says our white papa disappeared here off the cape. His boat capsized."

Ida scanned the water. She said, "Remember how Mrs. Muller was always nicer to us? Now I'm thinkin' it's cuz our skin was lighter than the others."

"Mamma said he was *Scottish*. I wonder where Scottish are from?"

Ida turned her gaze to Emma. "Anyway, I'm glad for you. But don't forget us just cuz yer with the big deputy man. We're still your family."

"I love you, Ida. I love you all, but I'm with Pierre now." She sighed dreamily. "I can't even believe I'm his wife! I don't know what will happen next."

"I know 'what next.' A *baby!*"

Emma stared at her sister. She'd been feeling strange for almost two months but hadn't told anyone, even Pierre. Now she looked at her sister as though she had a shaman's power to see this deep secret. "How did you know?"

"I didn't know, I only *guessed*."

"Oh Ida, I am so happy and scared."

"Tell Pierre to take you to hospital in Port Angeles where the white women go, in case you have trouble. He can do that for you Emma!"

Their sleeping arrangements were the same as the night before but Emma felt different now that she was Pierre's "wife." She curled contentedly up to his back side, and lost no sleep.

The trio woke to curling waves breaking on the beach. They packed up quickly, hoping the conditions wouldn't worsen. They clung to the canoe, waiting for the calmest series of waves to cast off into. Emma and Ida hiked their long dresses and slung their boots over their shoulders by the laces and held the canoe by the gunwales, waiting for the moment when they ran headlong into the wave. Emma laughed when Pierre boarded prematurely. She teased him for his unmanly launch but it didn't seem to hurt his pride, he just hollered, "Wayward ho!" and they were off for Neah Bay.

❧

It was nearly two months after their return from the cape that Pierre noticed something different about Emma. He was trying to concentrate on his reports, and Emma kept crumpling newsprint and rubbing the glass lantern chimneys until they squeaked. He looked up to ask her to stop and noticed her silhouette. He looked down again to his paperwork. He thought it had to be a trick his tired eyes were playing. When Emma lit the clean lamps and the room glowed golden, he looked again.

"Emma, it looks as though you are getting a bit of a tummy, no?"

"I was gonna tell you soon if you didn't notice. I'm gonna have a baby!"

She patted her tummy, looking proud. Looking happy. His pencil fell from his hand. "*Sacre bleu!* How did this happen?" He wondered if he looked as ill as he felt.

"Why Pierre, I think you know how babies are made! Are you not happy to be a papa?"

Pierre was mute. Somehow fatherhood had not figured into his plans. True, in an impulse of passion and romance he had given her a ring and asked her to be his wife. But already with autumn here, and the reality of another bone-chilling winter of gray days, torrential rains, and biting winds, he was entertaining the thought of returning to Alberta. His body ached for escape from this place, back to the wide blue skies of the prairies. Then too, he could not deny an ever-growing attraction to Emma's sister, Ida, her bright and animated ways and those sparkling eyes. Oh! That was certain trouble. Now, the sight of Emma's swelling belly seemed to have congealed the gathering ill vapors of his soul.

Even to his own ears his voice sounded like it was coming from a tunnel. "*Ma cherie*, I wish I could sing out in joy for this occasion but I am sorry. I am surprised and need time to think about what is best."

"What is best?" Emma paced the floor in front of him. "Do *I* have a choice about 'what is best'? I *know* I'm having your child. This is the ring you gave."

He felt ashamed. "I am a pathetic excuse for a man and I am sorry. But I feel a call to leave this god-forsaken land. I feel sure death will come to me if I stay."

"Then I will leave with you."

"Well Em, it is not so easy, you see, I must find work, I don't know where. Maybe I can go and send for you. But there is so much I don't know. I can make no promise."

She told him she would not believe any promise he made, after this, and made him swear not to leave until her baby was born. Her anger moved him and he rose and wrapped his arms around her. He asked, "When is it to be born?" Her reply made him cringe.

"In February."

❖

Emma could not believe that Pierre was set on leaving without her. Perhaps, she thought, when he sees the face of his child, his heart—*if* he had one—would melt, but in the meantime his cold response tortured her.

Her mother was kind enough just to comfort her with hot clam nectar and a wool shawl, and Ida kissed and reassured her that *she* would love and help care for the baby.

Soon everyone knew that she carried Pierre's child, and yet none of the whites whose houses she still cleaned ever mentioned it. Emma knew how their minds worked. "A refined gentleman like Pierre needs to find himself a respectable white wife." Or, "A dirty squaw and a half-breed child will only hold him down."

She spent her winter in a fog that only lifted when Mae or Ida dragged her off for tea or sat with her knitting baby sweaters. She appreciated their effort to cheer her, but mostly it didn't help. As Pierre withdrew, Emma could not hide her disdain. In late January, Samuel Morse invited the entire white population to an evening at the school. The notice pinned up at Washburn's said "Agent Pierre Virginia will be honored and awarded for his years of work and dedication to the government." Well, she thought. They might applaud him for "taming the frontier" and saving them all from their savage ways, but when she saw him slinking about Neah Bay, she called him what he really was: a coward.

When her delivery time was near, however, Pierre did keep his promise and made arrangements to take her to Port Angeles aboard *The Snohomish*. Though her mother wasn't feeling well enough to travel, Ida was enthusiastic. Even if she knew next to nothing about giving birth, it would be comforting to have her.

She had already begun to feel the first pains of labor when, on a brisk February morning, they departed from Neah Bay. A hard north wind blew making for a jarring cruise, which, for Emma, was most uncomfortable. Maybe, she thought, it would have been better to have stayed put in Neah Bay. Ida sat next to her chattering with other passengers and Pierre spent his time with the crew. Emma sank into her own brooding reality. Nobody, not even Ida, could understand how alone she felt. But a slight tightening of her belly and kick from within reminded her she really wasn't alone. She spoke silently to her baby. "My Little One, remember, you may grow up not having a papa but I will love you enough for two or maybe *ten* papas. Who needs him anyway?" The more she defied Pierre, the braver she felt.

Her labor pains came closer as the boat neared Port Angeles, and Emma wondered if her baby would be born at sea. By the time she disembarked, a kind man noticed her discomfort and gave them a lift in his carriage.

Pierre spoke with the nurse in the hospital. Emma only heard her say, "Don't worry, those Indian girls give birth fast!" Then they took her to a cot in a drafty room. The doctor was in surgery and would check on her when he was through.

Pierre stood looking down at Emma on the cot. "Now they're going to take care of you," he said proudly. "And Ida can stay. I'm going to have a drink with everyone, *oui*? I check back soon."

It was long after dark before he returned. So how could he be so surprised to see a baby? He stepped timidly to her side and peered down at the bundle in her arms. Emma's first instinct was to tell him to go away but instead she turned the baby toward him and said, "You have a daughter and I've named her Hilda Mae."

Ida chimed in, "And look at her dark curls!"

Emma brought the baby back to her breast. "I wish she didn't but I think she looks like you." She looked at Pierre for a response. She was quite positive she noticed his face soften and his eyes grow moist.

Pierre's voice was gentle. "She is fabulous! Look how she stares at you. She has more curls than her papa." He fingered the still moist locks of Hilda's hair.

But that was the end of his entrancement. "Well," he said, "I see that you are well and happy, no? And Ida is here. So I get back to my friends and give news of little Hilda." He leaned and delivered a quick kiss to the new infant. He then turned and playfully picked Ida up and said, "And congratulations to you Auntie Ida!" Then he grabbed his coat and hurried off.

The room fell awkwardly silent; a silence made more poignant by the small sounds of suckling. Emma's eyes burned, and tears fell onto her perfect baby.

♦

Pierre left with no assurances, and Emma settled into the winter with her baby. "Go out," Mamma said. "Git some air. Ida and I can look after her." But Emma mostly concentrated on basket weaving. Because they now were in high demand, Mr. Washburn made a new "basket room" at the store. It was convenient not to have to send their work away. But because so many women produced weavings, his inventory was large. He usually did not pay outright but gave "basket credit" for anything she wanted. As frugal as Emma tried to be, it wasn't easy to save money. Often credit was all that kept them going.

By the time Hilda was two years old, she was energetic, inquisitive and in command of her world. Her innocence and radiance nourished Emma like no other thing in her life. Hilda's curly hair and light skin set her apart from the other reservation children, and Emma let everyone spoil her with candy and attention. But no matter how charming her girl was, she still ached from loneliness. Sometimes she just wished to walk into the sea, to join her real father in his watery grave.

One day Ida suggested it might be refreshing for her to leave and take a job with their cousin Mae at the hotel at Sol Duc Hot Springs.

"You know that mama and I will take good care of Hilda. What do you think?"

Emma's first impulse was to reject such foolishness, but as the idea sank in, she found herself imagining a completely different life, being with Mae and making money. A few days later as she and Ida sat in the doorway watching Hilda play, she finally answered. "Ida, maybe you're right. I should leave for a while. What can it hurt? Anything's gotta be better than the reservation. I know you'll take good care of Hilda."

"I think it's just what you need. Mama and me will love-up little Hilda. She won't even know you're gone!"

They got word to Mae, who replied a week later to say the Sol Duc hotel was still hiring. And so within three weeks, Emma was leaving. She showered Hilda with kisses, but Hilda only smiled and waved happily as she paddled away. By canoe, buggy, and ferry, Emma traveled through Port Angeles and across Lake Crescent.

The resort was part of a big new *babaʔid* development right at the Makah's sacred waters. The hotel had more than a hundred rooms, a steam laundry, a dairy herd, and they grew all their own vegetables. Billiards, bowling, golf, tennis *and* a theater! It was a place for rich white folks, and Mae had been earning lots of money.

Now, Emma thought, she could make the life she really wanted!

◆

To Ida, it was a cruel coincidence when Pierre arrived without warning the next week. He looked relaxed when she told him that Emma was away working. He said he had business to attend to, and thought he might see Hilda Mae.

Ida went to fetch Hilda from the house. Pulling her along by the hand, she nudged her toward Pierre. "Hilda, this here's your papa, Pierre. Can you say hello?"

Pierre, smiling, had pulled a cloth doll from his rucksack, but when he saw his little daughter, he scowled. "If I'd known she wore such rags, I would have brought her a dress instead of a doll."

How dare he, thought Ida. "Well, at least Emma's off working to support her with no help from you."

"Of course. I apologize." He patted Hilda's curls. "I have been working hard, too. Maybe your mama can watch Hilda, and we can walk together? I'd like to tell you about Alberta."

Later, as they walked down the beach, he told her about a boom town called Macleod, where he'd been building sturdy sandstone buildings. She was surprised by how infectious his excitement was. "Look at these muscles!" he flexed.

Ida gave the rock-hard bulge a pinch and couldn't help squealing. It reminded her of touching a snake. Pierre laughed and pulled her to him.

Ida shoved him and slid away. "How unfair you are to Emma!"

Pierre looked down as though ashamed. He spoke softly, "I cannot explain this love I have for you, is different from anything I felt for Emma. A man cannot ignore his feeling for years." He looked up with pleading eyes. "Emma knows we can't be together. Please sit here by me?" He patted the drift log as if it were a loveseat.

Like warming sun rays melting a frosted morning, all empathy, as well as anger, drained from her. As he kissed her, she sensed his caution and determination, and, though she wanted it to continue, she pushed him away. Now she could hardly look at him. "What are we doing? *This* is truly why you came?"

Pierre sheepishly admitted, "Truthfully, I think I came for you, but it also pains me to see Hilda in this foul village."

In days to come, Pierre did spend time with Hilda and also slyly pulled Ida aside for kisses when no one was looking. Ida began to feel as effectively claimed by his kisses as a wolf claims his territory. Pierre's scent lingered and her skin still tingled from his touch long after his boat pulled away from Neah Bay.

When Emma finally returned, it was nothing as Ida had imagined. She was certainly glad to see Hilda, but mostly she wanted to talk about her new friends and the rich hotel guests she had met. She'd begun smoking, and had smuggled back a bottle of whiskey and happily pulled it out every so often. She had difficulty understanding Hilda's words.

"What? Say it one more time to mama. What?"

Hilda repeated with beaming eyes, "I saw 'papa Pierre'!"

Emma looked quizzically at her. "Did I hear her right? What'd she say?"

Mama walked over and lifted Hilda from Emma's lap and said, "It's time for little girl go to bed."

Ida didn't want to tell Emma the news, especially while Emma was drinking, but the longer she waited, the worse it would be, so she confessed that Pierre had arrived and of his plan to take Hilda to Canada. She did not divulge their romance. That could wait.

Emma greeted this troubling news with only more drinking and a long spell of silence. Finally she lay her head on the table and let out an anguished cry. "I don't deserve her anyway! What kind of mother have I been? I hardly thought of her at all…the whole time I've been at Sol Duc juz party every night! No! No! Oh! Ida I'm bad. I juz don't miss this place at all. I like my life away from here. Mae too! We love it there. Am I bad Ida?" She wailed on as Ida patted her back and reassured her.

Come morning, Ida was surprised to find Emma bright and happy. Emma looked at her calmly. "I oughta be mad but I'm not, you know if Pierre wants to be a papa to Hilda, well, maybe she *would* be better off. And you, Ida" She put her arm around her. "You need to spread your wings too."

Ida could not believe Emma's change of heart. Later that day she fanned out dollars for Lucy. "I've been working hard, Mamma, and this money is all for you. I'm taking Hilda to Washburn's today and buy her a brand new dress." She then turned to Ida. "And any money left over is for you." She swept Hilda onto her hip and was off to the store.

Ida's pangs of guilt from not telling her sister the full truth were made more painful by Emma's generosity. Also, when she saw Emma spending her last days quietly with Hilda sitting on the beach or curled up with her in bed, she understood it wasn't that Emma didn't love her girl. It was clear she did, but the whiskey seemed to have become an even greater love for Emma, causing her behavior to swing like night and day. Luckily, Ida thought, Emma's one bottle had not lasted long. It also appeared to be the reason Emma was ready to leave before her scheduled day. She grew edgy and short-tempered.

The morning she left, Ida stood on the beach holding her niece's hand waving goodbye to Emma. It seemed almost perplexing to see her sister's enthusiastic waves and kisses blown over the water to Hilda. Could the doors have opened any easier for her to pursue Pierre? Ida blew kisses back.

✦

Pierre was due to arrive on the steamship *Whatcom*. Ida felt she was about to burst like the salmonberry blossoms and raucous bird song all around the village as she braided Hilda's hair and told her that her papa was coming. It was not easy to make a neat braid because Hilda herself was excited and fidgeting. Ida's heart beat like a potlatch drum as she trotted with Hilda out the new pier as the boat puffed into the bay.

Pierre seemed more impressed with the new pier as he stepped out to greet them. "Neah Bay is looking good! Are you sure you want to leave?" He teased.

"I forgot to tell you! Mr. Washburn built it. But yes, I think I can leave even if there is a new dock!"

Hilda put out her arms and said, "Papa, I want to hug you."

Pierre scooped her up and gave her nose a small pinch. "I hope you are happy to come live with me?"

It was clear to Ida that Pierre was impatient to be away to Alberta as soon as possible. "But what about Emma? She doesn't even know yet that I'm leaving with you. Please can we wait for her to come? We owe her that."

"I think we can get word to her and bid our farewells in Port Angeles. However long that takes, I'm willing, but tomorrow would not be soon enough!"

Ida quickly arranged a meeting with Emma while Hilda spent much of her final days enjoying her grandmother's lavish attention. On their last day, Hilda insisted on holding her hand as they walked all the way from their home to the dock. Ida pried Hilda's hand free as tears fell from the eyes of all three of them.

Ida had no more of a concept than her niece of the changes they were diving headlong into. She had only known her tribal family and the lapping shores of the bay, the smell of the sea and the giant trees of the forest standing guard all around. She and Hilda both watched with anguish as they pulled out of the bay.

Ida dreaded the meeting with Emma in Port Angeles. Her guilt had gnawed at her for the past year. She could feel her palms sweat as she and Pierre and Hilda all walked toward Emma. Emma knew the truth in the first moment. Ida herself could not understand why it wasn't Emma leaving with him for Alberta.

Emma avoided Ida's burning shame by burying her head in Hilda's arms. She spoke to Hilda, softly, like in a confession booth. Then she reached into the bag she carried and pulled out white straw bonnet with a long, lavender ribbon. She placed it atop Hilda's black curls and said, "There you go Baby. You look beautiful! You go now. Be a good girl and don't grow up too fast before I see you again."

Emma turned toward Ida and Pierre. Ida could not bear the pain she saw on her sister's face. She wanted to embrace her and beg forgiveness, but fear of rejection kept her motionless.

Finally, it was Emma who, through pursed lips and a trembling chin, managed to say tersely, "Take good care of my baby." She turned and hurried off. She did not look back at her pretty little Hilda Mae, standing with the silk ribbon of her hat blowing out on the spring breeze.

✦

From Port Angeles the boat continued on to Seattle. Ida could see isolated settlers' cabins along the coast. Occasionally there would be a small mill town or a cannery. She imagined how lonely it must be to live without a village or neighbors. But she was not prepared for what she saw as they approached Seattle that night. The city blazed with electric light! Not even the starriest sky, not even the glowing phosphorescence in the black water at night could compare with the glitter of this city. Pierre pointed out a light high above the others. He said it was the Smith Tower, under construction. Ida was awestruck at how far the city sprawled. She was glad that Pierre was their guide. She felt they could be swallowed alive in such a place.

With their one steamer-trunk of possessions they were delivered into the busy streets. Ida's legs were rubbery as bull kelp. It didn't help that she was also carrying Hilda, who had fallen asleep. They took a room in a cheap hotel on First Avenue and by dawn the next morning they were on a train bound for Spokane and Canada.

Hilda was timid in the confines of the train and clung to the folds of Ida's skirts. Ida distracted her with the passing scenery. Now as they traveled through the gorge, the steep hills became less treed and rolled in waves of lush green grasses. The hills plunged steeply to the river's edge on either side, and when Pierre returned from the lounge car he told them they were following the Columbia River. He seemed kind and attentive to

Hilda. "This gorge, *ma cherie,* is like a secret passage through the snowy mountains," he said as he bobbed her on his knees.

As the train continued, the country opened and became drier. Ida saw a small herd of antelope spring across the dry sage landscape. She felt like she could see forever.

The last big depot was Spokane. At the train stop, Ida saw through the window an Indian family on a bench. They sat motionless as if they were a painting; the grandfather with his waist-length braids and the old woman wearing a stained felt hat and a plaid wool blanket as a shawl.

Hilda saw them too. "Auntie, that look like Grandma. She look sad."

Ida agreed. They looked out of place with the hustle of energetic white people all around them. A young boy, also with long braids, sat in her lap.

"Auntie, where's the boy's mama?" Hilda tried to get the little boy's attention. The train left the station but Hilda wanted to know who they were, where they were going and where they came from. Ida couldn't answer. She only knew that the Indians here looked as sad as the ones back home.

The train climbed the western flanks of the Rocky Mountains. The sun had almost set now, throwing its last rays of electric orange against the mountain's blanket of snow. Ida had never seen such brilliance. The train trundled east through the Porcupine Hills and into the vast rolling grasslands of southern Alberta. The prairie stretched like an ocean under the full moon. And like the ocean, it seemed there was no place to hide in this naked land. How could people live here? It would be like floating in a canoe on a never-ending sea.

It was late evening by the time they ended their long journey in Macleod. A driver offered them a lift in his Ford. Pierre directed him to a cottage on the outskirts of town.

Ida lit a fire in the small stone fireplace. She was still chilly from the ride, and Hilda fussed. In the flickering firelight, she looked around at the bare little cabin. It seemed very bleak, but Pierre was exuberant. "Beautiful, no? Wait, just you wait until the light of day when you see, and best of all is the location. I think you will love it!"

✦

Except for their waking in the morning and lying down at night, everything was different. Ida felt like a fish out of water, so far from her ancestral home. Her solace was indeed the Oldman River so near to them. In such a desolate land, the river seemed like life itself.

Pierre enjoyed his work as a mason. Every morning just before dawn, he rode off jauntily on Cut Ear. The spotted gelding was his pride and joy. Most evenings, when he returned, he was bone tired.

Ida knew that Pierre worked hard. In spite of her own isolation and loneliness she tried to be sunny in his presence, and to please him by keeping the cabin clean. She'd brought a burlap bag of seed potatoes from Neah Bay which she wasted no time planting, and some of the families here had given her seeds and onion sets.

One day Pierre decided to surprise them with a trip to town. All three of them climbed onto Cut Ear, who balked and pranced when Pierre urged him with his heels, but finally accepted his load. Soon they were stepping along at a nice pace. Birds flew up from the fields as they passed, and Hilda pointed to the dipping flight and long tail feathers. "What's they called Papa?"

"Magpies, *ma cherie.*"

Soon, Ida saw Hilda's head nod out to the side in sleep, but Pierre had her firmly between his arms as he held the reins.

Compared with the endless days of silence at their cabin, Macleod was exciting! Pierre tied the horse at a hitching rail between two parked cars, and led them into Sam's Chinese Restaurant. They sat near the window and Pierre ordered chow mein. When it arrived, Hilda sucked the long noodles until they slapped her nose, and they laughed, and Hilda giggled too, and did it again, and soon they were almost choking with laughter.

Ida noticed a gaggle of white women on the walk outside. They moved in unison, their hems dusting the street like a flock of earthbound birds. White sashes across their chests bore the big black letters: *WCTU.* She asked Pierre what the letters stood for.

Pierre scoffed. "The *Women's Christian Temperance Union.* Oh, they have bees under their bonnets! They have been gathering signatures for their petition for months now. They want to keep men from drinking."

As they passed, one of them noticed Ida in the window. She held up her petition and motioned to Ida to sign it. Whatever Pierre thought of them, to Ida it seemed like a good idea. Pierre might be right that it was foolish—after all, her own experience at Neah Bay showed how hard it was to stop anyone from drinking, even when drinking was illegal. Yet she could hardly imagine women with the kind of power to think they could prohibit men from drinking. She wanted to sign. But what would Pierre think? She looked at him, and the women looked at her, and then, after a flurry of conversation among them, they turned and walked away.

Pierre seemed relieved. "They saw you weren't a white woman. Indians can't sign no political papers, not even *metis.*"

Ida was embarrassed and angry that she had been so dismissed.

After that, Pierre toured the two around town. He showed Hilda the newly renovated building where she would one day go to school. He showed them the bank he was helping to build, and introduced them to Ernest, the foreman. He seemed nice enough, Ida thought, until he told her that she was "lucky to be married to a white man" or she'd need a pass to get off the reservation. She did not bother to explain that her people were the Makah and not from Canada.

After they left, she grumbled to Pierre.

Pierre only said, "Ernie, he puts food on our table. So do not give him anything but a pretty smile. Do you understand?"

As Pierre was lifting Ida onto Cut Ear, an Indian man approached and spoke to Pierre in soft tones. "You might want to come to the big Indian Jubilee next month. For now we're callin' it the 'Jubilee' so that Dillingworth and the Priest don't shut us down, but if they leaves us alone we will hold the Medicine

Lodge Ceremony instead. Don't tell no other whites. Jus thought since you are like brother to us Bloods and you have a squaw wife, you might want to come."

As Cut Ear trotted them toward home, Ida asked, "Who was that?"

"Peter Stands Alone. I bought this horse from his uncle." Pierre told Ida that unlike the Makah who could still fish for their own food, the Canadian Indians were not free to hunt. The buffalo had been gone for over thirty years, and without guns, they could not even hunt small game. They were reduced to a diet of stingy rations of rancid flour and poor quality beef, and even those could be ruthlessly denied. He said that back in the day when he had worked as an Indian agent on the Blood Reserve, he'd won their respect by arguing in Ottawa for more rations and guns and ammunition, as was promised to them in their *Treaty* 7. When he had complained of their unjust treatment, he was dismissed. It was after this that he had come to Washington.

Pierre tried to look over his shoulder to Ida. "Is a little better now in Canada. Last summer I went to the Calgary Stampede. It was breathtaking! Maybe, I take you and Hilda."

Ida wrapped her arms tight around Pierre's waist and rested her head against his back. She hadn't known these things about him. "Now you really are my hero!" She looked forward to seeing these mysterious and distant relatives.

The invitation inspired her to make special preparations. She sewed Hilda a red mother-Hubbard bonnet and matching pinafore.

"Since we don't own no umbrella, you'll be glad for this hat. Besides, it looks real pretty on you!" Ida said as she held Hilda at arm's length, admiring her handiwork.

The next project was to build a smokehouse. Ida had reconciled herself to the fact that there were no salmon in Alberta but there *were* fish in Oldman River and she knew how to dry and smoke them! Hilda was Ida's perfect helper. Together they fashioned a makeshift smokehouse out of old doors and the floorboards of an old buckboard wagon. She felt especially clever when she fastened one of the wagon wheels to the ceiling of the smokehouse so she could hang her fish from its spokes. All that was left to do was to jig up fish and that was the best task of all.

Every morning they were off as soon as Pierre had trotted away. They used a crude fishing pole strung with modern line and hooks that Pierre had brought them from town. From the bank of the river Ida pulled in Rainbow and Cutthroat, Bull and Brown Trout and Whitefish. Hilda made a squeamish face but dutifully threaded the gutted fish onto stout sticks.

"Look how pretty with all their spots and colors! And the best is when we eat them, right?"

Ida realized she'd discovered a new passion. She had been raised among a people immersed in the harvest and commerce of fish and yet she had never herself been *the* provider of fish. That had always been her papa's job. And never had she even seen fish pulled from a lively and feisty river. It was thrilling, but, she learned, it also required skill.

At first, Pierre thought she was too ambitious. Ida was happy to prove him wrong the day he rode home and caught a waft of smoked fish on the air.

He let out a loud call, "I smell something delicious!"

He left his horse in the paddock and came to see. He laughed proudly as she showed him the rickety smokehouse in full function. That night, when she served him the sumptuous fillets, he had to admit his error.

Finally the day came to leave on their long ride. Pierre borrowed an old mare from the Stands Alone family to use as a packhorse but Ida insisted on riding it as well. Even though she often fell behind and the packs flopped around, she decided she enjoyed being in command of her very own horse.

They made for a happy trio, Ida thought, as she looked at Hilda with her red bonnet sitting pretty as a pileated woodpecker, and her papa sitting tall behind her. That evening they made camp in the lush grasses along Pincher Creek.

Late the next day they began to see more and more people

traveling in all manners of conveyances. Many gave "Agent Virginia" a warm greeting. Those who didn't know him averted their eyes until they noticed her and Hilda.

At last they saw the gathering site. It was above the plains, in the rolling hills. Views of the Rockies loomed tantalizingly near. Hundreds had already arrived, many from just over the border in Montana. The Medicine Lodge was already standing.

Ida helped Pierre select a campsite and set up a light-weight tripod. They put down the bedrolls, and Pierre set off to find old friends and to admire the fine horses while Ida and Hilda sat and watched the others arrive. All stripes of Indian were here, from lowly families in ragged clothing to regal Chiefs and young braves in finely decorated buckskin war shirts and leggings. In the middle of an expansive area of grass stood the large, round branch-covered arbor that was the Medicine Lodge. Hilda could hear the heartbeat-like drums sounding from within and was curious to have a look.

Ida said, "Go peek inside, then come back and tell me. I'll be right here."

Hilda summoned her courage and Ida watched her run, light-footed through the grass, her pinafore fluttering. Her black curls and innocence made the old women smile as she flitted past. She peeked around one of the upright arbor poles to see the scene within. Ida watched her dip her knees to the drum beats. The drumming and singing didn't seem to frighten her. Of course, she had cut her teeth on just such sights and sounds as an infant in Neah Bay. Even though this place was new, it was the first familiar activity she or Hilda had seen since coming to Canada.

At last she made her way back to the little family tent.

"So what did you see?" Ida asked sincerely.

"I first just seen the mens drumming, then I looked up and at the top of the pole I seen a buffalo skull hangin'. It was hangin' there with some of its fur hide still on it. I think I also seen the three mens that are going to dance. They marked their faces and colored their skin. Come and look!" she said as she tugged.

"No, I'm waiting for Pierre. When he comes, we'll go around together."

It was dusk and the ceremony was underway when Pierre showed up with Peter Stands Alone. Ida put a blanket down for Peter to sit, and Pierre offered him a cigarette. Pierre had brought them for his old friends. As all three of them smoked and talked, Ida enjoyed Peter's quiet nature. His comments were spare but she sensed his depth. He told her the people here were known as *Niitsitapii* or "Real People." He pointed out a man wearing an eagle feather headdress.

"That's the head chief, Shot-Through-Both-Sides. He's watchin' over."

He said the center pole of the Lodge represented the center of the world, connecting heaven and earth. He told her of the middle aged Blackfoot woman named Suzette Bull Robe who had made the vow to pray and sacrifice in order for this ceremony to take place. Three of her male family members were dancing. The channels had been opened through her properly observed rituals for *Na'pi* to hear prayers for health and rejuvenation from *all* those who were gathered.

Hilda asked Peter, "What's 'Na'pi'?"

He replied, "*Na'pi* in English is 'Old Man or the Sun', Indian's god."

Hilda was delighted. "You mean 'Old Man' like our river where we catched all the fish?"

He nodded. "Yes. Same."

Pierre teased about being disappointed that horse racing wouldn't happen. Though he pretended to agree that the more somber call to prayer and ritual was better than the government sanctioned Jubilee, Ida knew he really would prefer the races over this solemn event.

Peter blew a plume of smoke toward the sky. "Well, we don't pierce the flesh no more but still if they catch us even doin' this, they takes our rotten rations and don't let us see our young ones at the boarding schools. We like racing too but we *need* this."

During the remaining days of the Medicine Lodge, Hilda ran with other children as imaginary herds of wild horses, neighing and throwing their heads. In the evenings, she went around to her new friends' camps, offering smoked trout. Ida noticed that the smoked fish was often met with indifference or even slight disgust. When she wondered aloud whether it was just her imagination, Pierre said that even though these people might look like her Makah relations, they were unaccustomed to eating fish, and thought of them as the spirits of their ancestors.

She considered this new idea, but could only feel that it was a shame for these underfed people to not know the pleasure of smoked fish.

Hilda had become especially close to a girl of her own age named Agnes Weasel Tail. When it was time to go home, Hilda was unhappy to learn that Agnes lived so far north that she would probably not see her again.

Hilda asked, "What about when I start school Papa? I'll probably see her there won't I?"

Pierre explained that the school in Macleod was only for white students.

"Isn't I Indian, too, Papa?"

"Only part of you *ma cherie.*"

Hilda turned over her hands and even pulled up her dress to see her legs, then looked up with true concern, "What '*part*' of me is Indian?"

Ida could only laugh.

✦

When Hilda started school, she rode with her Papa every day into Macleod. She felt very grown up, learning things she never knew before. She enjoyed practicing her spelling and math with Papa each day as they rode home. She could tell he was proud of her because sometimes she knew the answers and he did not.

She learned so much that she could even talk about the "Great War," which her teacher told her had erupted in the far off lands of Europe. But when she did, Papa got red in the face.

"It's a white man's war but the redman is dying. They join the Canadian Forces, just to be away from the reservation! And now grain and beef they need is sent away to England! Is criminal!"

He was so upset that she didn't bring it up again. Luckily, there was also good news that filled them with excitement. Suddenly, she had a little brother!

She loved being a sister. Baby Charles was sweet and handsome, and Hilda could look at him and hold him for hours. But after a while it seemed his legs weren't developing. They had no strength.

Papa especially took it hard. "How will he ride a horse? How will he get a wife? We must do something. Maybe I send you with him to Seattle, those doctors there can fix it."

Auntie protested, "What about the Blood Indian Hospital? I don't want to travel all alone to Seattle. It scares me."

But over time, Papa encouraged Auntie to be brave. They wrote and got appointments to a special doctor. Auntie went away with Charles while Papa stayed and worked, and she went to school.

She was only seven but still she could help her Papa by making simple meals. She liked having his undivided attention. Together they took care of the house, and by evenings they read to each other or played cards. Sometimes they talked about Ida and Charles. Hilda missed Charles most of all, his round face and rosy cheeks. A month passed before a telegram arrived.

WE ARE DOING WELL. DR STUMPED BY CONDITION. AM GOING TO NEAH BAY. FONDLY YOURS, IDA.

At first Papa was angry. He paced the floor. He cursed having not gone with her. Surely Charles was simply deficient of some vitamin or mineral. Had he not drilled Ida on what to ask? She had failed. And now they were going off to Neah Bay!

Hilda drew a sigh when he finally composed himself. His furrowed brow relaxed and he said, "Is OK no? We are getting by, you and me?"

"Yes, Papa."

The next day Hilda learned that her favorite teacher, Mr. Lowen, had left to join the war. He'd complained that the school trustees were docking his pay so much to help support the war effort that he "may as well go join." At first, she thought it was brave. But there was no new teacher to fill his place and suddenly the school was closing.

Papa cradled her. "Yes, *ma cherie*, they say it is the "War to End All Wars" but what a price! We will keep up on studies at home, don't worry."

When Ida and Charles finally returned, they made a colorful homecoming dinner with flowers and crepe paper streamers and steak. Ida was tired but brimming with stories. She handed Hilda an envelope from her mother Emma. Hilda barely remembered her. She had to read the short letter carefully as if she were deciphering hieroglyphics.

Darling Hilda my baby,

The beautiful hot spring lodge that I worked at burned to the ground and so I have returned to Neah Bay. I miss you and wish you were here. Ida says you are in school and you are smart. Ida said you helped her smoke fish you got out of a river. You must be big to help so good. Be a nice big sister to Charles. I hope I see you soon.

Always,
Your Loving Mother
Emma

Hilda went to her bed to lie down and contemplate these words. Looking up to the wooden peg from which her white straw bonnet dangled with its lavender ribbons, she could remember the dock long ago, and how her mother knelt and set it on her head. She saw her with a bottle tipped to her lips, laughing or was she crying? She saw her sifting sand through her fingers while they sat on a beach together. The one thing that each image had in common was that they seemed to be set against the same backdrop of a dark, dense green of towering trees. Yes, Hilda thought, I do remember my mother and Neah Bay.

She would have remembered more, but Charles climbed onto her bed and she began to tease and tickle him. It was so nice to have him back home!

✦

For Pierre, the year went from bad to worse. He lost his job. Every day the papers carried news of the war, and men came back broken, or didn't come back at all. An automobile struck and killed his beloved Cut Ear. When Spanish Influenza raged across the country, he kept his family home and they lived on what Ida had put up: turnips, potatoes, carrots, chickens, eggs and fish. Still, they grew rail thin, and his small savings was disappearing.

He read in the paper that 2,000 men were working in the ten big Galt coal mines at Lethbridge, and though he did not cherish the thought of the dirty work of a coal miner, he knew he was capable of anything for a stint, just to get them through the rough times. He traveled by train and arrived only to be told that production had reached its peak; there was no new hiring.

Pierre was still mulling when the train lurched out of the station. A man sat down across from him. He was well-muscled, with cool blue eyes and a pragmatic air. His large calloused hands sat undemonstratively on his knees as they watched dust-devils spin funnels of prairie straw up into flat blue sky.

He turned from the window and Pierre introduced himself. They shook hands. "George Fahrenkopf."

They talked about where they were going and the fellow said he was out of a job himself and on his way to Claresholm to see about ranch work. Pierre thought he heard a slight French accent as George Fahrenkopf explained that he'd grown up one of 14 children, and that he'd learned English at a Catholic boarding school and moved when he was twelve to the logging camps of Northern Ontario where he'd learned to speak French. He said he'd never been home since he was twelve, and had no affinity for his mother or his mother tongue.

Pierre was taken aback by his detachment but shared his own story, beginning with French missionaries in the Canadian wild of the 1600s, and generations of loggers after that, in Quebec. Though his father had died when he was ten, all his childhood memories were fond, and now, he said, he had a wife and two children, and the responsibility to keep them fed.

Pierre wished he'd thought of looking for work on a ranch. He was far more suited to riding horses and rounding-up cattle than being entombed, chipping away at a coal seam. He shuddered to think that he'd come so close to making that mistake. What a relief it was to imagine this different track.

Two weeks later, he took the train north to scout for work among the far-flung ranches. By inquiring around, he eventually found George at the Triple K Ranch eight miles from Claresholm.

George complained of his new profession. He shook his head, looking around. "It's the emptiest place I've ever been, and the cattle are all wild as hell!"

Pierre had to admit that this job and his new friend did not seem like a good match, but he was fairly certain that none of these complaints would be his if he could find similar work. Of course, having a family made Pierre's situation different. Most ranchers preferred loners, and none wanted to "put up" an entire family. For three days he followed empty leads.

As he kicked down the dusty streets of Claresholm, the tall grain silos along the tracks on the edge of town caught his interest, and he inquired. Luck would have it that they were in need of an operator. They were happy enough with Pierre and particularly with his well-calloused hands. His previous stone work and brick laying had etched on his body all of the work history they needed to know. He would run the conveyer belts and see to the cleaning and grading of the grain as it was delivered. They gave him a week to fetch his family and find a place to rent.

By the time his family was spirited away from Macleod on the ethers of his excitement, Pierre was happy to see that none were sad to leave. The cabin had begun to feel more like a prison to them with his absence and dwindling stores of food.

✦

Hilda was excited to live in an actual town. Papa had thanked his lucky stars when they'd found accommodations above Torkelsen's Dry Goods Store on Main Street. The living space was no bigger than the cabin, but instead of a hand pump outside, they had actual running water at a sink. Hilda turned the spigot off and on just to watch it flow so effortlessly, and Charles washed his hands and face without being asked.

Papa no longer had a horse or a reason to use one. His new job was just down the road. He could linger at home in the mornings, but his evenings stretched late by the time he socialized in the streets, smoking and conversing with townsmen. His new friend George met with Papa whenever he came to town. Papa said he liked the man but didn't approve that he had no shame in engaging with the women of ill repute. Papa always said that he himself, although a true admirer of the fairer sex, was not inclined to supplement his own feminine comforts. He was quite happy with Ida.

Hilda saw that her auntie was shy in Claresholm. The women sized her up, and stared curiously at Charles. She said in Neah Bay the people wouldn't act rudely just because a woman had a crippled child. Claresholm was nothing more than a wild-west town and since they were all newcomers, they ought to be on an equal footing. But Hilda did not mind running errands around town. Inquisitive eyes never worried her.

Hilda was often sent to buy a newspaper. In one, Ida read to her about a group of women who had tried to attend a trial of women accused of prostitution, and they were thrown out of the courthouse. The law said that women were not "persons" and had no place taking part in court proceedings. "Can you imagine, we're not considered persons! What are we then, cows?" Hilda liked seeing her auntie fired up. Still, what could she do? Even those town women who fought for their rights wanted nothing to do with her, to them she was a *metis*. Auntie walked to the window and looked down onto Main Street. Her eyes glazed as she scanned the scene below like a caged bird.

Hilda began her school year at the three-story brick school-house. She loved that she could walk to school, although on some of the freezing winter days when the winds howled, she wished she could be as fortunate as the children who rode all the way from the Ruby district in the wooden school bus. It looked comfortable but most of all it looked like fun, with its many windows and children riding all together.

In their second year in Claresholm, auntie decided it was time to take Charles and go back to Washington to visit her mother and sister. She seemed much more confident than she had when leaving Alberta the first time, and Hilda was enjoying school and glad to stay behind as before with her father.

Two days before Ida's departure, Hilda discovered, quite without warning, blood between her legs. She nearly panicked, thinking she was dying. Fortunately, Ida was still home and able to reassure her. She was a woman now, aunt Ida told her, though at almost 13, Hilda did not much feel like one. As a matter of fact she hated the whole mess and wished she could be a girl again.

When Ida left, Hilda took on the title of "lady of the house" with a mature attitude. She had reassured her auntie that she would do her best to have fixin's together for her Papa's evening meals and would keep his clothes laundered too.

Mr. Eilif Torkelsen, the proprietor of the Dry Goods Store downstairs, had grown fond of Papa and when family affairs called them back to Norway, they asked him if he'd manage their business. Papa could not turn down this opportunity, even if it meant giving up his job at the silos. He began training, and by the end of the month all seemed in order; the Torkelsons shook his hand confidently and were off on their journey.

Hilda enjoyed having her Papa working in the store. She studied in the early evenings by the potbelly stove, and learned to use the treadle sewing machine that sat shiny and new in the front of the store. She caught on quickly to the pumping rhythm of the pedal and was able to demonstrate to customers the smooth action of the machine, helping to make a sale within the first month. Most of the merchandise in the store consisted of fabric and threads of all colors but there was also an odd assortment of items like crockery, carpets and candles. One of Hilda's tasks was to make the flat folds of fabric neat and orderly before quitting time so that the store would be ready in the morning when Pierre unlocked the doors for business.

George Fahrenkopf dropped by for long visits with Pierre. One day she heard he'd been let go from the Triple K. "Seems free grass and open range are a thing of the past. No more herding and round-ups, the cattle are just being fed hay. I can work during threshing season and driving the cattle to market but I'm needing a place to live for right now. Maybe you could put me up? I could put a cot in the storage room."

Pierre did not object, and George became one more for Hilda to cook for, but he pulled his weight helping Papa. He helped bring loads of supplies from the train station. He could pack large bulky bundles of cloth on one shoulder while still stepping along fast. He would deliver the load and go back for more.

In the evenings he told stories near the fireside that both Hilda and Papa found interesting. One night he told of his younger brother Herbert's death in the Great War. He'd joined up after the Somme. George said, "I told him it was suicide but he wanted to prove himself. He was guilty about being German. He left here July 2, 1918 and died at Vimy Ridge August 8th. What a waste! He was only seventeen."

Hilda asked about his other brothers and sisters and was astonished to learn that he had five sisters and nine brothers and six more who didn't survive. Twenty-one times his mother had given birth! And the only one George had cared about was his brother Herbert, who went to war. He spoke as though he still could not believe this hard fact, shaking his head as his cool blue eyes burned a path to the hot embers of the fire.

Another story they hashed and rehashed by the fire was the robbery of the Canadian Pacific Railway by some local miners from up near Crow's Nest. It had been all over the headlines. And they liked to talk about the weather. According to Papa and George, the weather was the *only* thing that really happened in

Alberta. George told about ranch work during the bad blizzard a couple of years before, how all the cattle had gathered in the coulees as the wind howled out of the north, and they had died in droves, piled up in the fence corners. He'd ridden out in a storm so bad he could hardly see his horse's ears, and in one such pile of cattle he'd seen a steamy breath and found a nearly dead calf. He'd hauled him onto his horse and brought him home and nursed him back to health. He said those were the meanest conditions he'd ever worked in.

The winter of 1921 passed in this way, sharing meals and stories, working in the store and going to school. No word had come from Ida, and after a while Hilda began to worry. Papa explained that even though there were some telephones in Claresholm, Neah Bay was still about as isolated as any place on earth. One could only get word out by telegram. Finally, one arrived from her. Papa read it out:

CHARLES AND I ARE WELL. AFTER MUCH THOUGHT HAVE DECIDED TO REMAIN. PLEASE DO NOT BE SAD OR ANGRY. WE ARE HAPPY HERE. FONDLY, IDA.

Papa flew into a rage. He tossed a studio photo of Ida across the room and hammered his fist on the kitchen table top. Hilda had never seen her Papa so possessed with fury.

"I trusted that woman, I gave her freedom. How could she! Those damn Shamans put some magic on her. What was I thinking?" He picked up a silk parasol he had bought for her and threw it like a javelin. "I must go. I can talk sense to her if I just go there."

Hilda could only picture her own abandonment, and it was a chilling thought. "But Papa! What about me? What if you don't come back either?"

He stormed from their apartment and down the steps, and she ran after him. She trailed him to the lobby of the hotel where George was in deep concentration over the cards he held. Papa asked if he could have a word with him outside.

George looked concerned. "What's happened?"

Papa was almost breathless. "I must go to Washington to get Ida and Charles. Would you do me the kind favor of running the Dry Goods Store with Hilda?"

Hilda's heart sank. George was almost laughing, "No woman's worth that much trouble!" But then he patted Papa on the back and said, "In whatever way I can help, I'd be glad."

Papa made preparations to leave. He promised that in the unlikely event they decided to stay, George would escort her back to Neah Bay, and these words gave Hilda some comfort, but still she cried as he boarded the train for Seattle. He hugged and kissed her and consoled her, "*Ma cherie*, I will be back in a week or so. Do not cry. Be good, keep your studies up. George will take good care of you."

On Hilda's first evening home from school, she helped tidy up the store as usual while George closed out the till, but as she cooked dinner she began to feel uneasy and awkward. Typically there was conversation and small talk between her Papa and George, but now she just felt his eyes follow her every move. It was too quiet.

She tried to talk to him as she mixed the batter, but he barely answered. He just sat at the table looking at her. She felt like a rabbit being watched by a wolf.

On Sunday he offered to take her to the Cinema. A film company had come to Macleod the summer before and filmed a melodrama, *Cameron of the Royal Mounted,* and now it was showing in Claresholm. Everyone was talking about it, and there was a line around the block and the matinee was packed. They got seats toward the back. Hilda was spellbound by the film. Not only were there handsome movie stars, but she found herself on the edge of her seat through the Indian chase scenes, the train robbery and kidnapping of the beautiful Mandy, and daring pursuits on horseback through raging rivers. She left the theater feeling that her life was entirely dull by comparison. Though she supposed, since she wasn't even 13 years old, that there was still plenty of time for adventure.

That evening she found it hard to study. Her mind kept drifting to scenes from the film. Oh! The dashing Cameron! It was particularly romantic when he kissed Mandy. She was struggling in this way to concentrate when George walked in and laid himself right down on top of her! She couldn't believe it. She couldn't push him off. He buried his head next to hers and spoke into her ear. "Now, you can be the damsel."

He pushed hard against her and then pulled at the bloomers under her dress. Hilda tried to holler but George's large strong hand shoved her head into the bedding, muffling her cries. She kicked vainly as he forced himself into her, then gasped from the pain and humiliation. He held her head down and kept on until he moaned and lay still on top of her.

He whispered in her ear. "Nobody hears about this. And don't think you're not old enough either. It was just a matter of time before someone did it to you. It might as well be me."

When he was gone, she lay in shock and disbelief, not wanting to move, not wanting to feel between her legs. Her schoolwork still lay on the bed as if nothing had happened. She closed her eyes, remembering the time Papa had caught a coyote in a leg-hold trap by the chicken coop, and how she'd pitied the poor wild creature, and how relieved she'd felt when he shot it. Now she wished someone could do the same for her. Surely her Papa *would* want to shoot her if he found out.

Slowly she rose and made her way to the water closet where she stripped and scrubbed herself, crying as she washed again and again where he had touched her.

With morning came the reality that she would have to face George. How could she even look at him? She avoided him until he left, then tried to duck past the storefront on her way to school, but he popped his head out and called out, cheerily. "Good morning Hilda! See you after school."

Hilda's teacher that day complained about her torn and messy homework, and admonished her lack of attention. She didn't care. How could school matter anymore? She had far more urgent problems to solve than some mathematical equation.

She dragged her feet on the way home, wondering if other people could tell she had changed just by looking at her. She wanted to run away, to do anything but go to the Dry Goods Store. She reasoned, maybe a man doesn't do that sort of thing but once a year and so maybe he'll leave me alone and then Papa will return. That was the most hopeful thought she could muster. She went immediately to her chores. Customers came and went. She finished her work and went upstairs. Her heart pounded as she listened for his footsteps. When finally she did hear him coming, she backed into a corner of the kitchen, just like the coyote, in full panic.

"What are you doing? What's for supper?"

When she didn't respond, he got angry. He grabbed her by the arm and brought her to a chair. "Get this straight Hilda, it's completely natural what happened last night. You're no different than any other girl or woman. You all want it, you just pretend you don't. Now your job is to fix supper, so get to it."

Again that evening he pushed her to the bed and was on top of her. This time she was face to face with him, with her eyes squeezed shut. And this time she didn't cry, but rather drifted out of her body. She seemed to see herself from above, refusing to be in that poor girl's situation.

It was from this safe distance that Hilda endured George's full and frequent use of her until Pierre, Ida and Charles returned.

✦

Claresholm wasn't so bad, Ida thought, especially since Pierre was so exuberant to have her and Charles back at his side. However, both she and Pierre agreed they had some making up to do with Hilda. She seemed dark and moody. Ida could understand from Hilda's point of view why she would still be hurt about being left behind. But Pierre had only been gone eight days. She should get over it.

Because Charles' affliction kept her home, Ida decided she may as well make a wage by taking in laundry. She knew Pierre was not pleased to see their small apartment with lines stretching here and there across the rooms. But she also knew he wouldn't complain because working made her happy, and gave her spending money too! She appreciated that he endured and even seemed to grow used to strangers' undergarments and trousers always hanging overhead.

As Ida scrubbed away on the washboard one day, Charles remarked, "Hilda doesn't love me no more."

Ida stopped and looked at him, "That's not true Charley. She's probably just moody for female reasons and all the learnin' every day at school. Why don't we bake a cake and we'll have a little party for her birthday? She can bring her friend Tilly and invite George too."

Charles liked this idea and was sure it would help. But when Hilda heard about the party, she only said, "I don't want a party and I won't bring Tilly to this place!" and stomped off to her room.

Ida called after her, "If it's the laundry, don't worry, I'll have it all down." She followed and sat on the edge Hilda's bed. She said, "You coming into your womanly ways sure has turned you emotional. You had better shape up, young miss. I didn't come back to Alberta to add your poor behavior to my burden. If you're bleeding and got cramps, take care with a hot water bottle but don't huff around anymore. You hear?"

Hilda stared flatly at the ceiling. "I'm not bleeding any more since after you went to Washington. Maybe I've gone back to being a girl again."

"What do you mean? No monthlies since almost three months? That's not right. You can't reverse nature."

Ida reached over and turned Hilda's face towards her. "What's wrong with you?" A sudden dread filled her. "Have you been with a man?"

Still Hilda did not move but tears welled in her eyes and fell down her cheeks.

"*Have* you been with a man?"

"I didn't want to. It's not my fault. Please don't tell Papa! I didn't want to be left here. I didn't want it!"

"Who? What man?"

"George took me to the cinema but then he wouldn't leave me alone." Hilda rolled on her side and curled up like a pill bug trying to protect her soft and vulnerable self. "I didn't want to. It's not my fault. Please God don't let there be a baby in me!"

Ida's mind recoiled. How could George have stolen this child's innocence so cold and fiendishly? She put her head next to Hilda's and whispered, "No, you're not bad. Hush. Hush. It's not your fault." But her whispering seemed only to repulse Hilda.

Ida ran down to the store. When Pierre saw her face, he said, "What? What's happened?"

Ida could hardly believe her own words as they spilled out the poisonous story. Pierre reeled as he heard it. He looked sickened. He leapt to his feet and said, "You get Charles and finish up here. I'm going to find George!"

✦

Pierre knew that George had accepted a two day punching job along with a couple of Indians from the reservation. They were west of town up in the Porcupine Hills. He borrowed a motor car from his old boss at the grain silos and found George just before sundown.

Even though George stood there with a red hot branding iron, Pierre charged right up to him and threw a punch so hard to his left ear that George staggered in shock. The Indians released the calf they'd been pinning and jumped back.

"You son of a bitch, low down snake!" Pierre said. "You deflower my child when I trust her to your care? I'll kill you by God!" He lunged again but George waved his branding iron and kept him at bay.

George said, "It was just a moment of weakness. Look at that girl of yours. Any man would have answered the call."

"Answered the call? I'll tell you who's going to 'answer the call.' You're going to marry her and take care of her and that child." Pierre saw the surprise on George's face. "That's right, my daughter who is going to be thirteen years old on Sunday carries *your* bastard child! And *you!*" He bent down and picked up a large stone, making ready to hurl it at George. "How old are you?"

George shielded his face with his forearm and yelled out "Forty."

"Then the only comfort Hilda may receive is that you die when she's still young. But mark my word, you make her a good woman or I track you and shoot you like the dog you are."

He dropped the stone and got back in the borrowed car and drove away.

Pierre approached his Hilda now with the full understanding of what she'd endured. He found her in her room. She refused to come out. He brought a chair from the kitchen and sat with his hat in his lap while she lay turned away from him.

"Hilda, you will never know how tormented I am by having left you. But what happened we cannot undo. Now we have this baby coming. It is George's duty to marry you and provide, and to give your child his name. You have been gravely wronged but it would be far worse not to have a father for this child."

It was almost too much to bear, the pain of telling her that she must marry the man she despised. She lay before him, lifeless as a sack of grain. "Papa, leave me alone."

That night Pierre told Ida that he didn't think George would run, not because he was a decent man but because George had entrusted Pierre with most of his worldly belongings. He had his Marlin rifle and the sum of what he'd earned—saved in a cracker tin—since his arrival in Claresholm. Also, Pierre admitted to Ida, George did have some admirable traits, or they would not have become friends in the first place. George was the most fit and hardworking man he knew, despite his cold-hearted regard for women. "But perhaps," he said hopefully, "Hilda's sweetness could warm him."

When George showed up the following day, Pierre hoped he was right; George did seem to have come to grips with the gravity of his transgression. Pierre produced a bottle of bootleg whiskey and the two of them retired to the back room of the store.

They sat on crates, passing the bottle back and forth, discussing the situation.

It might have been the whiskey, but as the liquid went down, Pierre's admiration for his friend seemed to return. Perhaps he was attracted to the qualities George possessed that were so different from his own. George was a man's man, strong and independent while Pierre knew *he,* on the other hand, was a romantic. By the time the bottle was finished the two men embraced and a gentleman's agreement was sealed with a handshake. George would marry Hilda and do his best to support her.

They arranged the marriage quickly, before any obvious signs of pregnancy could cause a stir. George was not a man of faith but agreed to a German Protestant preacher to the north of Claresholm in Nanton, who would perform a simple ceremony. Ida sewed Hilda a silk wedding dress and Pierre liked the way it widened her hips and made her look older. Still, the tears he cried were not for joy as they married. Her new name on the document was Mrs. Hilda Mae Fahrenkopf, and the purposeful misinformation just above her signature was that she was of "legal age."

✦

During his years of cattle driving, George had come to know the prairie that stretched in all directions from Claresholm. He remembered seeing an abandoned herder's cabin out along Willow Creek, and found it still there. With Pierre's help, he put in new windows and patched the leaky sod roof. There was no running water but the creek was near. He figured he could make do here, at least until the child was born. For the time, it would keep them away from the attention of the uppity church-goers in town.

He used some of his savings to buy a 1908 Packard Model 30, and loaded his belongings. It was an unusually warm day, as the Chinook Winds blew down from the Rockies. George pulled the canopy back so he could enjoy the breeze, but it was clear that this was about all he'd be enjoying. Hilda's every look to him was daggers, even when he announced, as they sped along, that he'd teach her to drive. They were in a mess, to be sure, and he did not see the point of trying further to make her happy.

✦

Only two things brought fleeting moments of happiness to Hilda. First there was Willow Creek, which reminded her of the good days at Oldman River. She liked to sit by the banks on moonlit nights and listen to the beavers working and watch their glistening bodies as they swam back and forth; living and working together, as it seemed, good-naturedly. She envied them in their simple wet world. She also felt herself brighten at the movements of her baby. It was magical and mysterious, this small being inside her. Yes, she did dare believe, her feelings verged on joy at these signs of life.

Hilda was glad that George spent most of his days working for a dairy. Her heart sank each day when she heard his car returning and he never seemed happy to see her either. But he could at least count on a hot meal and an orderly home; that much she'd submit. He did not desire her physically as her belly grew taut and round. They slept in the same bed but about as cold and separate as a pair of steel railroad tracks.

Auntie and Papa helped arrange for a woman from the District Nursing Service to visit. These visits by the calm and confident midwife, as well as occasional visits by Ida, Charles and Pierre were the only other people Hilda ever saw.

The visiting nurse skillfully calculated the probable date of baby's birth and then came more often. She was there with a strong and reassuring presence when Hilda began labor. Hilda's reluctance at being married to George and forever tied to him by a child did not exactly provide her with the willpower to birth the baby. But at a given point, she had no say; the child emerged, crying out with shocking force from his tiny lungs.

She noticed George actually smile as he looked at his son, swaddled tightly in a blanket and peering out with large dark eyes.

"I will call him George Herbert for my brother. He looks Indian with that straight black hair. Not a curl from either of us. I guess if people are curious I'll claim you have Italian blood." He said this to her as if he'd just solved an important problem.

Hilda wondered what Italians looked like. She thought of her own birth for the first time. She couldn't really remember—what did her real mother look like? Did she have straight black hair? Did she look Indian? Was she happy when she gave birth to her? Did she love her? As she looked at her new son she thought her mother must have loved her because already she felt love for this helpless little one in her arms. She had not known if she would be capable of loving George's child until this very moment, when all doubt seemed to evaporate.

When Pierre, Ida and Charles came to meet the new baby, they seemed happy, even relieved to see that she loved her little George. Ida gave her breastfeeding tips while Pierre and George smoked celebratory cigars. Charles sat on the floor and Hilda placed her newborn in his lap, and Charles beamed. For the special occasion Papa shot three ducks that auntie roasted, and Hilda made a carrot salad. The greasy fowl tasted so good to Hilda that she devoured a single bird almost entirely herself. Ida encouraged her appetite because she'd said with concern that she looked thin and sunken-featured. She also advised that the longer she could nurse and provide milk for the baby, the better her chances of not having her monthly cycles and *that* will help hold off a second pregnancy. Hilda took this information to heart.

Over time, in their remote home, Hilda grew close to George as a prisoner might become to her captor. One thing they certainly had in common was in their admiration of baby George. He was their saving grace. His beauty and innocence brought levity to their hearts at unexpected moments. At times they would even spontaneously laugh together at his particularly cute or clever antics. Almost as quickly they would sink back into silence, battling their own dark thoughts about each other. When they spoke at all, their conversations were sparse and practical.

One other area of agreement was a mutual disdain for the sod-roofed cabin. It was deplorable, and Alberta's continuing drought compounded their sense of misery. The weather always seemed to be too hot, too cold, or too dry.

George grunted, "I got a mind to leave Alberta. Some place more abundant and profitable."

As much as Hilda did not even like this man, she surprised herself with unexpected emotion. Was he about to say he was leaving George and her? How could he just up and leave them? How could she make it on her own?

He continued, "Pierre has talked a lot about Washington State. He figures a man can make a good living fishing and logging there."

Hilda hoped that if he left, he'd have the decency to send home money.

"I was thinking," George went on, "I could move there and find a job and a real house and then you and the baby could follow up." He did not look to Hilda for a response; he simply pushed away from the table and said, "I'll take the train but I'll leave the Packard for you to get around. Then you can give it to Pierre and come on down by train."

Hilda sat dazed at this wholly new idea. What a concept! Pick up and leave? Together? But did she really want to go with him? She would be leaving Ida, Pierre and Charles, the only family she ever knew. Then, recalling that her real mother lived in Washington, she thought maybe she could find her. This new plan excited her.

Papa brought a map of Washington and he and George studied it together. They concluded that the new town of Anacortes, located on the north shore of Fidalgo Island, was a prosperous and promising location without the clamor of a big city, which George naturally shied away from.

If Hilda was being left alone, she insisted George give her the driving lesson he'd promised. He grudgingly began the next day. Hilda bundled the baby and put him on the floorboards by George's feet. There were so many things to try to remember at once. George had little patience for her lurching starts and for the numerous times she killed the engine and drove off the edges of the road. He grew red in the face and hollered so often that she became flustered and confused. She cried as they sputtered up to the cabin and with one final humiliating error, she stalled the engine. Hilda stomped into the cabin leaving George to carry in his son, who was also crying. They did not speak to each other for the rest of the night.

The next day, against Hilda's wishes, they embarked on another lesson. George admonished, "Don't be a quitter. I'll whip you if you don't get in that car! This time sit on a pillow and put one behind your back. Your feet will reach the pedals better and you can see out the window too."

Hilda, though ambivalent, found that the adjustments made such a difference that she ended her second lesson with a clean and perfect stop back at the cabin door.

The day that George left from the Claresholm train station, Pierre, Ida, Charles, Hilda and Baby George stood together on the platform to bid farewell. As the train pulled away, Hilda felt both free and completely at a loss. She didn't know what to do with her freedom. She spent the first night with her family above the Dry Goods Store. Charles relished his time with his little nephew, who was almost more ambulatory than he had ever been. Little George made mad dashes on all fours to every corner of the apartment. It took vigilance to keep him out of mischief. Charles made a good guard.

Still, she couldn't stay long. The Torkelsens, though good folks, still wagged their tongues in grave judgment of her, and there were disapproving stares all over town. She'd been a schoolgirl not long ago, and now here she was with a child! She could almost hear them asking themselves what the world was coming to. She soon tired of it and was glad to have her car and escape back to Willow Creek. When word finally came that George had found a home in Anacortes and was ready for them to come join him on the northwest Washington coast, she was almost happy.

♦

On the train platform, Hilda's eyes grew teary as she hugged her father, Ida, and Charles goodbye. Little George waved innocently to his grandfather.

She vaguely recalled her train travel into Canada as she left it behind. At the platform in Spokane she saw the same bench where the sad Indian family had sat long ago. She thought of the little boy with his long braids, and wondered where he was now, ten years later.

In Seattle she nervously clutched the itinerary George had sent her, and waited for her connecting Great Northern. A kind woman noticed her unease and asked if she would like to see the world's tallest building. Together they stepped out of the station and Hilda saw the dazzling white building with its pointed spire. It looked as though it could snag the passing clouds. Together they strolled until they reached the plaza, where her memory was jarred by a towering carved totem pole depicting powerful creatures standing one upon the other. At the very top stood a long-beaked bird, fanning its large wings. Shadowy images came to her of early days at Neah Bay, and she remembered old men with carved masks of long-beaked or winged beings, snouty-teethy wolves, masks with wild hair and rolled back eyes. She remembered how they had made her tremble. Odd, she thought, that it would be here, in this angular, alien city of walls, where she would be reminded of things so clearly from her past.

She re-boarded in time for the next leg of her journey and finally arrived in Mount Vernon, then rode the little "Galloping Goose" to Anacortes. The local train went North and then due west into a blinding setting sun. What a sight, to see the waters of the inland sea! After the dry, parched plains of Alberta, this world of water and green was like a dream. The train crossed a trestle over Fidalgo Bay and made a grinding halt in the lively town that was to become her new home. Even though it was dusk, children ran and bicycled in the streets. Shop owners sat in their doorways. She saw pool halls and a theater called "The Empire."

George was at the station to meet her. She wondered if he knew how his blue eyes sent icy shivers through her body, just as the carved masks had when she was young. She tried to look at him as someone else might see him. He was tall with thick curly hair and a very erect posture, perhaps handsome, but oh so old!

She handed George his son, relieved to have a break after so many hundreds of miles, and then George handed her a gift. It was a tube of deep red lipstick. He had never given her anything before.

"Put it on."

She'd never worn lipstick. She ducked into the station washroom to apply it neatly with the help of a mirror. She was impressed with the transformation, and giggled at her own reflection.

When she came out, he said, "There, that makes you look more like a woman."

He took off briskly down the sidewalk as Hilda trailed behind. They went south about a block and then crossed the tracks to a beach community of houseboats and rustic cabins built on piers.

Hilda looked at George in disbelief. "Is *this* where we're gonna live?" She had seen so many pretty little houses as the train pulled into town. She imagined herself in one of them, with their dahlias, sunflowers and sweet pea trellises. But now standing before this shanty town on the beach, she just about cried.

"This is it. Like it or get back on the train to Alberta."

She trudged behind him, climbing over beach logs, flotsam and foul patches of scum. They began to encounter the little homes, maybe fifty in all, none with a lick of paint. Sad-looking laundry was strung everywhere and children ran barefoot around the homes in sand that smelled of raw sewage. Was this a step up or down from her sod-roofed cabin?

The tide lapped against the house they entered. She discovered that they were luckier than most. They had running water. George made sure she knew that! They also had electric lights and an electric cooking stove. So it was not so bad, she decided. As the evening progressed, the house began to float. This rocking cradle, she thought, could take getting used to, but in a deeper reservoir of her being, she understood that she had come home.

✦

George worked at the Anacortes Lumber and Box Company, not far away at the foot of T Avenue. Many living in "Little Chicago" (as her neighborhood was called) worked at the same mill or in the canneries. George got up early and left for work with the rest of them. He told her to have a decent meal when he got home, and gave her two dollars to stock the kitchen. Hilda could hardly wait to venture out on her own. She felt dignified with her fresh lipstick, but as she approached the busy part of town, her confidence faltered. She felt conspicuous and used baby George as a barrier, talking to him rather than looking at the people who passed by. She found a friendly merchant in a market called Luvera's.

"Are you in town to catch the ferry to Canada?" he asked.

"No," Hilda said, holding the baby up near her face. "I live here now. I just got here yesterday from Alberta."

"Oh!" the man said, "I know an Alberta man here named George. Are you his daughter?"

Hilda blushed. "No, he's not my dad," she said in a muffled voice behind Little George. "I'll take three of these bananas, four onions and a bag of flour."

Hilda saw the grocer make a quick reassessment of her. He smiled and asked what her and the baby's names were. If this man was any example of the people, Hilda decided she'd like this town.

She toured the length of the business district until her arms were full of items. George slumbered in a leaden lump against her shoulder but she made it back without dropping any of her precious cargo. At first opportunity, she promised herself, she would send a letter off to Claresholm, telling all about her ugly home and her first venture out in Anacortes.

After George's return from work on the second day, he demanded Hilda succumb to his need for physical pleasure. When she resisted, he grew angry. He said, "There are plenty of women of ill repute in this town but I shouldn't need to spend my hard earned money when I already have you! Don't you deny me!"

Out of duty now, she endured his advances—after all, she was his wife—but retreated in her mind and hoped the baby would wake up crying so that she could pry George off.

It wasn't that he didn't work hard and provide. The house and electricity and food, all cost. She couldn't complain, but she was just as happy if he went to shoot pool with the other men at the end of the day. The hard part was listening to him when he came home. He'd hand her the liniment and ask for a rub down as he carried on.

"Our mill cut 200,000 feet of lumber in one shift today. If not for damn prohibition we could celebrate instead of drinking sodas. The cannery boys put together the figures for all five factories and figured they'd just put up 225,000 cases of canned salmon today! That's worth over a million dollars. Pierre was right. I might not earn much, but there's money and work all over town. Can you put a little more muscle into it? Down to the right!"

Though George provided for their necessities, he was otherwise tight-fisted. He wanted her home except to do the shopping. Still, she could not help herself from wanting to explore. She stayed away from the waterfront near the mill, so as not to be seen, but soon discovered Causland Park, the whole perimeter built of stone in swirling patterns and mosaics. Stones of one color twirled off one way, while stones of contrasting colors spun in opposite directions. She let baby George wander and explore while she lay on the mown grass. That night she got a lashing from George. He didn't believe her sunburn was from walking to the store and back.

Carnegie Library was the next place she discovered. She imagined herself to be important as she climbed the steep stone steps and passed through the grand pillared entry. Inside, she studied maps of the area, tracing her finger along the inland waterways. From Anacortes southwesterly, through the San Juan Islands and beyond to Juan de Fuca Strait, she slid her finger along the water until it bumped into the jutting coastline of the Olympic Peninsula. She found Neah Bay on the point of that peninsula: the place of her birth, the place where her mother lived. It seemed so close.

She was so excited, she said to George that evening, "If we took the ferry from Anacortes to Victoria, I could practically swim to Neah Bay!"

When George asked how she learned that, she had to confess her trip to the library. He smacked her and told her to stay home.

She tried to comply, because she did not like being hit, but she would not ignore friendly chats with her neighbors in Little Chicago. She felt drawn to a little old woman a few houses down, who looked Indian. Hilda liked it when she held baby George. The woman said, "He's dark like me. He got some Indian in him?"

Hilda was taken aback, but remembered to reply, "No, no, we're Italians."

The woman said, "I'm Salish Indian but my husband, he's white. I'm Lizzie and he's Clarence," she pointed to a lanky man on the beach. "Last name is 'House.' Did anyone ever say you look more Indian than Italian?"

Hilda saw she was teasing. It was no mystery to Lizzie that she was not Italian.

She smiled and said, "My husband said to say that. My mama is Makah. My Papa is French-Canadian. I'm Hilda Mae. You probably know my husband George Fahrenkopf. He don't like it when I leave the house."

Lizzie's eyes got soft and moist. "Don't be shamed of bein' Indian. I know it's a 'white man's world' but my man Clarence, he color blind. He don't care what people think about his love for me. Plenty of them whites disapprove all right. They never liked the Indian. We're just in their way. They floated in like weed seeds and got stuck in the soil here. My soil! They grew tall and there was more and more and we was just pushed aside. But at least I got my Clarence. He's a good white man." She handed the baby back to Hilda. "Just you remember, I'm right here and I'll watch after this sweet boy of yours if ever you need."

✦

Hilda didn't know she'd be calling on Lizzie's help so soon. She found her shaking a rug outdoors and was invited in. "I'm pregnant," Hilda said, before she even sat down. "George says he wants the baby born at home. I had a nurse midwife when I birthed baby George. It was hard. I don't want to do it all alone. Could you be with me when the time comes?"

"How can I possibly say no? You're a little girl havin' a baby!" Lizzie patted Hilda and said, "I'd be glad to be with you but still, *you* be doin' all the work!"

Hilda nodded. "Just to hold my hand and tell me everything is all right. I'd be happy if you would."

Four months before baby George's second birthday, his little sister, Mary Ann was born and she came with such force that even though Lizzie was there, Hilda suffered a tear. Lizzie had to convince George that a doctor needed to repair it.

Even then, she had such pain that the doctor gave her codeine. During the next two months as she healed, she had Lizzie pick up more and more. Hilda enjoyed a relief from the pain but also appreciated how much happier it made her. She marveled at her daughter's translucent skin and black corkscrew curls, and tended her and little George but felt less restless about getting outdoors. She seemed to float through the last weeks of summer and into the fall.

But at some point Lizzie said enough, and would not get her more. Hilda found herself falling into worse moods and fighting with George more and more until one night he turned on the electric stove and held her hand to the burner, yelling, "This! This is how hot I want my dinner! I do not work hard all day to come home to you being lazy and surly! Feel this heat?"

Her skin seared and smoked and she screamed but George kept her hand to the heat and didn't release it until George Jr. began howling in fear.

He pushed her. "Go take care of the kids and stop being a lazy good-for-nothing!"

When Lizzie saw Hilda's blistered hand she went off and got more codeine. As she bandaged Hilda, her voice was soft and soothing. "Maybe things could get better if you just try to meet his needs. And take heart that you got two beautiful children."

Hilda could not hear her. The words were dull and distant. But when Lizzie's tone brightened, it caught Hilda's attention. "This might lift your spirits," she said. "I wonder if you like me to try to find your mother and grandmother in Neah Bay? Us Indians here, we have connections to other tribes. I think I might find em. They don't even know you're here in Anacortes. Do they?"

"No, I don't think they know."

Lizzie warned that she did not want to give false hope. Still, Hilda was grateful.

Because of her injured hand Hilda was allowed to take the family wash to the Steam Laundry. At eight cents per pound Hilda spent forty cents of George's hard earned money per week just having diapers cleaned, and she thought: "It serves him right!" She kept her hand bandaged longer than necessary for the luxury of not having to do washing.

On certain Sundays when George was home, family life almost seemed harmonious. On one such Sunday Hilda convinced George that they should take an outing. She packed a picnic and they walked up the steep-bluffed peninsula close to Little Chicago, known as Cap Santé. From this promontory the view was breathtaking. The deep-blue-green frigid waters encircling the cape were alive with fishing boats and tugs with barges and log rafts coming in from Canada. They could see the cluster of rooftops of their neighborhood far below. "That little box is *my* house?" asked George Jr. in disbelief. The snow-covered volcanic cone of Mt. Baker stood majestically above the dark foothills of the Cascade Range. Looking north into Canada, more snow-tipped mountains seemed to wink their brilliance over all the miles as if to beckon, making Hilda slightly restless.

On their way back, the family walked to the waterfront along Guemes Channel so that George could show his son the mill where he worked. While they went around the pier, Hilda stood with Mary and saw a canoe coming toward the beach. A young white woman, not much older than herself, paddled it. Painted dragons adorned it. Who is that woman? Hilda wondered. What is she doing? The canoe ran ashore and a frisky dog jumped out and the woman followed and pulled her canoe out and turned it over on some logs. She seemed so confident, strong and able, so unencumbered.

When George returned and they began to walk back home, Hilda asked if he knew who the woman was. They could see her now striding up Commercial Avenue with her dog at her side.

"She lives on Guemes Island. They call her 'Bubble.' Some good-for-nothing artist-type as far as I can tell," George snorted.

Bubble, thought Hilda, even her name was fun! She lagged behind George, carrying Mary and feeling more than ever burdened, tethered and hopeless.

Hilda saw a chance at some relief when George announced that he was quitting the mill job and would be going for two or three months to Alaska for salmon season. Finally, Hilda sighed, she could spread her wings. She would have some freedom! Mary was coming up on her first birthday and Hilda was feeling old at sixteen.

When time came to leave, he threatened her grimly to behave while he was gone. Hilda only nodded. But when he left, she hardly knew how to misbehave if she wanted to. For her it was a great sin to spend frivolously on ice cream and movies, sodas and new Buster Brown shoes for the kids. Instead of cooking, she took them to the Oyster and Chop House some nights, and then was embarrassed when she realized she'd overspent her budget and still had a month to go before George's return. She had to borrow from Lizzie.

✦

When George returned he seemed pleased to see his children and was almost congenial with Hilda. He would not tell her how much he'd earned, but went right to the bank and squirreled it away. Now Hilda found herself more under his thumb than ever. He did not have a regular work schedule but took a part-time job installing street lights. Still, he was home far more than when he had worked at the mill. It was always a relief when he turned his critical eye away and told stories to George Jr. He'd sit with him on his knee and tell him of working the fishing nets, drawing endless fathoms in over the gunnels, heavy with salmon. He told him of whales and storms and working on diesel engines and taking his turn as cook in the cramped galley of the boat. One night she overheard George say he was satisfied with his work in Alaska and, though it was difficult, he looked forward to doing it again next season. Hilda perked up when she heard that, knowing she'd have another summer of freedom.

As the months turned dark and gray they found themselves once again at each other's throats. George hit. The children cried. Hilda sulked. George went off to shoot pool and then the routine began again. By the next fishing season, George was as happy to go as Hilda was to see him walk out the door.

✦

One night in Little Chicago there was a commotion. Hilda had already put the children to bed when she heard the thud of feet landing on the deck of her houseboat. She went out the door and saw a man in the dim light hunkered down against the outside wall.

"Shhh!" The man said. "Don't worry, I won't hurt you. The Feds are after me. Can I come in?"

He was a rum runner, Hilda guessed, and she agreed.

He sat panting for a while before he introduced himself as Blackie. They could see off in the distance the lanterns as men scrambled over the deck of Blackie's schooner, looking for evidence.

He said he had almost made it in from Canada when he'd been spotted.

"It really pains me to throw that good whiskey in the drink," he said.

It turned out that he'd saved one crate, and he brought out a bottle in payment for her hospitality.

For the residents of Little Chicago, moonshine and bootleg whiskey were just about as available as water, and Hilda was used to raids, but she had never had so much as a sip, George made sure of that. Now, with him away, the offer seemed irresistible. "The kids are in bed so I don't see why not," she said.

Blackie passed her the bottle. "Ladies first! Though you sure don't look old enough to have kids," he said.

Hilda put the bottle to her mouth and let it run freely until she felt the burn and then she abruptly stopped and coughed. "How does anyone drink that stuff?"

Blackie assured her that after a few more swigs, she'd understand. And it was true. They passed the bottle back and forth and soon Hilda discovered the taste did not bother her in the least. She enjoyed the sensation of being out of control and also enjoyed the thrilling fact that she was harboring a criminal. In her loosened state she found herself divulging to Blackie the sorry state of her life with George. She allowed herself to be comforted by this stranger in her house. She allowed him to put his arms around her and lay her on the floor. She craved to discover what real love was. She wanted the sort of love that she saw other couples sharing. She wanted to be held and adored.

Blackie was more than amenable, although he warned that he was probably not going to be her savior. But he *was* willing to fulfill her needs and desires for this one night. And, he admitted, he was comforted by the knowledge that her husband was a thousand miles away. He made love to her in a sweet and tender way she had never known was possible.

Hilda whispered sadly just before he left, "Will I see you again? Can you come back before summer is over?"

"I'm Canadian, but I'm in the business of running bootleg, so I just might see you again," he said with a wink. He left her with two bottles of scotch and was gone before dawn.

Hilda's head hurt the next morning. The encounter with her mysterious lover had left her sad and lonely and heady with transgression. To protect her tender condition, she sent the children to the beach to play with the other kids.

"You keep an eye on Sis," Hilda reminded George Jr. Then she pried up a couple of the old loose floorboards and hid away her bottles.

The children returned later, breathless with excitement. They had made a "sea dog" friend. All they and the other kids had to do was whistle and a seal would pop its head up looking for treats. They'd been feeding it scraps from the canneries.

When the seal did not show, there was still fun to be had. At low tide there was room for all of the kids to run and explore together. Hilda watched them make drift-wood forts or race little crabs against one another. The gnats, mosquitoes, and sand-fleas gave their playground the unglamorous name of "Bug House Beach," but they never seemed bothered. Hilda sipped from her whiskey stash and made full use of her last free weeks by joining her neighbors for impromptu parties and music. Two fiddle-playing friends often sat on the roof of their shack and sent their bright, uplifting melodies reverberating off the cliff walls of the boat haven, providing one more layer of atmosphere to the already colorful community Hilda had grown to love. One night these fiddlers invited fellow musicians from Bellingham to come play, and all the neighbors built a bonfire and roasted salmon, potatoes and squash on the coals. When the tide came in the party moved up into the homes and degraded to near debauchery. It was all in fun though. The children ran wild. Hilda felt so carefree that she offered up a bottle of her whiskey to the musicians. The fiddles sawed away and a banjo joined in. She sang along on the verses she knew to her favorite song, "Shady Grove."

Shady Grove, my little love
Shady Grove, my darlin'
Shady Grove, my little love
Goin' back to Harlen

Coffee grows on the white oak tree
The river flows with Brandy
The rocks on the hills are covered with gold
And the girls are sweeter than candy

Did you think my little miss
That I would live without you
I'll let you know before I go
I hear so little about you

As dawn came, she dropped to bed with pleasant memories of singing and dancing and did not wake until someone grabbed her hair and dragged her out of bed.

She screamed. It was George, come back from Alaska, and there she was, asleep, disheveled, and smelling of alcohol.

"You little tramp!" George stripped his belt and lashed her bare legs. "This is how you conduct yourself while I'm away? I risk my life fishing all season in Alaska just to have you back home making a fool of me?"

Hilda hopped around trying to evade his lashings and his hateful blue gaze, but somehow did not feel pain even as welts flared up across her thighs. Her mind was beyond this madness. She knew she could no longer live with this man and for that reason, in the midst of her punishment, she felt relief and release. It was as if an angel had come down and touched her or a dungeon door had swung open, throwing a glaring light onto her. She would now be free of this man and that could only be good.

Of course, knowing was one thing and doing was quite another. First were her babies. Where would she move with her children? How would they get by? She told herself that everything would fall into place if they could just get away.

That evening when things had quieted down, she told George she was leaving.

"Over my dead body are you taking the children. Look at them! They are dirty and unkempt. You are an unfit mother!"

"They've been playing all day on the beach. Of course they're dirty."

George's anger flared again. He shoved with his powerful hands. "It's more than their lack of cleanliness, look at Mary's legs! She's got god-damned rickets! Looks like you haven't fed her anything nourishing all summer! You've been boozing and not caring for my kids. I'm more than happy if you leave. Just get! But you're not taking them. And when you walk out that door don't you *ever* come back, not even to see them because I'll kill you if you do!"

Hilda felt weak. She trembled as she looked at Mary and George. It was true, she'd been neglectful, but not terribly so. Yet Mary's legs were definitely bowed and misshapen. Now she felt she truly was a bad person and a bad mother. She had made a mess of everything. She knew that George meant what he said.

A heaviness seemed to push the breath from her. She would die if she stayed. And she'd die if she left her babies. But now she had no choice.

Hilda called to her children and asked them to come sit in her lap. They snuggled close to her, sensing her sadness. She sobbed as she rocked them. She talked softly to them. "Mama loves you so much. Please don't ever forget me? Someday I'll have you back but for right now your daddy says you have to live with him. I will think of you two all the time and George Jr., you take good care of Sis. Don't let her fall in the water or get left behind by the big kids. You hear? Take care of her."

Choked with tears, she could say no more. She kissed their foreheads, packed her suitcase and walked out the door without once looking at George. Now she felt the sting of her lashing as she walked stiff and slow to Clarence and Lizzie's cabin and knocked on the door. When Lizzie saw her standing like the wrecked empty shell she was, she pulled her in and held her.

Hilda felt like a piece of trash thrown out of the house into the sea, floating directionless. If some powerful ebb did not carry her away, she was sure to sink to the bottom. This was not the feeling of elation she imagined once she was free of George.

Lizzie offered her enough cash to get her on the road and keep her from starving for a month or so. That was the best she could do. Hilda was so grateful. She hugged her and kissed her wrinkled soft cheeks and left Little Chicago early the next morning.

As she passed the fiddler's house she stopped and asked for the names of their friends in Bellingham. They wrote names and numbers in a song book and wished her well.

The most difficult part of leaving was the next few steps she took. Her heart felt stuck in her throat as she passed her little houseboat where George Jr. and Mary were still sleeping.

Could this really be her life? She felt as though she were in someone else's body, some *other* tall, rail-thin seventeen year old.

She guessed that she must be on her way, by ferry to Bellingham. Yes, that must be where she was going.

✦

George's boat had an exceptionally good season in Alaska. His profits were generous enough, he decided to move out of Little Chicago into a quiet neighborhood. He felt he'd been made a laughing-stock. He had no way of knowing just what-all went on there while he was gone. He trusted no one.

And there were those damn friends of Hilda's, Lizzie and Clarence. They seemed to be spying on him as he packed his kids and household items in the back of a borrowed truck. They even followed him as he drove and parked in front of his new rental house on 6th Street. He ignored them as they watched him moving his belongings into the house. So worthless, he thought. Have they nothing better to do than snoop around?

George set into a regimen of cod liver oil treatments to cure Mary's rickets. He could hardly bear her shrieks of protest each time the liquid was forced into her mouth. He also bought plenty of vegetables and meat. The children whined when he refused to buy them Juicy Fruit gum as their mama always had and they complained when he would not buy Cypress Ice Cream or Bubble-up sodas. Now it was more apparent just how Hilda "cared" for his children. It was obvious she'd fed them nothing but garbage!

George was not accustomed to being in charge of his children on such a continuous basis. It was not long before he put an ad in the *Anacortes American* and a couple of weekly papers down-sound. The ad read,

NEEDED, A QUALIFIED NANNY FOR TWO
CHILDREN IN ANACORTES WASHINGTON.
POSITION TO COMMENCE WITH THE SUMMER
ALASKAN FISHING SCHEDULE OF '27.
REPLY BY POST AT: GENERAL DELIVERY.
CARE OF: MR. GEORGE FAHRENKOPF.

A wide range of local women responded, from giddy girls to perfumed retired Ladies of the Night. He took on a lame woman for a trial period while he worked as a substitute deck hand on a local ferry, but though she seemed good and sincere, she could not adequately perform the necessary chores and had to be let go.

George ran the ad again; this time he hired the first respondent. He had a fairly positive feeling from the letter she had sent. When she arrived for her interview George saw that she was a matronly, gentle-natured lady. She had come from a farming community near the small town of Monroe, Washington. She introduced herself as Nettie Welsh and explained that she had already raised her three children to adulthood but was forced to divorce her hopeless alcoholic husband and support herself. George felt that he could relate to her tale. She had the natural, easy way of a country woman and was at ease around George Jr. and Mary. She exuded calm, which appealed greatly to George.

She returned a few days before the fishing season and settled into becoming acquainted with George Jr. and Mary.

George walked into the house and caught Mary asking Nettie earnestly, "Where's my momma?" But before Nettie could reply Mary cried, "I want my momma! You're not my momma!"

George Jr. put his arm around her and calmed her. "It's OK sis, Momma's just gone for a little while and this here lady's just helping Daddy 'round the house, with chores and all. Don't cry."

George instructed the kids to go out and play. He warned Nettie not to baby his children. He did not want them manipulating her. "They'll adjust. They're strong. And it looks like George Jr. will help keep an eye on Sis."

Nettie looked confident and unruffled by her new charges. And so, with peace of mind, George left the following day for Alaska.

✦

Nettie felt positive about her new job in this new town. She was unsure about the father but her heart ached for his children. Brother and sister often sat on the front step, whispering softly to each other and looking lost to the world. One day she baked them cookies and they all sat on the step and ate, and soon she had them talking to her.

George Jr. said he missed his momma and his buddies on Bug House Beach. He scowled when he looked out at the tidy new neighborhood. Nettie reminded him about the school, where he would be starting in the fall. She spoke brightly, telling him how he would learn to read and write and best of all, there would be many kids his age. Her strategy worked, for soon he became curious about what school was like and asked many questions.

One day there was a knock on the door. An old woman stood with kind eyes and asked if she might come in. The children recognized her and both ran to her when she came in. Nettie poured a cup of tea for her guest and then waited to see what this woman had come for. After a sip or two she introduced herself as Lizzie House and began telling Nettie the story of young Hilda Mae. She told Nettie that she had been the midwife at Mary's birth and had been very close to Hilda and her kids. Lizzie had brought the children each three molasses cookies and a little glider aero plane, and she suggested they go toss it around outside. When they went out, she continued telling Nettie of the many difficult details of Hilda and George's relationship, and finished by saying that she'd promised to keep Hilda informed about her children.

Nettie touched Lizzie's hand. "Thank you for sharing this with me. It seems none of our lives have been easy. I left a marriage made hellish by a lousy drunk and here I am starting my life all over at almost 50 years of age! When I saw the ad for a nanny, I thought this might be just what I needed to get away and start fresh. And then the most peculiar thing occurred. It was right before I had come up to Anacortes for the interview, that I had a vision. I hadn't even laid eyes on the children yet. It was as strong and vivid as you are sitting here before me. An old Indian woman appeared and said, 'Care for those two children, they need you.' Those were her only words and then the apparition faded. I knew right then and there it was my calling to be here with them. I still get chills when I think of that Indian woman. She looked a lot like you, but I thought of her as the kids' grandmother and now that you have told me about Hilda's Makah family, the image of the old woman makes sense!"

Lizzie was nearly crying when she spoke again. "You, Nettie, truly are a godsend. You like a light for these children. It's a sad situation. Sometimes I can't sleep thinking of Hilda. But the other day she wrote and said she'd found a home in Bellingham. She's made friends with a group of musicians. When I got her letter, I knew I had to come meet you so I could tell Hilda about you. Now, I'm happy to tell her, you're an angel. She wants to see her kids but George forbids it. If we can think of a way for her to see them later this summer, would you help?"

"Yes," Nettie agreed. "We can find a way." As she ushered Lizzie out, she thought of what a godsend this woman was as well. When Lizzie started to walk away, the kids saw her and ran to the sidewalk and embraced her. Nettie hoped they would love her as much someday.

George Jr. and Mary soon warmed up to Nettie too, and even demanded her as their playmate. She was fun-loving and carefree by nature and being around them reconfirmed her love of laughter and play. She was not bashful about rough and tumble activities. What did she care if the neighbors thought she was not ladylike? She'd throw the ball in the park for the kids and people would point at her. But even she had to admit that when she jumped rope or hop-scotched with Mary, her large unharnessed breasts swinging freely might be a bit of a spectacle.

Nettie also loved to cook. She shopped for the best deals at the produce and meat markets and then prepared succulent country-style meals that the kids grew plump on. She knew her own ample girth was due to the fact that she loved her own cooking as well.

The biggest challenge of each day was hair brushing Mary's astounding mop of curls were quite the envy of mothers around town but obviously, *they* didn't have to brush them. Every day was the same routine. Mary ran when she saw the brush, and once Nettie got her hands on her, the best strategy was to give her a paper doll to dress while she freed the tangles into charming little corkscrews.

❖

On July 1st Lizzie stopped by again to request a favor. "Would you bring the children to the park on July 4th, after the parade so that Hilda can see them?"

Nettie wanted very much to help the poor young mother reunite with her babies, but she had a real concern. "What if the kids tell their father? I would be in trouble, and Hilda too, if George was serious about his threat to kill her. You can't expect children that age to keep such a secret. They're too innocent."

Lizzie agreed it could be risky. Then she had the idea that it would at least give Hilda great comfort to see her children, even if they did not see her. To this plan, Nettie agreed.

Hilda would be coming into town on the passenger boat from Bellingham on the 4th. Lizzie said she would tell Hilda to wear a big hat or scarf so that the townspeople wouldn't recognize her so easily. She told her to go directly after the parade to Causland Park. If she stood up in the bandstand behind a pillar, she could see out into the park and observe her kids playing and having a picnic.

Nettie agreed to the plan. On Independence Day, she packed a basket full of fried chicken drumsticks and potato salad, as well as a ball and the kids' favorite book, *Grimm's Fairy Tales*. After the excitement of the parade, she shuffled the kids along to the park, and while they played, she kept an eye on the bandstand. After about a half hour the stage started filling with the members of The Juvenile Band of Anacortes. About 15 of them were getting ready to perform. Then Nettie worried that Hilda would not be able to use the pavilion as planned.

She started looking nervously in all directions until she spotted someone she was sure was Hilda. She stood just left of the stage. Even with a head scarf hiding her hair, she still looked persuasively like Mary, only tall and slim.

So many families had thrown down blankets to relax on during the show. As the band blasted trumpets, trombones, French horns and drums from directly behind her, Hilda looked anxiously out to the crowd. Nettie stood and wagged her arm in the air. Onlookers must have assumed she was waving at her son in the band, but soon Hilda saw her and timidly waved back. Nettie gathered the kids. She positioned Mary and George straight towards the stage and gave them each a plate of food.

Nettie saw Hilda almost stagger and then she seemed to be wiping away tears. She knew she must feel conspicuous and awkward standing with everyone looking towards her on the stage. Soon she sat on the step and did not take her eyes off her children. Nettie asked the kids if they could tell her which horn was the trombone. She was glad as they each stood and tried to decide, because Hilda got a much better look at them. She was not surprised when Hilda dabbed her eyes again and walked away. It had to be torture!

Nettie told the kids, "Sit tight and finish your salad."

She circled the edge of the park. Hilda was already halfway down the block. "Hilda!"

The young woman stopped and turned and Nettie huffed and puffed her way to meet her. She reached out to touch the young girl. "I am so sorry for your loss. I'm a mother too. I know how difficult it must be for you. I just want you to know I love them dearly. They are fine children. You must have raised them well. Please know that we can meet like this again whenever George is fishing. I am happy to help you see them."

Hilda hung her head. "Thank you, Nettie. I really was not a good mama to those kids. You're good for them. They look so different! You are feeding them well." She broke into tears. "I should have done anything to stay with my children but I can't turn back time. Lizzie said you are kind and this comforts me." She said, "I may want to see them again even though it is so painful to not hold them. Thank you. I've got to go."

"It's not your fault. Forgive yourself," Nettie said, and hugged Hilda and let her go.

❦

Nettie set her sights on making ready for Mr. Fahrenkopf's return by deep cleaning the house. She had been pretty casual about that until now. She also tried to prepare herself mentally for being in his presence. It was one thing to be living in his house, raising his kids while he was away, but what would it be like to have him in the same house? It was understood that she would stay on if all were amenable, but as yet, she did not have her own separate quarters. It made her uneasy, hearing from Lizzie about how Hilda had suffered at his hands, and how he'd stolen Hilda's childhood from her.

George seemed pleased when he returned to a sparkling clean home and was dumbfounded when he lifted his children to greet them. "They look radiant! They've gained a lot of weight! You been feeding them bricks?" He turned, giving her a quick hug and thanked her repeatedly. This did not seem like the man she'd been warned of, thought Nettie.

That night, she bedded down on a cot in the children's room. It was all right temporarily, but being rather wide of build, she felt the need to discuss a better remedy to the situation. When she nervously brought it up to him, the next morning, he said in a very matter of fact tone, "Well we could 'remedy the situation' by getting married."

She hadn't yet seen his "bad side," and thought she ought to take it slow. She said, "The cot will suit me fine for a little longer while I think on your proposal Mr. Fahrenkopf."

"Please," he said, "Call me George! I know it's sudden to think of marriage but I admire your way with the children. I'm a hard worker and good provider, and I'm no drunk! Think about it, Nettie. We might make a good team."

Nettie lay on her uncomfortable cot that night and she did think about marriage. She wasn't sure she liked the way George used the term, "good team." It made her feel like an ox or a mule. She thought about the young children, and the apparition of the Indian grandmother charging her with their care. She thought of her rundown farm in Monroe, and this new lively town of Anacortes. She believed George was accurate in his assessment of himself as a hard worker. His body was lean and muscular for a man of forty-seven, and then too he was German. A stubborn, working breed! With all of this to mull over, it took half the night before she was able to fall asleep and when she finally did, she dreamed.

Nettie dreamt she was being chased by her ex-husband. He had a gun and was stubble-faced, dirty and drunk as he stumbled along shooting at her but the bullets whizzed by. When he couldn't hit his mark he went back into the farmhouse and grabbed their young daughter Hester and lugged her under his arm to the well. He dangled her over it while hollering for Nettie to bring the bottle she had hidden from him. Nettie ran to them, but as she battled, Hester slipped from his grasp and fell, and Nettie fell after her, together to a grim death down the well shaft.

She awoke in a cold sweat, and lay in the dark remembering those horrible years. Alcohol had turned a fairly decent man into a hideous demon who could on many occasions have killed her or their children, if it had not been for her own quick wit and strength. Compared to that hard life, maybe George would not be half bad. She did have skills and strengths that poor Hilda never had a chance to develop. She imagined that George would treat her more as his equal even if he seemed inherently incapable of much warmth. At least to have a spouse with a work ethic would be a novel and refreshing experience.

By morning, with the kids bouncing all around her bed, Nettie felt haggard but resolute. Mary took her hand and led her out. George already had a strong cup of coffee waiting for her and a stack of pancakes with strawberry jam. He was clearly trying to woo her, she thought as she sat. The others joined her at the table.

When Nettie finished her pancakes she said, "I have an announcement to make." Addressing the children she said, "First, I would like to know from you two if you would mind if I was your full-time nanny? From now until you're all grown up?"

The children felt important being asked ahead of their dad about such a matter. They looked at each other to see if they were both going to give the same answer. They each smiled broadly and nodded their heads enthusiastically.

Nettie said, "That would make me very happy!"

She then turned toward George and said, "I think if I'm going to be with Mary and George until they are all grown up then maybe we *should* get married!"

She watched George's face soften and relax, almost breaking into a smile. His direct gaze made her uneasy. She was broad as a house and nearly old enough to be his kids' grandmother, she hadn't even taken the time to brush out her fuzzy braids, yet he said, "Nettie, I like your character and spirit. And neither of us are in our prime but I think we can make a new life together."

✦

George worked at odd jobs around town through the fall and winter, saving money to buy a truck, and come the time to head north on the purse seiner, he was chomping at the bit. Not because of troubles at home; everything was peaceful and pleasant there. Perhaps precisely due to the domestic peace, he was ready for the wildness of Alaskan salmon fishing.

He loved the journey: the pristine rivers, waterfalls and misty fjords. He wanted to explore them all, but salmon fishermen had no time for sight-seeing. He enjoyed the skill involved with closing a whole school of salmon into the purse-seine net. After the captain hustled to jockey his vessel to be first in the line-up of fishing boats, he would motor out to drop his net in the path of the migrating salmon. The next maneuver was to bring the net around in a large circle. As the boat closed the circle tighter and tighter, George guarded the opening by slapping the water with a metal cupped plunger on the end of a long pole. The popping sounded like seal flippers slapping the surface of the water and helped scare the fish away from the only escape route. As they drew the purse closed at the bottom, the salmon would start roiling the surface; only then would the crew know if they had a good haul. Then they hauled the net aboard, dumped the catch in the hold, restacked the nets and rinsed the fish slime from the decks. Through the long bright days, they repeated this process many times.

When George returned to Anacortes in the late summer, he was well ready for rest and peace. He was ready to see his children, and dare he admit, his wife. He still had responsibilities with boat work. There were fathoms of net to mend, and the boat to clean but at least now he was sleeping in his own bed. Not only that, but he'd done well that summer and had hatched a plan for how to use it, but it all depended on Nettie's willingness to support it.

He waited for a quiet evening to broach the subject. She'd settled into mending when he said, "You've told me so much about that farm in Monroe I thought maybe since your divorce is final we might move onto your five acres and work the land. Raise animals. Milk a cow. Be independent. What do you think? Could you live peaceably near your ex?"

Nettie looked contemplative and then spoke. "I've become pretty fond of the convenience of living in town. And it would take a lot of work to patch that farmhouse up. But the fences and barn are sound. If Jim keeps to his half of the land and leaves us be, it might work. We might take a Sunday drive there. It will give you a notion what'll need fixin'. The land *is* beautiful!" she said. "It scares me though to think of what might come back to haunt me."

The following Sunday George packed Nettie and the children into the car and drove. His children had never left Anacortes, and on the two hour drive, he pointed out migrating snow geese covering the Skagit Flats and the mountains of the Cascade Range marching white-capped in single file to the north and south. Even for George, this route south was new to his eyes. He drove slowly to take in the beauty of the wide Skagit River and the beautiful green Stillaguamish. Turning eastward, they crossed the Snohomish River, and got out to stretch their legs at Pilchuck Creek. The kids threw sticks and stones into its lively waters before resuming their drive. Less than a half hour later, he was pulling up the long driveway to Nettie's farm.

George got out of the car, stretched and looked out across the fields. He could almost taste the succulent richness of the land. The farmhouse was simple but not as dilapidated as he'd feared. It only needed some roof work, window replacing, screen doors to re-hang and the deck to be shored up. Nettie's ex, Jim Walsh, had already built himself a small cabin on his five acres and was nowhere to be seen, a relief to both George and Nettie. The kids explored the chicken coop while he poked around in the barn. He saw old cobweb-covered milking buckets and stiff leather harnesses. Moldy hay still lay in the cow stanchion.

After Nettie had showed them everything she could think of, right on down to the tool shed and the outhouse, it was time to head home. The entire drive back to Anacortes, his family talked excitedly about the prospects of living on the farm. Nettie told the children about the small Wagner school, and promised them they could each have whatever kind of pet they wanted once they moved to the land. George Jr. said he wanted a dog and Mary wanted a rabbit. George thought Nettie seemed excited, but also sad.

"What do you think Nettie? Can we swing it?" He asked earnestly.

"Seeing that place again brings back so many memories. But it's easier now to imagine going back there. I think I can do it."

George decided that the children ought to finish out the school year. In the early spring he went to turn the soil for planting. He had no plow animal yet to pull, so he turned the whole garden by hand, and then took on work with a strawberry farmer near Anacortes, on March Point. The man promised him all of his extra runners. On the weekends George took his son to the farm to help with planting the strawberries.

"This, son, is the *real* life. Look at this soil would you!" George could not help the excitement welling up in him as he sensed his new beginnings of a life with his hands in the earth.

✦

On one of the weekends that George was away, Nettie and Mary walked to Lizzie and Clarence House's. While Mary went down to play on the beach, Nettie told the old woman that they were moving to Monroe, but wanted to keep the line of communication open for Hilda's sake.

Lizzie, looking pained, said, "I got bad news and I'm sorry I never come to tell you about it. Hilda called a few months ago sounding awful bad. She had a baby boy, you know after she went to Bellingham, and when she called she was callin' to say the baby got killed in a car wreck on Chuckanut Drive. He was only about a year old. So now I'm afraid it might have put her over the edge. I tried to calm her then, and when I called her back friends said she'd left for California and they hadn't heard no word from her. Poor child! She's had a hell of a life!"

There was nothing for Nettie to do but give Lizzie her address in Monroe and draw her a map. Shaking her head, she said, "I sure hope she'll be okay. Too much suffering for one soul! Please tell her kin at Neah Bay this information if you have contact. I don't want to stand between these kids and their blood relatives. It's important they know where they are. If Hilda, bless her soul, disappears from the face of the earth it's even more important that someone out there knows."

Nettie hugged Lizzie and thanked her again for her steadfast support of Hilda, but resolved not to tell the children until they were old enough to understand the complexities.

Within the week after school let out, the car was loaded and the family left Anacortes for their new life on the farm. George Jr. and Mary were happy that they each got their own rooms and Nettie allowed them to decorate in any way they saw fit, "as long as it doesn't cost money." George Jr. wanted to put pictures of cars from magazine covers and ads on his walls. Mary wanted flowered wallpaper but settled for some flowered fabric curtains instead.

It seemed almost like magic to see her homestead come back to life. George set right to work making the necessary repairs. He'd bought a new ax, shovel, pitchfork, manure fork, bow saw, a carpenter saw, a rock rake, hoe and a hammer. What a world of difference between George and Jim, she marveled. George managed his money so well he'd even had enough left to buy a nice freshened cow and a work horse from the local auction. He was indeed a worker beyond compare! He oiled the leather harnesses and filed the rusty plowshares. He toiled tirelessly, showing little humor but no discontent either. She'd never seen anything like him before.

Nettie found that if she just kept the man fed, he was content to stay busy until darkness drove him indoors. She, meanwhile, scrubbed, painted, and cooked. She also set herself to the task of making large oval braided rugs from factory wool scraps. Her daughter Hester worked in a Seattle garment factory and so was able to keep her mother supplied.

Hester visited often on weekends. Nettie gave thanks for the sweetness of her daughter. She could have been mean-hearted or in some way broken from the bad influences of Jim. George's kids loved her and called her "Auntie." She brought *Boy's Life* magazines for George, and pretty printed fabric scraps for Mary, and then often sat and helped her design and sew doll clothing.

Nettie's son John had some time ago fallen into the drinking habit right alongside his father. The two of them were quite a pair of ne'er-do-wells. They hollered and fought so loud that at least once a week, they could be heard from the back acreage. They shot bullets into the sky and at beer bottles until their ammunition was gone, but later in the week they'd get more, and the Wild West shoot-outs would start up again. They were ornery and malcontent most of the time but they knew they were outmatched by George, and never dared cross him. Nettie's second son, Irving, lived in Monroe. He was a good man, but caught up in a bad marriage that consumed his energy, and she rarely saw him. Nettie clearly saw that this second chance at raising a family was a blessing.

The children were expected to work five days of the week. Their chores were simple but time consuming. Nonetheless, it was important to George that they do their share. Weeding the strawberry patch and the potato patch was their first job. Nettie tried to protect them from being worked too hard. She thought George seemed out of touch with what he was asking of his youngsters. She particularly tried to dream up excuses why she needed Mary's help in the house. Mary was always thankful whenever she got a break from the field and could instead help bake or sweep.

After they baked a pan of muffins, Nettie liked to hang the pan back on the wall with the muffins still in it so that she could dole them out to the children when their father wasn't looking. She always had Mary open the doors to fan out the aromas of the baked goods. "Your father is overly concerned that you kids will become fat and lazy if you eat too much. But we know that's not going to happen, right?" She'd wink at Mary, who giggled over their little secret.

Nettie knew that George was not without his thoughtful moments, like the day he brought home a puppy, a white rabbit and a brood of young chicks and gave them to his son, daughter and her respectively. The kids thought they had died and gone to heaven, to have their very own pets.

Yes, thought Nettie, the farm was coming back to life! With their milk cow "Bell" and the fine, well-trained young gelding called "Mister," life felt in order.

In October came the frightening news of the stock market crash. As the situation worsened and it appeared quite a calamity was at hand, Nettie and George realized how fortunate they were to be on the farm. City people had lost their jobs and the banks had lost all their money. Soon people were living in the streets hungry, angry and desperate. If they had still been living in Anacortes or if they had not had access to the farm, where would they be now? Nettie and George both gave thanks and kept their noses to the grindstone while much of society crumbled around them.

One day, in the midst of these hard times when not so much as a traveling salesman bothered to come by, a knock came on the farmhouse door. Jesus was about the only thing people were trying to sell these days and Nettie didn't need any proselytizing religious folk trying to get her to join a church. She almost didn't answer but, peering through the curtain, she realized they were Indian women. She greeted them kindly and invited them to come in, but they preferred to remain on the porch. They introduced themselves quietly as Emma and Lucy Bell from Neah Bay, the grand and great-grandmothers of Hilda's children. Lizzie House had told them how to find the farm. They explained that for the first time, due to a new road, they were able to drive from Neah Bay out into the world.

Mary stood shyly behind Nettie as she and the Indian women conversed. Nettie understood Mary's fear; they were dark and unfamiliar to her. They kept glancing at Mary and then talking to each other.

Nettie encouraged Mary to step forward. She said, "This is Mary, Hilda's daughter. She is seven years old. Her brother George is out in the barn with his father. He's nine."

The women touched Mary's curls and smiled. "Looks like Hilda!" Emma said. "You know we're your grannies?" Lucy asked. Mary shook her head, looking confused.

Nettie did not want to offend the women but she was concerned with what might happen if George were to see them there. She left Mary on the porch and escorted the women back to the car. "I am so happy to meet Hilda's actual kin! But please tell me how she is. Where is she?"

The women said that she was singing in nightclubs and on radio stations, and as far as they knew, she was doing reasonably well, although they too knew of the loss of Hilda's third child and her addictions. They thought she might be in California but were not positive. They explained that they had to see their grandchildren and be reassured with their own eyes that they were being cared for. They had heard about Mr. Fahrenkopf through Lizzie and so, not wanting to cause trouble for Nettie, they bid their goodbyes. They also promised they would get word to Hilda that all was well with her children. They waved from their car to Mary as they pulled away.

When Nettie returned, Mary said, "Mother, were those women my real grandmas?"

Nettie put her arm around Mary. "Yes, those are your real grandmas and they only came to see you and know you and brother are in good hands."

Mary looked relieved. "I love you and I never want to go off with them ladies even if they are my true kin!"

✦

A year or more later, things had gone from bad to worse in the country. Life on the farm was not luxurious by any stretch of the imagination, thought Nettie, but they had their basic needs. Hester told her about a woman she'd met at a dance marathon who had two sons living in an orphanage. "Is it possible," Hester wanted to know, "for the boys to come live on the farm?"

Nettie brought the idea up to George, of boarding the brothers in exchange for some extra help on the farm. Her heart was already sold on the idea of helping the unfortunate lads. She knew she was not suffering as so many were, and felt they were in a situation where they could help in some small way.

George was at first opposed. "Why," he shouted, "would I want two more mouths to feed? I work harder than a damn machine just keeping us fed!"

Nettie continued cautiously, "That is precisely why I think it would be a good idea to have the boys. Look at that grain field full of mustard weed." She pointed to the tall yellow blossoms poking their heads up throughout the field. "They've gotten ahead of you even though you never stop working. A chore like that would be perfect for the young brothers. They would also give Mary and George companionship while they're working. I'm afraid you'll work our two young ones to death. Let's try the boys! It's no trouble for me to cook an extra two helpings."

George fumed for a few moments and then said, "All right. We can give it a try but if they are a couple of dandy city slickers who can't pull their own, then they're out of here! I don't want to be no charity outfit!" He grumbled to himself as he wandered off to the barn. He called back over his shoulder, "They got to be healthy. And I want to meet them before I give an absolute 'yes'!"

When Nettie told the children of the brothers who might come to live with them, they were excited. They felt sorry for the city boys who had no daddy and a momma who couldn't afford to care for them. George was particularly ready for buddies to play with, while Mary seemed a little disappointed. "Can we get a girl from the orphanage too?" she asked. "I want to share my bedroom and dolls with some girl that's got none."

Nettie shook her head sadly.

Mary said pensively, "Mother, did my real mama leave me and brother because she couldn't afford to take care of us too?"

Nettie ruffled Mary's curls. "All I know for sure is your mama loved you and it was very hard for her to leave you. I think you'll see her someday but I don't know when."

Nettie was delighted to report back to her daughter that all was clear on her end. She talked to their mother Irene over the telephone, and reassured her.

Irene said, "My sons are my life and it would mean the world to me to have them in a loving home. I'm living in a shanty and working as a cleaning lady but can't seem to make headway. I hate to see them in an orphanage. This opportunity is a blessing for them."

Nettie said, "Don't you worry. I'm sure everything will work out. I'm happy to share my home and give you some peace of mind as well. Hester will be in touch with you to arrange the day to bring them."

The day Hester said they should expect the arrival of the brothers, Nettie was so deep in her meal preparations that she almost did not hear the car pull in or the dog barking. When she finally realized they'd arrived, she ran out to greet them. As she suspected, they were just fine and simple folk. She learned their names and then invited them into the house and asked the boy to ring the triangle on the porch.

She knew that George would be wondering what kind of mess she had gotten them into as he sat down to the table, noisy with chatter and the clattering of dishes. She could see him itching to eat and get back to the fields. He eyed the brothers critically and questioned them. She felt uncomfortable for them, but they eyed George right back and answered brightly. Nettie rather doubted they spoke the truth about having work experience but George took them at their word. He must have decided they looked able-bodied enough. He rose to leave and told the boys they were welcome to stay on the farm. He said he had to sharpen a tool but then he wanted Mary and George to be ready to get back out and finish their weeding job. When he walked out everyone glanced around the table at each other and glowed at the success.

Mary lingered as long as she could and complained about going back out to the field. "You'd better go," said Nettie sympathetically. "Father and brother are already walking out. We'll come out onto the porch so you can say goodbye."

They all went out the door. Irene called out to George, "Thank you Mr. Fahrenkopf! You'll like my boys. They'll be good!"

Mary whispered in Nettie's ear, "Why's the one brother wearing that funny leather hat and goggles on a hot day like this?"

Nettie replied quietly, "Hush now and get goin' or Father'll be mad."

Grudgingly, Mary picked up her hoe and trailed after them. Nettie saw her turn and look longingly back. She shyly waved to the group standing on the porch. The older brother, the one wearing a strange leather hat, was the one who waved back.

My uncle George and mom in Anacortes, WA.

My uncle George and mom in the days after their mother Hilda was run off.

ABOVE: My mom and her brother and my dad and his brother on the farm in Monroe, WA. (Back row: Uncle George, Buddy, my mom, my dad —with the flight helmet. Front row are two unknown neighbors.)

My Grandma Nettie and Grandpa George Fahrenkopf in Monroe, WA.

My mom and her
brother George.

A joyous reunion, the day
my mom's real mother,
Hilda Mae found her.

My mom and Hilda Mae and
my dad and me on
the reunion day.

Paddling Around and on
from Cape Caution

THE WHALES THAT HAD USHERED ME into this remote
beach on Cape Caution and sparked thoughts of my mother's forebears were still present and busy stalking their prey, or
perhaps at play. Whatever they were engaged in, this had to be one
of their favorite places to congregate. I studied their immensity,
while they rolled and spouted. It seemed impossible to compre-
hend the audacity of the Makah, who actually harpooned these
beasts by primitive means.

My mother had inherited ample shares of tenacity from her
German, Makah, and French-Canadian ancestors. But from her I
also learned simplicity and humility. I never remember her wanting fame, fortune or even middle-class comfort. All she demanded
from me was that I find happiness. I certainly could not be happier than I was now, paddling onto the sands of this, no doubt,
one of Earth's wildest places.

A re-evaluation of my chart that evening made me think that perhaps I was not at Blunden Bay. It seemed I was just north of Neck Ness Point. Wherever I was, it was magnificent! I rejoiced at having made this landmark. It was not named Cape Caution by seafaring explorers without good reason.

Here was yet another note scrawled on my chart, where the psychic had predicted I would encounter wildlife. Of course, all along the way I'd had my encounters, but if you could name the Earth's supreme living creatures, the whale would surely top the list. At this precise place, my whale encounters would have to qualify as yet another accurate reading of the supernatural energies. Also, I continued to see evidence that I shared the beach with large numbers of wolves, or, rather, they shared it with me. I would have been happy to hear their songs, but the deafening surf overwhelmed them. I toasted to my success so far with a beer as I studied the star-encrusted sky, and sent up a silent prayer for safe guidance on tomorrow's voyage around the cape. I lay awake knowing I would have difficult paddling ahead, but feeling ready for the challenges *and* the gifts to come.

Getting off the beach in the morning was messy. I stood at tide's edge, the bow of my loaded boat pointed into the curling surf. I'd need all my strength and finesse to pierce the waves and make it on out into the big swells. With paddle in hand, I shoved my boat forcefully and jumped in ready to paddle hard and straight. Instead, the boat was thrown sideways and I was swamped. While sponging out my boat I cut my hand on some broken glass. So with a bloody hand I pushed on through the breaking waves on my second try. As I left the bay I looked down and realized I was paddling directly over a humpback whale. It blew and then lay at the surface near me before it dove again. Oh! Thank you my mother's ancestors for being at my side!

The next eight miles were some of the most strenuous miles of my paddle as I rounded Cape Caution. In fact, most of that distance was death-defying. All I could do was breathe hard, moan, pray, and fight to stay in control. To compound the difficulty, the fog was so dense it was hard to see where the shoreline was. I had to try to stay near enough to see land yet far enough away to avoid the churning waters near shore. The sea was big! I felt as if I was paddling up mountainsides of seawater and as often as I paddled up them, I also had to tumble down. Doggedly and repeatedly I climbed these immense swells with my bow pointing toward the sky only to be thrown recklessly down their backsides, requiring rapid-response paddle bracing. By the time I reached Long Beach, I was almost too tired to make it into shore. There, I was confronted with a beach as wide as any I had seen. From the edge of the forest to the tide line was 300 paces, and each trip seemed like miles as I trudged back and forth, carrying five loads of gear, then finally, exhausted, dragging and carrying my kayak.

When Stewart had told me to look for a cabin right inside the forest here, I'd scoffed about wanting anything more than my tent, but now it looked like absolute heaven: a darling cabin, made from hand-hewn cedar shakes and salvaged beach wood. Inside it was comfortable, with a good sheet metal stove, sturdy bunk bed with soft foam mattress, a small table, stool and tiny library shelf.

I made a piping hot fire, stripped my wet clothing, made and ate pancakes with honey, preheated my sleeping bag by the stove, crawled in and crashed. What ultimate comfort. At this point I did not care if I went one inch further on my sojourn.

For the next two days, I stayed away from the salty brine. My home in the woods was neat and clean. It was obvious that it had been lovingly built and maintained. The wooden door of the cabin was short, like a hobbit entry, with wooden hinges and a wooden latch. There were useful items like a crab cooker and candles. The stove sat beautifully installed on a framed-in hearth of sand, the wall protected by metal flashing. From the look of the cabin's journal, few visitors made it to this location. Only one person had made an entry this season, on June 13. Now it was July 20, and I'd been paddling for 22 days. Besides Ivory Island, this was only my second real day of rest, and I had not the slightest bit of guilt. In the cabin library I found a book, *Miles From Nowhere—Around the World Bicycle Adventure* by Barbara and Larry Savage, and I spent the day reading, inspired. Their great adventure made mine seem puny by comparison, but at least I knew we were kindred spirits. I finished it only to learn in the epilogue that after surviving all their epic travels, Barbara had died in an accident back home in the states. That night I lay in my bunk, lulled by the crashing surf in the distance.

The next morning, I was ready to explore. I walked along the fog-enshrouded beach and found no treasures but came across an odd sight: stuck straight down into the otherwise unblemished fine sand of the beach was a stick, protruding about 3 feet. From a distance away I saw tracks of a hopping raven. The tracks came right over to the stick where they continued around and around the stick in tighter and tighter concentric circles. What was that about; a dance, a ritual? I never could imagine.

As I walked further down the long beach, the pounding surf was like a taunting trickster, daring me to take up my paddle once more. I tried not to listen. It was so easy and pleasant here. Then again, those lashing waves, like the protruding tongues of recess bullies, daring me to chase them. Okay! Okay! I finally decided, perhaps I *could* move on the next day. Surely the most arduous stretch of coast was behind me. I fell asleep that night to waves that now sounded caressing, massaging my doubts like a drug.

The next morning, the clash of the sea was as rambunctious as it had been the day before but today it was sunny and clear. A good day to go. I took a line of sight reading on my kayak compass as I pushed into the sea from Cape Caution. It was provident of me. Soon after I cast off, the fog settled back in and the coastline vanished. I was able to follow a true course until I came to Slingsby Channel where, in big swells and thick fog, a whale fluke stood on end very near me and then disappeared. Then again it emerged right in my path. I sang, "*Way hey and up she rises…*" and hoped that she wouldn't, at least until I was past.

I often sang as I paddled. Typically I sang one of the scores of "Earth Circle Songs" which I shared with my community on Lopez. These simple songs of natural earthly elements and love served to bind us. We sang together at every gathering: for deaths, celebrations, births, for any occasion or no occasion. We just sang. Now, here alone, steeped in the very elements those songs honored, it was fitting and empowering to sing them. One new chorus, now circling in my head was *not* one of the "circle songs," but the old Cat Stevens song, "Miles From Nowhere." Since reading the book in my little retreat cabin, I couldn't shake the song of the same title. I changed a few words to match my own sentiments, and during that day, it became my mantra:

Miles from nowhere
I think I'll take my time…to get there!
And my body
Has been a good friend
And I'm gonna need it when I reach the end
Miles from nowhere
I think I'll take my time…oh yeah, to get there!

I felt vulnerable in the fog white-out. I knew that here, at Slingsby Channel, was a wide gash of open water with a few islands sprinkled about, but I could see none of it. I just knew I had no more coastline to follow and I was uncertain where the opposite side of the channel was. I decided to follow a 140 SE heading and hope to bump into land, maybe Fox Island. In the distance, I could hear the melancholy drone of a diaphone, which I imagined helped keep me oriented, because at this point I did not feel trusting of my compass either.

A fishing boat appeared out of the mists. I talked to the pilot, hoping he could help me get my bearings, but he seemed as befuddled as me. After looking at the chart some more we figured we must be on the SE side of Braham Island. His problem, he said, was that he usually fishes more out to sea. If we were accurate, all I had to do was find Skull Island and wait out the fog, which seemed to be dissipating. I did and it did, and soon I was able to paddle on to Shelter Bay for a total of about eighteen miles that day.

The next day's travel was a relatively short distance. I paddled to Blunden Harbour in four hours. This is an old Indian, or as they say in Canada, "First Nations" village site. It's in a nicely protected area with a pretty shell beach. The ruins of big houses—massive beams that once served as ridge poles and roof supports—are now flat on the ground. Pottery shards and other semi-modern artifacts put occupancy of this site into fairly modern times. I lazed on the beach as evening approached, and a few large cruisers and sailboats came in to anchor for the night. From one of the boats I made a call to Gregg. I only got an answering machine message. He had left the message just for me and it said that he and Raven would leave on the 29th.

From the beginning of my serious plans to embark on this journey, Gregg had decided that he and my son Raven would meet and camp with me for a few days. That time was drawing near, now that I was coming into the inside waters between the BC mainland and Vancouver Island. It was feasible for them to catch a ferry from Lopez, drive up Vancouver Island and throw a skiff in from the island's northeast side. From there they would motor out and rendezvous with me at a predetermined location. This message from Gregg meant that I would need to kill about nine days in order to meet them in the area where we had agreed.

Here in Blunden Harbor, I began to have a hankering for social interaction. The boat people came to shore in their skiffs and dories to run their dogs or dig madly through the deep beach sand in search of old glass Russian and European trade beads. I myself was not above keeping a bead if it revealed itself to me at the beach surface. But some of these folks were going about it wholesale, mining with shovels. Eventually they all went back to their boats and right when I was feeling that I would be dining alone on my same old rations, a skiff came buzzing across the water straight to me. Maryanne and John Beverage had come to invite me to dinner aboard their 1940's vintage yacht, the *Nika*. I thanked them and said I would be right out. First I spiffed myself up.

This couple looked like they might be in their mid-forties. They had been married for 25 years and had one son they called Tig. They moored their boat in Maple Cove near Nanaimo. Maryanne had owned an antique store for years and so their vintage live-aboard was made homey with a lot of antique décor. They served me a delicious dinner of pork chops, gravy, potatoes and broccoli. Plenty of cookies and tea followed. We talked on into the evening after that, and they gave me lots of friendly advice and helpful suggestions, along with my first detailed chart book. It was outdated, but better than anything I had. These folks were jewels; I appreciated their kindness and generosity so much at this stage of my journey! At last I thanked them, and they sent me off with a bundle of cookies.

In the morning I dug clams to have later for dinner and found one glass bead that I gave to Maryanne. Another couple came to the beach to bead hunt, and out of the goodness of their hearts gave me two lovely blue-faceted Russian beads. The kind gestures of humans seemed never-ending.

I left Blunden Harbour early the next morning in flat conditions, though a persistent rain fell, and paddled steadily all day, about twenty-two miles in eleven hours. I was soaked to the bone and cold by the time I reached what was supposed to be my rendezvous point with Gregg. An acquaintance had recommended this place as a great camp, but all I saw were rocks. Somehow, I must have missed the recommended site but now I was worn out.

Yet another yacht, the 44′ *Argonauta* and her kind crew of six took me in for a cup of coffee. I hadn't been trying to solicit charity from these mariners; I only meant to ascertain my whereabouts, but when I paddled to their anchored boat to ask them, I can only imagine I was a pitiful sight, drenched and weary. When, over the cup of coffee, they learned my story and how I had probably eight days to wait before I met Gregg, they invited me to spend the night aboard and motor with them to Alert Bay the following day. By now it was too late to search for a camp in the rain, so I took them up on their offer. They were a jolly bunch of friends from the Seattle and Portland areas. They insisted I have a glass of wine and a shower. The glass of wine I figured was for my enjoyment but the shower may have been for *their* enjoyment! After all, it was fairly tight quarters. I didn't truly think this, though, because I loved my daily plunges in the salt water. I was no doubt cleaner on this paddle than I would have been back home, slaving in my garden!

The next day I went along with my kind saviors. We motored through the heavy rain, around the south side of Malcolm Island to the much smaller Cormorant Island and its village, Alert Bay. I thanked them from the bottom of my heart and paddled from the village marina down the island until I came to the shore-side youth hostel called the *Pacific Hostelry*, a place I had heard about while traveling. Here I spent $10 (Canadian) to use their nice facility, but I still pitched my tent out back. From the hostel I talked to Gregg and told him of my early arrival and we made plans for a new meeting area. He encouraged me to stay as long as I wanted at the hostel, after I told him my concerns about spending the money.

For the next two days I stayed put, enjoying the young travelers at the hostel. I walked with a German chap all over the predominately native community of Alert Bay. We saw the world's tallest totem pole, the Gator Gardens, and a museum. Later that evening, the hostel keeper and his sisters invited me to go with them to the Nimpkish Pub to shoot pool. I enjoy pool and even have a natural eye for the angles but had few opportunities to play. I drank beer and shot with all the native guys, one of whom guessed that I was a kayaker because I "looked strong." A rock and roll band from Nanaimo played but not a soul danced. I never could stand still when I was around music. I had to dance! Not only did I inherit the name Irene from my Dad's mom, but I also inherited her love of dancing. I could only guess that she, like me, felt it was almost a sacred obligation to move our feet in time to music. I wondered too, if I'd been hard-wired to fall in love with a drunk as she also had. I knew better now though, and steered clear of the intoxicated that night. The walk back to the hostel was star-lit and I began to feel impatient to be back on the water. Gregg and Raven were making their way north and I could hardly wait!

✦

I had not really gained headway on my journey by diverting to Alert Bay, in fact it probably extended my route a little, but at any rate, I took off the next morning on my new, slightly adjusted course. I was heading for the Village Island group, specifically to the old village site known as Memkumlis of the tribal band Mamalilaculla, where I now planned to meet up with Gregg and Raven. I was so happy to be paddling again.

I thought of my thirteen-year-old boy as I struck out. My plan of passing him around at birth perhaps had paid off; he is the quintessential well-adjusted child, bright and full of humor. My heart felt joyful at the thought of seeing my loving son.

I paddled Johnstone Strait until I turned north into the narrow pass between Hanson and Harbledown Islands. The current, in this constricted channel, was powerful, like a raging river that boiled and whirled chaotically in all directions. I could see that it would be a "whole new animal" in these narrow waterways. It was a challenge to even bring myself to look down at the wild whirls of water that tossed my kayak about. Here, *Iakim*, the mythological undersea beast known to the aboriginal Kwakwaka'wakw, still stirred the waters into freakish upwellings. I could almost imagine the hairy arms or tentacles of this monster reaching up through the depths to overturn my boat. I decided to keep my gaze straight ahead. Now, as I recalled the fishing boat that had capsized not far south of here while I was motoring north on Patrick's boat, my mind sharpened like a developing photograph. I pushed on with more effort. Giving it all I had, I was barely able to make headway; instead I was being swept back towards Cracroft Point. After an hour I finally did succeed, but I was too exhausted to continue across Blackfish Sound. A passing fishing guide in his motorboat told me it would be six hours before the tide allowed me to continue and so, not really wanting to be saved but also not wanting to be kept from my goal, I accepted a wild tow around the point. He told me about his floating fishing lodge, where clients paid thousands to stay, and invited me to come eat and visit if I wanted to paddle over during my stay in the islands. I thanked the fine fellow for his offer and paddled off to a small islet near Mound Island where I pitched my tent on a high grassy point. From here I looked southeast, straight down Indian Channel towards Village Island where my boys would arrive.

The next morning I decided to paddle first over to Mound Island, just to check it out and to fish. When the wind came up suddenly, I decided to sail to Memkumlis, but there must have been trickster spirits at work, for in this short four-mile sprint, the sheer force of the elements prevented me from tacking. So as I looked longingly in Memkumlis, I was swept onto the shores of a village site called New Vancouver. What a cruel fate that I should be kept apart from my loves! Surely they had arrived by now, but it was too far off, out of sight around a headland, and there I was, stranded on shore by the wind, only gazing out on the water in the hope of spotting them in their skiff. The waves and wind were wild enough that I even feared for *their* safety. Finally I decided to put all fears aside; "be here now" seemed to be the lesson of the day.

There were no obvious ruins from the old native village site at New Vancouver but I found a small group of natives there who were preparing to rebuild the site that they claimed had been occupied until 1965. That was hard to imagine, but then Nature reclaims quickly in this rainy, lush land. I wished them luck and went to camp.

The wind pounded the beach all night, making me wonder whether I would be marooned the next day as well. But when it did finally die just before sunrise, I dashed around packing up. The weather radio at 5:00 A.M. issued a "supplemental forecast" warning of more gale-force winds. I thought to hell with that, and made my break from the beach in fifteen minutes.

The light was still dim as I paddled into Memkumlis. I was disappointed because I could see no sign of the guys. But as I drew nearer, there they were! The white-hulled skiff was almost invisible against the shell beach, the green bow pulled right up into the vegetation. It was very quiet so I knew they were still asleep in the tent. Silently I snuck up and scratched at the tent walls, growling. Gregg yelled and threw open the tent door, with eyes as big as saucers. He really thought I was a bear! Then we were bear hugging, so happily reunited.

We caught each other up on all news. Raven had brought a bouquet of flowers, and many funny and loving notes from my beautiful tribe back on Lopez. We then walked up to see the remains of the village. The people who had once thrived here were like cousins of my coastal kin, or perhaps enemies, but both had suffered the same fate. It was hauntingly quiet now. The beautifully carved cedar house posts were still standing, too big to wrap my arms around. In their scale and grandeur they seemed no less impressive to me than the columns of Greek temples. A mossy wolf totem seemed to lurk and snarl from the vegetation where it lay. Oh, to have seen this site in its heyday! We were exploring when we heard branches breaking above us, and looked up to see a black bear literally out on a limb in one of the old apple trees, stretching to reach the red fruit. This was the first bear that I had seen on my paddle.

In the following days together we explored and fished. We found a burial site with old steam-bent boxes still containing bones, kept dry and protected all these decades (if not hundreds of years), under a rock overhang. It made me remember my trip to Yakutat for a memorial potlatch for a close family friend, where my father was also honored. I had taken his ashes and spread them there in waters that reflected Mount Saint Elias. I was glad that his remains had not been confined in one of these small boxes, all folded up in a fetal position. In my mind, he seemed better off as ash on the water and in the wind.

We went to see the village of Health Bay and were surprised to find that it was not a ruin but a thriving native community. We decided just for fun to get a taste of the local scene by asking if they had a store. "Yes," was the answer. "Ask at the purple house." Soon a teenage girl came, complaining that it was "not her job." She opened the store, which seemed to sell only candy bars and dish soap. We felt bad that we had made the girl open the place for us so we each bought a candy bar. Then we thought of asking if the café was open, to which the same person said, "Ask at the purple house." Pretty soon out came the same teenager, saying under her breath that "it wasn't her job," but she opened the café.

It was a bright, neat establishment. We ordered from the simple menu: two coffees, one milkshake, one bowl of ice cream and a plate of french-fries with gravy. It seemed a challenging task. Perhaps the normal workers were away. In the end, it seemed nearly half of the population came in to prepare our order but at least *we* had fun! And the total bill was only $7.50.

Of course, we much preferred *real* food. Gregg had brought vegetables from my garden, and in one fishing session I caught a mammoth ling cod. It must have weighed twenty pounds. I had actually caught a little fish first, which the ling took hold of. The ling wouldn't let go of its bite, and for days after that we had fried cod, cod spaghetti, cod ceviche. When the man from the fishing lodge saw us out fishing again, he brought us a salmon, and we raced it back to camp and filleted it for dinner. We played cards each night and laughed at Raven's perfect sleight-of-hand card tricks. He really was the trickster spirit for whom he was named!

After four days of perfect sunny weather, the morning we parted was foggy, gray and damp. The change of weather seemed to reflect our sadness. We kissed, hugged and kissed and hugged some more and then went our different ways into the mists.

❖

After leaving the guys, I started down Canoe Passage on the south shore of Village Island, but looking down its length, I thought I could detect a sandbar. Since it was low tide, I judged it best to turn back. I stopped at yet another abandoned village site that we had not discovered in the past few days. Here I picked the most fragrant deep lavender rose that had been growing all on its own for who knows how many decades since some native woman lived there and planted it. I stuck it in my hat.

Now I took the course of paddling down Turnour Island. The day cleared and soon the heat of the sun had me stripping. I'd heard about a place called Lagoon Cove on Cracroft Island, and decided to investigate. Here I took a rejuvenating hot $2 shower.

I then took off around the island, carried by a swift current, and by 6:00 P.M. I had paddled twenty miles and made it to a pristine pre-contact village site called Matilpi. Its beach was steep and deep with shell. Here there were no old shoes, glass beads, iron chunks, pottery shards, wringer-washer parts or broken glass, just clam shells and a stream at one end. Not that this site was not covered in refuse, because it was. Many of these sites had thousands of years of occupation before the arrival of the whites. Their organic debris built by increments beneath them. In some cases twelve feet of rich black, shell-laced soils were all that was left to show for a people's existence in a location. I wish that could be said about us now, by those living in the future, but sadly we seem to be leaving a much worse mess in our wake. This beach was almost too clean. In fact there was not one stick of wood, so I lit my stove for the third time on the trip. Usually, I enjoyed the comfort and ritual of making a real fire each night and morning to cook on.

It had now been forty-seven days since I left home. The next day I paddled about sixteen miles and arrived at Port Neville at about 2:30. The only services were a dock and post office. Here I ran into the Grizleys, not the biting, scratching kind but Jack and Maureen Grizley, a kind English couple I'd already met at Lagoon Cove. They invited me aboard for dinner. They fixed a salmon ceviche and I stir-fried the last of my garden vegetables and we had a lovely evening.

The wind blew so hard all that night that the front stakes that anchored my tent pulled out and sand came through the door screen. With so much wind the next morning, I was in no great rush to get out into Johnstone Strait. I took tea and toast with the postmistress, Lorna and her young daughter Erika. Their life here at Port Neville was very secluded, so it probably was not my imagination that they seemed to enjoy my company. By 9:30 the wind seemed to have calmed a little, and I pushed off the beach, but when I got out into the straits I found it as raucous as ever. I tried not to let it frazzle me, but the big followings seas kept me on my toes. It was better to try to surf on top of the waves than to wallow in their troughs, but it meant fast and hard paddling.

I turned into Sunderland Channel, but still had very little protection. When I came to a narrows with a whirlpool, I was ready to charge right through, but then I noticed other large boats were anchored in Forward Harbor, and when I talked to a tugboat operator waiting to pull a raft of logs through, he said it wouldn't be slack until 6:00 P.M. I waited, and finally passed through and made camp. After eighteen miles, I was ready to quit, and so tired that I didn't care about the black bear that seemed to be sharing my beach. When I saw it, I called out to it, just to let it know I was there. It looked up, startled, but then we pretty much both did our own thing. I didn't lose a wink of sleep, and it was still there in the morning, flipping rocks on the beach, looking for delicacies. At this stage in my journey, I probably looked too tough to even consider dining on.

Paddling down Wellbore Channel in the morning, I rounded a headland and saw my first madrona tree, signifying that at least botanically speaking, I was nearing home! The Arbutus, as they are called in Canada, was solitary and lonely looking amidst the fir trees on the bank. I did not see one more of its kind for the rest of the day.

Two hours later I reached the notorious Green Point Rapids. I'd carefully calculated that I should not attempt to paddle through until 1:20 P.M. But the actual rapids, when I arrived, didn't appear threatening. I looked questioningly at a passing motor boat and the man gave me a very enthusiastic "GO" sign, so I went and perceived no effect whatsoever of the rapids. So much for my brilliant calculating! It could have been, however, that there was not a significant tidal exchange that day.

Paddling along Cordero Channel, I came to a positively out-of-place scene: a little German restaurant. I thought to myself, was my mom's maiden name "Fahrenkopf" or not? Yes! So I sat and ate bratwurst und apple strudel und coffee. I had actually been told about this place from two couples who had done this same journey. One couple was Mary and Steve Gropp from Orcas Island and the other couple were the Ashenfelters. The proprietors still remembered with fondness these adventurous couples.

As I relished my hot coffee and refills, I thought about my own stern German grandfather. Only after my real grandmother made her shocking reentry into our lives (at which point Grandpa

Fahrenkopf was in a nursing home) did I start to learn what had happened in my mother's family. In the last years of his life, he had lived with us, so I'd known him only as a very old man who loved to grow things. From him and with him I learned my first gardening skills. We played endless games of cribbage. Though my mom and uncle had few good things to say about him as their father, except that he was very hard-working, I only learned later that he was a child rapist! It was difficult for me as a youth to see this frail relic of a man as anything but harmless. Perhaps within each human there is the seed of evil and the seed of good. Depending on which seed is nourished and which is neglected we become lovable, repugnant or somewhere in between. I felt fortunate that he could share with me his love of growing food and flowers. In our large family, I may have been the one on which he left that truly positive mark.

I said "auf Wiedersehen" to my warm German hosts and told them their restaurant was "ausgezeichnet" and "danke Schön" and "Schönen Abend noch." By the time I left they were probably relieved to not have to act impressed with mein schlechtes Deutsch!

Burping bratwurst, I paddled off to position myself just northwest of the Dent and Gillard Rapids. Beyond those lay the Yuculta Rapids. It would be important for me to be poised and ready to paddle across the first of these potentially dangerous rapids at the precise moment of slack tide, which would be at 8:10 A.M. the next day. Near that destination I ran once again into the tug boat man and other tug boats all waiting with their rafts of logs to go at the morning low slack. Just beyond the tugs I rounded Horn Point and paddled wearily into a small quiet bay. I was searching for a place to pull out but all I could see was marsh grass. I was exhausted after this twenty-mile paddle, but was almost resigned to paddling back out when a big black dog came bounding out through the shallow water barking and wagging its tail. I thought to myself, nice dog probably means nice people. I decided it wouldn't hurt to ask if I could camp at the edge of the woods.

Here I met a woman of about my age, living with her eight children in a rustic home. Her husband was away working a construction job for a month. Anna wore a scarf wrapped around her head like a babushka, but was young and pretty. She told me she was Russian Greek Orthodox, born in China, and raised in Brazil. She had moved to Oregon and then to Alberta and had lived for two and a half years in this remote location. And her husband was born and raised in Turkey. She could have been straight from the old country with her soft, low Russian-accented voice. Her children ranged in age from two to twenty, and all lived at home but for the eighteen-year-old, who had married two years ago and moved in with her Greek Orthodox husband. Their house was sturdy but had no electricity. All of the children were bright, kind and inquisitive and each spoke Russian and English. There was a teeny travel trailer parked next to the house which the little girls used as their "Barbie playhouse." Good naturedly they ran out to clean it up so that I could sleep there. Anna fixed fresh-baked buns and tea. I let one of her boys, Terry, paddle my kayak. It was their mother's 38th birthday the next day, so when Terry brought me a kerosene lamp that evening, I gave him the two Russian trade beads that had been given to me in Blunden Harbor. With these, I suggested, they could make their mom a pair of earrings for a gift. He was really happy about that plan.

Rain pounded the tinny roof of the trailer through the night but I was able to sleep in until about 6:30. When I went into the house, Anna was already cooking a big breakfast for me, of fried potatoes, fried spam, fried eggs and instant coffee. Her head scarf was off and her hair now hung in long braids, as did the hair of all of her daughters. When it was time to leave, she and many of her kids came to the water's edge to wave good-bye to me. I was very charmed by their innocence and generosity.

As I paddled away, I reflected on my own choices as a parent. I know nothing of Greek Orthodox belief, but my concern about the environmental impact of unchecked population growth makes me feel that no religion should continue to encourage unlimited childbearing. There must be room for the bear, the wolf, the salmon and *all* creation. Still, Anna's simple and loving ways felt familiar to me, and her minimalistic lifestyle was not unlike the one I'd chosen. At one point, I had even turned off my electricity and sold my vehicle. Growing up, I'd never equated status or wealth with success, and though I came of age during the time of Women's Liberation, I never questioned the importance in my own life of childbearing and childrearing. When I was faced with single parenting, I chose to live on food stamps so I could stay home and parent my children, rather than taking a low-wage job and sending them off to child care. Being with my children was of supreme importance. To me, raising a child—whether we give birth or take on the responsibility for another's child—is one of the highest callings and most enlightening experiences any woman (or man) will ever undertake. The most studied person still knows next to nothing if they have never studied under the holiness and majesty of an infant or youth.

The night's rain had ended, and I paddled all morning through the mist. I timed the Dent and Gillard Rapids perfectly, but if I wanted to stop in Big Bay and do laundry, I'd have to wait until the next high slack at 3:00 to go through the Yuculta Rapids. And I did want to do laundry! I could hear the line-up of tug boats chugging behind me. They definitely were not going to miss their shot at all three rapids.

But I paddled in to Big Bay where I did my laundry and took a shower and ate cherry pie and bought jars of peanut butter and jam. It's funny the things you crave on an adventure like this. I burned so many calories that I needed oils and fats. I had always despised "power bars" of any sort but I had talked Golden Temple Bakery Inc. into sponsoring me with their Wah Guru Chews, which I never grew tired of. I had boxes of these nutty bars. The pie, coffee and beer cravings just were to add much-needed variety to my diet.

By 2:30 I was like a horse at the starting gates of the Yuculta Rapids, raring to go. These were the biggest, wildest ones yet. I tried to test the waters just slightly in advance of slack and found that even then it was impossible. As I sat in my kayak waiting, I saw a large hog of a boat power-up its engines and try to plow through the rapids, but even this boat got spun and spat back out.

Finally it was time to go, and when I popped out the other end of Yuculta it was like I had been released from the dark mountain kingdom of a distant land, and into a world where things were again familiar. I could almost smell home! The sky opened up and as far off as I could see to the southwest, islands and land masses were gentler and lower in elevation. The Yuculta Rapids were like a magical threshold, my final gateway home after slaying the seven dragons and crossing the boiling waters. There were still plenty of miles ahead, but I had a true sense of elation at having surmounted the real challenges of the journey to this point. I paddled for miles down the channel, and every so often I looked back and shuddered at the sight of the dark cloud-enshrouded terrain I'd come from.

♦

I was now in Calm Channel and, just as the name indicates, it was calm; that day at least. Nine miles beyond the rapids I had started praying to the spirits for a little place to rest my head, when around the very next point on a small island I came to an old, dilapidated but story-book-cute farm house. It was built of vertical logs that were listing decidedly southward. The remains of a picket fence, with some sections still standing, and blooming gladiolas gave the old homestead the unmistakable look of a place where once love dwelled. Not only was it homey here, but a feast lay in the shallows: oysters for easy pickin's—the first of my journey.

The morning brought its own feast. I picked a pot of blackberries and simmered them with honey and then made buckwheat pancakes and smothered them with my berry syrup. Squirrels chattered loudly from high in the broadleaf maple as I ate.

I was looking forward to my next destination across Galley Bay to Zephine Head, some sixteen miles away. My best friend's sister-in-law and her husband, Claudia and Rick, had agreed to take me under their gentle wing for two days. First, though, I paddled in sunny, warm conditions over to Refuge Cove, where I bought beers so as not to arrive empty handed. By the time I left the cove a southerly had picked up, making my five mile

rossing a challenge, but I was determined. It took me two hours
and fifteen minutes.

When I pulled ashore on the 180-acre homestead, Claudia and
Rick were there to greet me. I had met and visited them here in
the not so distant past, and they were like family. Their land had
been an early 20th century homestead and then was bought by
the Bloom family, where it was a commune and place of refuge
for American draft dodgers. It was not long after these glory days
that Claudia and Rick met, moved here, and became shareholders
with the Blooms and others. Claudia and Rick had remained as
the primary occupants, but other shareholders and guests often
dropped in. It was rarely as lonely a place as it might appear in its
wild environment. The tall old orchard trees were still very pro-
ductive, and the original sturdy farmhouse had been well cared
for through the decades, and in all directions were views of dramatic mountains and mystical inlets.

The only thing marring this beauty, and the largest trial for
Claudia and Rick, was the boat traffic. Pleasure cruisers to the
count of about 15,000 boats per summer make this their destination, so their bit of paradise had a price, but they'd adapted
with good grace. Rick worked for the Provincial Parks, running
his skiff around Galley Bay, and Claudia, who made hand-dipped
candles, had a trade going with a restaurant in Oakover, where she
offered to take me out to dinner. There we had the best seafood
I had ever eaten. I'm sure she could not have imagined what a
gift this meal was after my unending beans and rice. Rick blasted
us all back in the skiff, but cut the engines midway so that we
could take in the flaming sunset simultaneously with the rising of
a cool, fat gibbous moon. What rapture!

Claudia and I sat up late talking. Her brother Mark was a dear
friend of mine who had moved to Lopez with his wife Doreen.
We'd became fast friends. I was at the birth of both of their
daughters and became "goddess-mother" to them. Mark had died
tragically of a genetic blood disorder that ran strongly in their
family, and that night we remembered his Dylan-esque mop of
curly hair and his beat-poet sensibilities. He had been ethereal in
life and now was one with the ethers. We both missed him.

On August 10th, I thanked my friends, and set out for Texada Island, but after a tiring day of paddling and with steel-blue thunderclouds bearing down in my direction, I pulled in at the northeast point of Harwood Island. This island was conservation land, and also the party beach for the local Powell River youth and Silammon natives, lying directly across the two mile wide Malaspina Strait. Camping was technically prohibited, and after hearing on the local radio station the day before that a teen-aged girl had been shot and killed here, I didn't *want* to stay, but at this point, nothing could have made me leave. For this night, I would have to abide the newly released spirit of that poor soul and sleep as best I could. I made my dinner fire and pitched my tent quickly, hopping into the tent with my warm meal just as the thunder shower cut loose. As fatigued as I was, I probably could have slept peacefully on a battlefield of massacred soldiers.

I was on the water by 6:30 the next morning. The strange impulse we humans have for straining our necks to see a wreck on the roadside also had me scanning the longer east-facing beach of Harwood as I paddled by. This is where I imagined the girl had been shot, and my intuition was confirmed when I saw a cross stuck into the sand and draped in fresh flowers. Teens can and do get themselves in trouble in every demographic, but native communities suffer in profoundly greater numbers. I couldn't help but think of the pain and shame that were so much a part of my grandparents' and parents' legacies.

I paddled against a headwind along the east coast of Texada Island, with one quick stop in the small town of Vananda where I bought some chicken drumsticks to grill for dinner. Then on again through high evening winds and whitecaps. After eleven hours and twenty miles, I landed in a pounding surf to make camp amidst baseball-sized rocks. By now my dreams of grilling marinated chicken seemed too ambitious. By the time my camp was made, the best I could do was throw them in a pot for soup.

My next day was longer, perhaps 24 miles, less strenuous, but high adrenaline. With the current in my favor and a stiff tailwind,

I raised my sail. For a while, I tried trolling while moving at this pace, and ended up with a baby salmon on my hook. I decided to sacrifice the small fish and use it for bait, but never lured a larger one, and finally had to drop my sail as the following seas built higher. By 3:00 I had made it around the southern point of Lesqueti Island and continued across to my camp on little Sangster Island where I fried my tiny bait fish and ate it with beans and rice.

I was now perched and ready to pounce on the crossing of the northwestern end of the Strait of Georgia. I would be paddling toward but avoiding Ballenas Island, just off the mainland of Vancouver Island. Ballenas Island is a military torpedo test zone. It would certainly ruin my whole day if I were caught in "friendly" fire!

When I left the beach the next morning, the Strait of Georgia was already rockin'! I almost considered not going, but decided to try it anyway. Strong winds blew me off course in a sweeping northern arch, making my crossing to Schooner Cove that much longer. During my arduous hours in this open stretch, working hard to reach the cove, I sang to keep my spirits up.

The river is flowing
Flowing and growing
The river is flowing
Back to the sea.

Mother carry me
Your child I will
Always be.
Mother carry me
Back to the sea.

I was spent but elated when I reached the marina, where I did my laundry, showered, drank coffee and called Gregg. He was happy I had made it to the east coast of Vancouver Island. By 5:00 P.M. the winds had died enough that I could venture out again. I was told of a nice little island to camp on, a mile and a half from the cove. I found it to be sunny and beautiful, covered with Garry oak and madrona. A whole chorus of crickets made their sweet music all night long. I again found oysters to eat and bedded down contented with the accomplishments of the day.

Stormy weather marooned me the next day. Shiver me timbers! Aaarg! I only had about twelve miles to go before I would be in the more protected waters near Gabriola Island but the tremendous waves crashed all day. In my eagerness I felt like a horse to the barn, and remembered a favorite horse of mine named Babe. She was so easygoing that I could ride her right into the bar and around the pool tables, and when the police once tried to arrest me for being flippant, I'd jumped on and used her as my getaway vehicle, galloping down alleyways. In my early days on Lopez, when the ferry service rules were more relaxed, I could ride her directly onto the inter-island ferry to go for rides on Orcas Island. Like most horses, she could find her way home from anywhere, and always trotted along with much more enthusiasm on the home stretch, so I certainly could understand her sentiments, as I was reined in here on this rocky perch.

In the meanwhile, being hostage to the elements allowed me the time to take notice of the beauty surrounding me. There were little gardens of kinikinik, yarrow, mossy rocks and succulents in comfortable niches with views out of the wind. Kingfishers buzzed and vultures circled. I called out to the vultures reminding them that I wasn't "dead *yet!*" And there was always the background song of the crickets. As in Galley Bay, north of here, the waters were much warmer, hence also the night temperatures. This was better habitat for the oyster and the cricket, both of which are rare in the colder environs of Lopez Island and the rest of the San Juan Islands.

Finally on August 15, with a shift in the winds, I was able to paddle off eighteen miles to False Narrows between Gabriola and Mudge Islands, thereby avoiding the turbulent waters of Dodd Narrows. False Narrows was like paddling down a tree-lined boulevard. Neat little cottages lined the beach. I noticed a pay phone and was able to pull ashore easily to give a call to my mom to wish her an early happy birthday. I was certain a telephone would not present itself to me so effortlessly the next day. I only got her answering machine but it nonetheless felt good to send my love to her.

I camped that evening on a lovely little parked-out island, open and sunny. It had a sampling of trees: a beautiful juniper, some twisted Garry oak, fir and madrona. The whole understory was short-grazed grass, dry and comfortable for camping. It started to pour just as I finished making my dinner of pesto pasta, so I ducked into my tent to enjoy my meal while peering out of my vestibule.

I left the next morning at 7:30 and had a calm easy go of it for the first ten miles, but once I entered the channel between Valdez and Galiano Islands, the waters grew squirrely and jumpy. Then, with a headwind and a back-eddy both working against me, I saw a sign on a government wharf that simply read, "Hamburgers." Now, I didn't really desire a burger but I also was not having fun in the conditions, so I tied my boat and went up the steep flight of stairs to find a surprisingly fun store, stocked with exotic foods, fresh veggies, baked goods, organic eggs and fresh milk and run by a stand-up comedian type gal by the name of Kate. I whiled away two hours there, waiting for a break in the weather, and found a pair of secondhand silk pants and treated myself to a homecoming gift at the price of $1.00. At last the wind died. By then, the flood tide was against me, but the back-eddies were in my favor, and the second ten miles of my day were relatively quick and painless.

I made Montague Harbor on south Galiano by 6:00. I'd passed up alluring white shell beaches, but since it is a Provincial Park, no camping was allowed there. The official campsites were in the harbor. After two months of soloing in the wilds, the idea of being sandwiched between hordes of late summer vacationers held no appeal. Instead, I made a low-profile bandit camp in the woods on the point, threw my brown nylon tarp over my kayak, used my camp stove instead of a fire, and hoped I wouldn't run into Ranger Rick. I made my dinner of ham and eggs I'd bought from Kate's store, and once again ate from the shelter of my tent as the rains began. This was waterfront dining at its best!

I left my bandit camp and paddled into a brilliant morning amidst ferry traffic between the islands of Mayne, Galiano, Saturna and Pender, and then through Navy Channel. The day was calm, with winds only at the headlands. I came through Plumber Channel, the exit of the Canadian Gulf Islands to look across the glassy-still Haro Strait and Boundary Passage. I would be in the San Juan Islands by the afternoon!

Haro Strait can be harrowing but the spirits that guided me now granted a most benign crossing. Tankers ran these waters like a superhighway, and two passed through when I was about a third of the way across. I saw another in the distance. These ships moved fast, and having seen the first two pass, I could roughly calculate that this third one would come quite close at the rate I was going. I poured on the coals in hope of not being mid-channel when the monstrosity plowed through. It never would have noticed little ol' me out there. In fact it did come a little too close for comfort, but I already had my sights set on Waldron Island, its long sweeping sandy beach ready to embrace me like a loving arm. After nineteen miles of paddling I pulled onto the shore of my friend Laurie Glenn's charming and funky little beach-house property. I was back in the US of A!

Two friends of Laurie's were on the beach and were probably a little shocked at my bold and half-naked landing right at their feet. Soon they and eight visitors of Laurie's were on the beach welcoming me. They had not known I was coming and in fact the friends were gathered for a send-off to Laurie who was about to sail north with her partner for two months. My timing was impeccable. If I'd come a day later not a soul would have been there. As it was, before I was even out of my kayak, I was handed the juiciest, fattest fig I had ever seen. It was just plucked from the tree and very ceremoniously given to me with a deep, reverent bow. Even though they were not expecting me they knew instantaneously that this was a momentous occasion for me. These people were part of my extended tribe. They are people that we Lopezians celebrated special occasions with. Waldron has no ferry service, so these people are fringe of the fringe. My people!

That night, their house glowed like a lantern as the send-off party swung into full motion. Joyous laughter pealed, but my energies were depleted and I bedded down for the last night of my journey under a starlit sky. I had called Gregg to tell him that I estimated arriving at Odlin Park on Lopez at about noon, and that night I hardly slept.

In the morning, I loaded my boat, tucked my lifejacket (still not worn once) in its place behind me and pushed off quietly from the soft sands of Laurie's beach. There was not a peep from the house. I had about fifteen miles to paddle to get to Lopez and I could see right off that I was really going to have to work hard to prove I belonged there. My eyes watered in the sharp headwind. I crossed President Channel and rounded Orcas Island to its southern shoreline. Here I experienced the heaviest boat traffic of my 750 miles. Power boats between Orcas and Shaw Islands ran like a pack of rats back to their homeports along the coastal mainland. It was August 18th. Summer was drawing to a close and we, one and all, needed to get back home! I dodged their nasty wakes and pushed on through the unrelenting wind, thinking of my many encounters with magic and mystery, with obstacles great and small. I thought of the endless acts of kindness bestowed on me by the very humans of whom I had grown to be cynical. I knew that all of this had come my way because I had opened myself to trust and faith in the power and loving guidance of my ancestors. I was carried by my understanding of their actual lives; lived in undoubtedly harsher times along this coast. Their lives and struggles were omnipresent, a great source of inspiration when I needed the courage to press on. My father and mother had both suffered much in their lives, and only ever wished for me to be happy. The wisdom of their uncomplicated love and advice was and had always been a great and empowering source of motivation.

One of the final predictions from the psychic had been that this journey would reveal a "strong metaphysical connection" between my father and me. I could not deny the accurateness of her otherworldly readings; it was one more level of the magic that had aligned to guide me on this spirit quest. There's no way she could have known about the white hummingbird–spirit-of my-father, who initially lent me the reassurance to proceed with my daring dream.

Now, I was coming home reaffirmed in my desire to commit to my tribe, the close and supportive community we lived among. I was thankful for the love and support of my beautiful family and community for having helped to give me the permission, the courage, and the faith to make my desire into a reality. I thought of how our society at large lives in fear. How can we teach our children to love and care for the Earth when they are afraid to be out in the magic of her wilds? My solo journey had reaffirmed above all my yearning to live an ecstatic rather than a fearful life.

As I drew near to Lopez Island I could hear faint sounds of drums reverberating and a saxophone squawking joyful rifts. Yes! There was my tribe; there were my loves! They lined the beach. Children ran this way and that. Friends sang and shouted out. I stopped mid-channel just to cry. I then paddled with all my strength, driving my bow up onto the sandy shore to the tremendous embrace of my community and family. I jumped from my kayak and first kissed the ground and then kissed my man, my daughter and my sons and looked to the blue sky and gave a thanks to the spirits of my ancestors. I was home!

✦

My return to Lopez.

Me with my children. Cody, me, Raven and Summer Moon.

Acknowledgments

SO MANY TO THANK: Top of the list is my husband, Gregg Blomberg. When I read aloud my first excerpts, he cried and said, "Keep writing!"

Karen Fisher for her ever-wise counsel, reassurances, kind heart, sharp eye, speed and wit! Fishtrap Writer's Conference, for awarding me a Fellowship. For Amon Burton, an attendee at Fishtrap, who offered praise as well as a grant to pay for editing. Also my gratitude to these early readers who, offered feedback, encouragement and funds: Summer Moon Scriver, Steve Brown, Carol Burton, Doreen Kana, Patty Prichard, Leslie Redtree, Sona Woolworth, Janet Yang and Pamela Maresten. Kip and Stanley Greenthal, Diana O'Daugherty and Matt Hummel and Amy Shipman. A special thanks to: Milla Prince, Edi Blomberg, Chris Carter, Diana O'Daugherty, Alice Acheson and Aviva Kana for their more thorough reviews. To Adriene Bowechop for her help with Makah language spelling, to Keri Eggleston, for her help with Tlingit language spelling, and to Nancy Low, volunteer book narrator at the Washington Talking Book and Braille Library. To these and many more in my community who chipped in funds because they believed in my project.

In addition, I'm so happy to say what a gift it was to find Dede Cummings at Green Writer's Press. She is "my people" and everyone she surrounds herself with, are my people, too. I'm very comforted to know we are everywhere! Thank you for believing in my book and working so hard to bring it into reality.

And to the continued family lineage of my beloved children: Summer Moon, Cody, and Raven.

And to the children of my children: Cosmos and Rio. Finnegan and Oliver. Wren. Also, to the in-laws and "in-loves" of those children: J'aime, Tessa, and Kelly.

And with love to my siblings: Gail, Mary Kay, Sally, Donny (RIP), and Tim.

Also with extended blessings for my step-children: CedarBough, Karjam, Zack, Eirene, and step-grandchild Juniper.

CPSIA information can be obtained
at www.ICGtesting.com
Printed in the USA
LVHW040842140623
749612LV00005B/475

9 780998 701240